# "NO ONE AVOIDED DANGER"

# PEARL HARBOR TACTICAL STUDIES SERIES

J. Michael Wenger, Robert J. Cressman, and John F. Di Virgilio, editors

With nearly three-quarters of a century having passed since 7 December 1941, it seems counterintuitive that no comprehensive, tactical history exists for the Japanese attacks on the island of O'ahu. It is only within the span of the last two decades that much of the material and documentary evidence relating to the attacks has become generally available to historians and researchers. This material not only spans far-flung repositories in the United States and Japan, but also bridges a vast chasm separating two very different cultures, complicating the material's use.

The Pearl Harbor Tactical Studies series seeks to fill this wide gap in military history by diving down to the lowest levels of practical, personal, and tactical details. The goal of these works is to promote a deeper understanding of the events of 7 December 1941, and to convey the chaos and magnitude of the disaster on O'ahu, as experienced at an individual level. Compilation of such a series has been possible only through a careful survey of the widest spread of records and accounts from both sides, resulting in comprehensive accounts that document the epic American-Japanese struggle on and over O'ahu, and the intensely human tragedy of that day.

NAS KANEOHE BAY AND THE JAPANESE ATTACK OF 7 DECEMBER 1941

# "NO ONE AVOIDED DANGER"

J. MICHAEL WENGER, ROBERT J. CRESSMAN, AND JOHN F. DI VIRGILIO

NAVAL INSTITUTE PRESS

ANNAPOLIS, MARYLAND

**This book has been brought to publication with the generous assistance of Marguerite and Gerry Lenfest.**

Naval Institute Press
291 Wood Road
Annapolis, MD 21402

ISBN: 978-1-61251-924-1
ISBN: 978-1-61251-925-8 (ebook)
Library of Congress Cataloging-in-Publication Data is available.

♾ Print editions meet the requirements of ANSI/NISO z39.48–1992 (Permanence of Paper).
Printed in the United States of America.

23  22  21  20  19  18  17  16  15          9  8  7  6  5  4  3  2  1
First printing

Most photographs are U.S. Navy official, from the collections of the National Archives and Records Administration (NARA II or NARA, St. Louis), the Naval History and Heritage Command (formerly the Naval Historical Center) (NHHC), National Personnel Records Center (NPRC, St. Louis), National Naval Aviation Museum (NNAM), or are from private collections. Photos marked 71-CA, 72-AC, 80-CF, 80-G, and 127-GS can be found at NARA II in College Park, Maryland. The NHHC's photos are distinguished by the NH prefix. Photos with a USAR prefix are from World War II Valor in the Pacific National Monument. Photos loaned or given by individuals are indicated by the donor's last name. Photos marked BKS can be found at the War History Library (*Senshi bu*) of the Japan Defense Agency, War History Office (*Boeicho Kenshujo Senshishitsu*).

*To the "Klippers" of Kaneohe, the forgotten heroes of 7 December 1941*

# Contents

# Preface

Of the major American military airfields on Oʻahu that came under attack on 7 December 1941, none lay farther away from the U.S. Pacific Fleet at Pearl Harbor than did Naval Air Station (NAS) Kaneohe Bay on the island's windward shore. Situated on Mōkapu Peninsula approximately fifteen air miles east-northeast of Pearl, the station seemed something of a backwater, isolated by distance and the jagged Koʻolau mountains. A historical byproduct of that isolation is that the events of 7 December 1941 that unfolded there receive, at best, superficial coverage in most accounts of the attacks on Oʻahu. Hence, comparatively little is known regarding the battle that took place along the picturesque shores of Kāneʻohe Bay.

Like many of the wartime facilities in Hawaiʻi, Kaneohe remains an active military base—currently Marine Corps Base Hawaii. Among the hangars and parking aprons at what was once NAS Kaneohe Bay, however, Americans battled the attacking Japanese with courage and resolution that matched that of their adversaries. One of the great, but inevitable, misfortunes that occur in the aftermath of war is that the valor and heroism of brave men comes to be remembered dimly with the passing of generations. The American soldiers, sailors, and Marines—still living at the time of this writing—who were the object of the attacks on Oʻahu feel this phenomenon keenly. We hope this work will bring to life the story of the valiant defenders of NAS Kaneohe Bay on 7 December 1941 and ensure that their story will edify and inspire those who read it.

J. Michael Wenger,
Robert J. Cressman,
John F. Di Virgilio
1 August 2015

# Acknowledgments

A book such as this is necessarily the product of the supporting labors of many, from trained archival specialists to friends and colleagues in the field and those who lived through these momentous events. Some no longer work in the archives in which we began our research, but our feeling of indebtedness lingers as we remember assistance rendered. Many veterans with whom we talked or corresponded, sadly, have died.

In particular, this work stands on the shoulders of two individuals without whose resources any work dealing with the Pearl Harbor epic would fall woefully short of the mark. Dr. Gordon W. Prange's papers remain an unparalleled source of information. We especially thank Jennie A. Levine at the University of Maryland and Dr. Donald M. Goldstein, Marianne Kasica, and Michael Dabrishus of the University of Pittsburgh for making Dr. Prange's materials available. Similarly, Walter Lord's work is practically synonymous with the attack on O'ahu. Access to his interviews, questionnaires, and correspondence came to us via archivist Curtis Utz of the Naval History and Heritage Command.

Archivists and reference specialists provided help and guidance at a number of institutions and repositories. The National Archives and Records Administration (NARA II) in College Park, Maryland, has provided access to records over many years, and we thank Jim Trimble, Holly Reed, Theresa Roy, and Sharon Culley of the Still Picture Branch; Nathaniel Patch of the Textual Branch; and Andrew Knight and Alice Rosser of the Cartographic Branch for their assistance. The generous staff at the Naval History and Heritage Command (formerly the Naval Historical Center) in Washington, D.C., helped the authors for more than the span of a generation, particularly Charles R. Haberlein, Agnes F. Hoover, and Mike Walker. Hill Goodspeed at the National Naval Aviation Museum (now a part of the Naval History and Heritage Command enterprise in Pensacola, Florida) gave generously of his time, resources, and materials. Randy W. Hackenburg of the United States Army Military History Institute provided access to the Denver Gray collection of photography. Lisa Fox of North Texas University supplied copies of interviews from that institution's oral history program. NAVFAC Hawaii assisted in locating architectural plans. Our research at the National Archives and National Personnel Records Center in St. Louis, Missouri, would not have been possible without the energy and advice of Scott A. Levins, Bryan McGraw, Barbara Bauman, Whitney Mahar, Eric Kilgore, Donna Noelken, Amy Reckmann, Angela Miller, Mary Parker Biby, and Jaclyn Ostrowski.

The following individuals assisted with translation of Japanese documents, books, articles, and monographs: Dr. Kataoka Hiroko, formerly of North Carolina State University, Oka Akio, Sugahara Kan, Dr. Kawamoto Minoru, Sam Tagaya, and D. Y. Louie. In particular, Mr. Sugahara was instrumental in evaluating the authors' translation of the Japanese aircrew rosters from the attacks on O'ahu.

Shibata Takehiko and Kageyama Kōichirō at the War History Office of the Japanese Defense Agency offered expertise, documents, and analysis and served as our liaison with Japanese veteran groups.

Access to U.S. Marine Corps service records at the National Personnel Records Center would have been impossible without the help of Annette D. Amerman of the Marine Corps History Division and Jill Glenewinkel at Headquarters U.S. Marine Corps, Personnel Management Support Branch.

Fellow historians and researchers extended generous offers of assistance. Capt. Roger Pineau and Cdr. Chihaya Masataka proved instrumental in helping with Wenger's research in Japan. Other individuals provided documents, materials, and valuable advice, including John B. Lundstrom, James C. Sawruk, Kamada Minoru, John W. Lambert, William M. Cleveland, Todd Pederson, James Lansdale, Norm Richards, Jessie Higa, and Richard F. Barnes. Eric Mitchell kindly provided access to the photograph collections of VP-11 veterans Clifton W. Dohrmann and Robert C. O'Connor. John W. Lambert provided his correspondence with Abe Yasujirō. Dr. Timothy P. Mulligan made available copies of the fragmentary code books recovered from Japanese aircraft wreckage. Institutions and individuals in Japan supplied documents and photography: War History Office of the Japanese Defense Forces, Murooka Yasuo of *Maru* magazine, Todaka Kazunari, Tanaka Shoichi, Fujita Iyozō, Murakami Fukuji, and Kamada Minoru. Osamu "Sam" Tagaya secured pictures of Japanese aircrews from Dr. Izawa Yasuo. Other individuals provided photography: Russell J. and Anita Crownover, James W. Curylo, Angelina and Stephen Engel, James F. Evans, Ed Horky, John S. Kennedy, Walter Lord, Al Makiel, Jerome McCrimmon, Charles P. Muckenthaler, Michael Perucci, Dr. Lisa L. (Petriccione) Neumann, Dr. Gordon W. Prange (via Dr. Donald M. Goldstein), Paul Van Nostrand Jr., Harriett Tracey, William Watson, Kathy Weeks, and authors J. Michael Wenger, Robert J. Cressman, and John F. Di Virgilio.

The authors were fortunate to have interviewed and corresponded with key American and Japanese attack participants. Americans included Capt. Charles P. Muckenthaler, USN (Ret.), Capt. William P. Tanner, USN (Ret.), Capt. Benjamin H. Troemel, USN (Ret.), and AEC John S. Kennedy, USN (Ret.). We contacted the following Japanese aviators who contributed materially to an understanding of Japanese ordnance, tactics, and the events of 7 December 1941: Abe Zenji, Fujita Iyozō, Harada Kaname, Satō Zenichi, and Ushijima Shizundo.

Beth Oldham Design assisted with maps and graphic overlays.

The following individuals on the staffs of World War II Valor in the Pacific National Monument and Pacific Historic Parks have supported the research and work of the authors on a continuing basis: Tom Shaw, Marjorie Shaw, Marge Nordman, Alison Akau, Ray Sandla, Edean Saito, Daniel Martinez, Scott Pawlowski, and Patty Brown.

The officers, men, and families of Marine Corps Base Hawaii displayed intense interest in this project and offered enthusiastic support and gracious hospitality during our visits, particularly former commanding officer Col. Brian P. Annichiarico, USMC, and his wife Carla.

Finally, we wish to thank Richard Russell of the Naval Institute Press for his continued interest in the authors' work and in the story of NAS Kaneohe Bay.

# U.S. Navy and Japanese Aircraft Names

The U.S. Navy, by and large, did not often use the popular nicknames approved in October 1941 for its planes. The Imperial Japanese Navy designated its types of aircraft in a particular way, so we refer to them as it did. The reader, thus, will not find the anachronistic "Val" or "Kate" in the text since those names would not be used until November 1942, nearly a year after Pearl Harbor.

**U.S. Navy**

Douglas SBD-2, -3 Dauntless

Consolidated PBY-1, -2, -5 Catalina

Vought OS2U-1 Kingfisher

Grumman J2F-1 Duck

**Imperial Japanese Navy**

Aichi D3Al Type 99 carrier bomber (*kanbaku*) ("Val")

Mitsubishi A6M2 Type 0 carrier fighter (*kansen*) ("Zero")

Nakajima B5N2 Type 97 carrier attack plane (*kankō*) ("Kate")

# Japanese Names

All Japanese names are rendered as in Japanese fashion, with the surname first and the given name last. Romanization of Japanese names from *kanji* characters is an inexact science. After translating the names herein, the authors consulted with historian Sugahara Kan of Japan, who offered many corrections and alternative readings. Owing to the nature of Japanese personal names, there will never be a last word on this matter. With the help of Mr. Sugahara, however, the rosters of the Japanese participants are as authoritative as practicality allows.

# Hawaiian Place Names

All Hawaiian place names are rendered in native orthography, except in names of military bases and quotations from contemporary correspondence.

# National Personnel Records Center

For two generations, the term "National Personnel Records Center" has been synonymous with the former Page Avenue facility in St. Louis, Missouri, that held all the Official Military Personnel Files (OMPFs) from the World War II period and other eras. In recent years, however, with an increasing volume of records being released for public use, the facility in St. Louis is no longer a monolithic entity. In reality, it is two institutions in one building operating under the umbrella of the National Archives and Records Administration, each with its separate research room and procedures. One institution, the National Personnel Records Center, administers nonarchival records (those closed to the public), while alternatively the National Archives administers archival records (those open to the public).

For the sake of clarity, when citing primary sources from "St. Louis," closed material accessed through the research room in the Records Center will be cited as residing in "NPRC, St. Louis." Open material accessed through the research room in the National Archives will be cited as residing in "NARA, St. Louis."

# Glossary

**Miscellaneous Items and Abbreviations**

AA: anti-aircraft; acting appointment, when used as a suffix to a chief petty officer rating

A–V(G), USNR: commissioned aviation officers holding the designation as naval aviators, qualified for general duty afloat or ashore

A–V(N), USNR: commissioned aviation flight officers, detailed to active duty in the aeronautic organization of the Navy immediately following the completion of training and designation as naval aviators

BAR: Browning Automatic Rifle

BOQ: Bachelor Officers Quarters

BuNo: bureau number

CarDiv: Carrier Division

CEC–V(S): commissioned civil engineer

ChC–V(G), USNR: commissioned chaplains qualified for general detail afloat or ashore

*chūtai:* Japanese aviation unit of six to twelve aircraft, usually three *shōtai*s

CinCPac: Commander-in-Chief, U.S. Pacific Fleet

CinCUS: Commander-in-Chief, U.S. Fleet

Com 14: Commandant, 14th Naval District

ComAirScoFor: Commander, Aircraft, Scouting Force

ComPatWing: Commander, Patrol Wing

D–V(G), USNR: deck officer, commissioned or warranted, qualified for general detail afloat or ashore

D–V(S), USNR: commissioned deck officers qualified for specialist duties

F–4–C: Fleet Reserve class, wherein men who were serving in the regular Navy 11 July 1925 or who re-enlisted under continuous service immediately thereafter are transferred to Fleet Reserve upon completion of sixteen years

HC: Hospital Corps

IMI: request to repeat message

Jig: request to repeat message and verify

*kankōtai:* Japanese aviation unit of Type 97 carrier attack planes

kg: kilogram

M1917: Model 1917

MAG: Marine Aircraft Group

MarDet: Marine Detachment

MC: Medical Corps

NAP: Naval Aviation Pilot

NAS: Naval Air Station

NCO: non-commissioned officer

OOD: Officer of the day (or deck)

OpNav: Office of the Chief of Naval Operations

PA: permanent appointment, when used as a suffix to a chief petty officer rating

ROTC: Reserve Officer Training Corps

SC-V(S): commissioned supply officers, qualified for specialist duties

*shōtai:* Japanese aviation unit of two to four aircraft, usually three

T.H.: Territory of Hawaii

USMC: United States Marine Corps

USN: United States Navy

USNR: United States Naval Reserve

V-6: Naval Reserve class, wherein enlisted men are required for mobilization, in addition to other classes of Volunteer Reserve

**Standard Nomenclature for U.S. Navy Ships**

AD: destroyer tender

AG: miscellaneous auxiliary

AKS: general stores–issue ship

AM: minesweeper

AO: fleet oiler

APD: high-speed transport

AT: fleet tug

AV: seaplane tender

BB: battleship

CA: heavy cruiser

CL: light cruiser

CV: aircraft carrier

CVE: aircraft carrier, escort

DD: destroyer

SS: submarine

ZR: rigid airship

**Squadrons**

VB: bombing squadron

VP: patrol squadron

**American Ranks and Ratings**

Adm.: Admiral

ACMM: Aviation Chief Machinist's Mate

ACOM: Aviation Chief Ordnanceman

ACRM: Aviation Chief Radioman

AEC: Chief Aviation Machinist's Mate

AMM1c, 2c, 3c: Aviation Machinist's Mate, 1st Class/2d Class/3d Class

1st Lt.: First Lieutenant (USMC)

AOM1c, 2c, 3c: Aviation Ordnanceman, 1st Class/2d Class/3d Class

AvCdt: Aviation Cadet

BM2c: Boatswain's Mate, 2d Class

Bug1c: Bugler, 1st Class

Capt.: Captain (USN and USMC)

CCStd: Chief Commissary Steward

Cdr.: Commander

ChCarp: Chief Carpenter, a warrant officer

CPhM: Chief Pharmacist's Mate

CM1c, 3c: Carpenter's Mate, 1st Class/3d Class

EM1c, 3c: Electrician's Mate, 1st Class/3d Class

Ens.: Ensign

F3c: Fireman, 3d Class

Gen.: General

HA1c: Hospital Apprentice, 1st Class

Lt.: Lieutenant

Lt. Cdr.: Lieutenant Commander

Lt. Col.: Lieutenant Colonel (USMC and Army)

Lt. (jg): Lieutenant (junior grade)

Maj.: Major (USMC)

MAtt1c: Mess Attendant, 1st Class

Midn.: Midshipman

P3c: Photographer's Mate, 3d Class

Pfc.: Private 1st Class (USAAF and USMC)

Pharm: Pharmacist, a warrant officer

PhM1c: Pharmacist's Mate, 1st Class

Prtr3c: Printer, 3d Class

Pvt.: Private

Rear Adm.: Rear Admiral

RM1c, 2c, 3c: Radioman 1st Class/2d Class/3d Class

SC2c: Ship's Cook, 2d Class

Sea1c, 2c: Seaman 1st Class, 2nd Class

SK2c: Storekeeper, 2d Class

Vice Adm.: Vice Admiral

Y1c, Y2c: Yeoman, 1st Class/2d Class

## Japanese Ranks and Ratings

The Imperial Navy's aviation ratings did not correspond with those of the U.S. Navy. For commissioned ranks, American equivalents are used. For the sake of simplicity, Japanese non-commissioned and enlisted ranks are presented as follows: WO (warrant officer), PO1c, 2c, 3c (petty officer 1st, 2d, 3d class), and Sea1c (seaman 1st class). See the table with corresponding Japanese terminology and translation below:

| | | |
|---|---|---|
| Adm. | *Taishō* | Admiral |
| Vice Adm. | *Chūjō* | Vice Admiral |
| Rear Adm. | *Shōshō* | Rear Admiral |
| Capt. | *Taisa* | Captain |
| Cdr. | *Chūsa* | Commander |
| Lt. Cdr. | *Shōsa* | Lieutenant Commander |
| Lt. | *Tai-i* | Lieutenant |
| Lt. (jg) | *Chū-i* | Sub-Lieutenant |
| Ens. | *Shō-i* | Ensign |
| WO | *Hikō Heisōchō* | Flight Warrant Officer |
| PO1c | *Ittō Hikō Heisō* | Flight Petty Officer, 1st Class |
| PO2c | *Nitō Hikō Heisō* | Flight Petty Officer, 2nd Class |
| PO3c | *Santō Hikō Heisō* | Flight Petty Officer, 3rd Class |
| Sea1c | *Ittō Hikōhei* | Flight Seaman, 1st Class |

# Notes on Ship Names and Times

Unless otherwise specified, all USN ship names will be understood as being preceded by USS (United States Ship); a USN ship's alphanumeric hull number will be used only when it is first used in the course of the work. All times and dates are those observed locally by a ship or station unless otherwise specified and are rendered in "military" fashion (i.e., 1000 for 10:00 a.m., 1300 for 1:00 p.m., etc.).

# ONE

## "IT WAS LIKE THE TIME OF YOUR LIFE"

"Crossroads of the Pacific," the subject of many a serviceman's snapshot. (Weeks)

Kau Kau Korner, the well-known restaurant that once stood at the intersection of Kapiʻolani Boulevard and Kālakaua Avenue, lay on the boundary separating Honolulu from Waikīkī. The garish signpost nearby, "Crossroads of the Pacific," caught the eye of many visitors. Hyperbole aside, the sign spoke succinctly of Hawaiʻi's strategic importance and reinforced the notion of the thousands of servicemen in the Territory of Hawaiʻi that they were indeed on America's front line . . . a remote, yet strong and well-guarded outpost on the Pacific frontier.

Long-range aerial patrols and reconnaissance figured prominently in the defense of Hawaiʻi. Increasing congestion on the aprons and waterways at the Fleet Air Base on Ford Island made it imperative, however, that large-scale expansion of patrol plane activity on Oʻahu would require additional facilities. Consequently, the Navy looked to Mōkapu Peninsula and Kāneʻohe Bay as the site for a new naval air station on the island's windward shore, about three miles northeast of the village of Kāneʻohe, twelve miles from Honolulu (over the Nuʻuanu Pali), and fifteen air miles from Pearl Harbor.[1]

After obtaining approval on 10 August 1939, by declaration under the authority of the First War Powers Act, the Navy purchased Heleloa on the north shore of Kāneʻohe Bay, mostly beach and agricultural property, from Mr. Harold K. L. Castle of Honolulu.[2] Contractors

A view of a portion of the tract of land taken over by the Navy for the new air station at Kāneʻohe Bay. Note the location of the bulkhead, which defines the large fill area required for the hangar line, parking aprons, and landplane runway. (NARA II, 71-CA-156D-13067)

Kaneohe's temporary buildings along the thoroughfare that became Avenue D. Note the crushing plant at far right. View looking southeast on 28 March 1940. (NARA II, 71-CA-156D-13556)

commenced work at the base in September 1940 and continued through February 1941, completing numerous buildings along with roads and the landing mat.[3]

Cdr. Harold M. "Beauty" Martin arrived on 29 November, and the first group of thirteen sailors arrived shortly thereafter on 7 December. In late January 1941 Maj. John C. "Jiggs" Donehoo Jr., a native of Steubenville, Ohio, arrived to take command of the Marine Detachment. No officers quarters were prepared, so Donehoo took up residence in an empty room on the second deck of the soon-to-be-completed Barracks Building 7, just north of the Marine Barracks.[4]

Harold Montgomery Martin—a native of Bay Mills in Michigan's Upper Peninsula—received his appointment to the U.S. Naval Academy in 1915 and graduated with the Class of 1919, entering service early, in June 1918, due to World War I. Then-lt. (jg) Martin reported to NAS Pensacola for flight instruction on 16 May 1921. He transferred

Construction progress on the station's enlisted barracks as seen from atop the unfinished Administration Building on 29 August 1940, showing the covered walkway that connected the barracks buildings with the Mess Hall just out of the picture at right. On 7 December 1941, these three barracks buildings housed (l-r) VP-14 (Barracks 6), "Ship's Company" (Barracks 7), and the Marine Detachment (Barracks 8). The two barracks out of the photo to the north (at far left) housed VP-11 (Barracks 4) and VP-12 (Barracks 5). (NARA II, 71-CA-156A-13879)

Construction of Kaneohe's seaplane ramps and apron is well under way in this 29 November 1940 view. Note the Maintenance Hangar at right center and the ramps at left center. (NARA II, 71-CA-156D-14001)

into patrol aviation on 13 March 1934, when he assumed command of VP-10F. Promoted to commander on 21 July 1939, he received orders on 2 November 1940 to oversee, and eventually take command of, the new station under development at Kāne'ohe Bay. Martin reported on 29 November 1940, bringing with him his wife Elizabeth and son David and a diverse range of experience in aviation, administration, and command. The men liked and respected Martin, who presented a down-to-earth, rugged, and unpretentious character and a kindly appearance with eyes that were always smiling. AMM1c Walter J. Curylo, an NAP from VP-14, said that he never heard a single unkind remark about his skipper. Martin was "strict, but fair, and went by the book." Soon after Martin arrived at Kaneohe,

Cdr. Harold M. Martin addresses the men of NAS Kaneohe Bay during the base's commissioning ceremony on 15 February 1941. Behind Martin are (l-r) Lt. Cdr. Robert C. Warrack, executive officer; Maj. John C. Donehoo Jr., commander, Marine Detachment; and Lt. Cdr. Wilbur E. Kellum (MC), senior medical officer. (Kennedy)

The Navy Band strikes up "The Star-Spangled Banner" while Platoon Sgt. George L. Spence of the Marine color guard raises the flag during Kaneohe's commissioning ceremony on 15 February 1941. (Kennedy)

Three PBYs from NAS Pearl Harbor execute a dramatic flyover during the commissioning ceremony at NAS Kaneohe Bay. (NARA II, 80-G-410182)

he sat down on his typewriter box, "rolled up his sleeves and went to work."[5]

Although NAS Kaneohe Bay was far from complete, an allotment of 115 men arrived during mid-February. Although the seventy rates represented specialties required by the station, of the remaining men, forty sailors were relatively new enlistees at the rank of Sea2c, which left room for growth in the ensuing months, both in terms of numbers and experience.[6]

The new arrivals reported just in time to participate in the station's commissioning ceremony, which commenced at 1500 on 15 February 1941, at which time the station's ten officers and 118 enlisted men mustered at the base of the flagpole in front of the Administration Building, forming a hollow square with Cdr. Martin and the officers facing north, the Marine Detachment

west, the Navy enlisted men east, and the Navy band south. Martin opened the proceedings, reading relevant dispatches from the Secretary of the Navy and the commandant of the 14th Naval District and orders issued by the Bureau of Navigation. Following Martin's recitation, Lt. Cdr. Robert C. Warrack—the station's first executive officer—passed the national ensign to the color guard. Platoon Sgt. George L. Spence raised the colors just as the band struck up "The Star-Spangled Banner." From the direction of Kāne'ohe Bay, three PBYs from NAS Pearl Harbor flew in formation over the assemblage, dropping garlands of hibiscus. Martin set the watch, putting Kaneohe into business, after which Maj. Donehoo took command of the Marine Barracks.[7]

Less than a month after commissioning, air activity began at the station when, on 6 March 1941, Kaneohe received its first airplane, a Grumman J2F-1 (BuNo 0190), a veteran of four years of service at the Fleet Air Base and utility unit, and fresh from a major overhaul at NAS Pearl Harbor. As the runway to the west would not be ready for four months, the only way for the small, single-engine

amphibian to land and take off was via the dredged channel in Kāne'ohe Bay. Accordingly, the station commander's Duck made the inaugural flight, taking off from the water south of the aprons on 8 March 1941, just two days after its arrival. Large-scale operations started two days later, when the first Consolidated PBY-1 from VP-24 under Lt. Cdr. Dolph C. Allen set down in the blue water and taxied north to the seaplane ramps at 1145 on 10 March 1941. Beach crews hauled 24-P-1 up and onto the ramp, and the Catalina's crew clambered out and came on board the station, greeted by Cdr. Martin.[8]

On 15 April, the arrival of VP-26 (redesignated as VP-14 on 1 July) under Lt. Cdr. William T. Rassieur doubled the number of patrol aircraft at Kaneohe. More notably, that unit flew the late variant PBY-5s, the first

The first PBY arrives at 1145 on 10 March 1941, as crews prepare to move 24-P-1 (presumably Lt. Cdr. Dolph C. Allen's aircraft) onto one of the seaplane ramps at NAS Kaneohe Bay, greeted by the welcoming party at right. Note the three other PBYs in the distance, one under each wing and above the fuselage of 24-P-1. (Kennedy)

BuNo 0190, assigned to Cdr. Martin, makes the first aircraft landing on the partially completed runway at NAS Kaneohe Bay on 8 July 1941. Note the Maintenance Hangar in the distance at center right, as well as Hangar 2 then under construction. (NHHC, NH 96662)

such planes to be based on O'ahu. The squadron's complement boasted twelve of the first thirty-two such aircraft to roll off the assembly lines at Consolidated Aircraft Corporation from November 1940 through February 1941. Although the newly arrived –5 variants were the harbingers of many to come, it would take five months for the Navy to re-equip the other squadrons on the windward shore.[9]

By mid-July, the PBY-1s of VP-11 (formerly VP-23 as of 1 July), transferred from NAS Pearl Harbor to NAS Kaneohe Bay, flew east from Ford Island, landed in Kāne'ohe Bay, and turned north toward the beach-

ing parties waiting near the seaplane ramps. The assignment of that unit set in place PatWing 1's complement of three squadrons.[10]

The months of October and November proved a time of significant transition at Kaneohe. By the fall of 1941, the Consolidated Aircraft Corporation plant in San Diego stood ready to deliver late-model Catalinas to Rear Adm. Patrick N. L. Bellinger's Hawai'i-based patrol wings.[11] Such a change entailed substantial logistical difficulties. So as not to lay Kaneohe bare in the face of the demands of patrols and training on O'ahu, only one of its three squadrons was to undertake the ferrying mission to the West Coast at any given time. Such a movement also required a great deal of preparation of both planes and people. The aging PBY-1s from VP-11 and VP-24 were all due for exchange stateside, as were the older PBY-5s of VP-14.

Hangar line at NAS Kaneohe Bay looking north on 1 October 1941, just prior to VP-11's departure for San Diego two days hence. A complement of thirty-seven PBYs lies on the aprons, with VP-11 having thirteen aircraft assigned rather than the customary twelve. Close examination of the original print shows that seven of VP-11's PBYs (east and south of Hangar 1) have light-colored vertical stabilizers, although none of the aircraft present are in the experimental camouflage that appears nine days later during VP-11's absence in San Diego. (NARA II, 80-G-279362, cropped)

The first squadron to take delivery of the PBY-5s was VP-11. Following maintenance and preparations for the twenty-plus-hour flight to San Diego, the squadron departed en masse from Kāne'ohe Bay at 1030 on 3 October 1941. The exhausted crews settled into quarters for three days of rest, after which skeleton crews transferred the PBY-1s to training units in Texas and Florida. After taking civilian air transportation to San Diego, the crews began familiarizing and testing their new planes, and after fifteen days the men of the squadron loaded their gear and boarded their new aircraft for the return flight to Hawai'i.[12]

With the large seaplane tender *Wright* (AV-1) and the seaplane tender (destroyer) *Ballard* (AVD-10) acting as plane guards out from O'ahu and San Diego, twelve PBYs from VP-11 took off separately starting at about 1330 on 27 October, with the planes proceeding independently to O'ahu, arriving at Kaneohe during the forenoon watch of 28 October. Simultaneously, six crews from VP-12 (the future VP-24), having received their aircraft during the first week of August, took off at approximately the same time, bound for NAS Pearl Harbor.[13]

ACMM Edward Lupenui, circa 1942, PBY crewman and in-flight chef during the 27/28 October 1941 flight from San Diego to Kaneohe. (O'Conner)

Lt. (jg) William F. "Red" Raborn Jr. while posted to VF-5B on board the carrier *Lexington* (CV-2), circa 1 August 1934. (NPRC, St. Louis)

During the return flight to Kaneohe, the crew of 11-P-5 (BuNo 2426), under Ens. Norris A. Johnson, A-V(N), enjoyed a sumptuous midnight feast courtesy of AMM1c Edward Lupenui, a native of Hawai'i and culinary expert, who had arranged for a package of steaks to be shipped on board. At approximately the midpoint of the flight, he fired up a hotplate in the small galley near the navigation table. With steaks ready singly or in pairs, the aroma of the seared beef wafted through the drafty aircraft for quite some time. Having already immersed himself thoroughly in the "uptown" Kaneohe lifestyle, Ens. Charles P. Muckenthaler, A-V(N), the junior pilot and navigator, savored the meal, remembering it as "quite an event." Lt. William F. "Red" Raborn Jr. (future ordnance officer on the staff of Cdr. Knefler "Stuffy" McGinnis, ComPatWing 1), a passenger on board 11-P-5, was similarly impressed, as the in-flight steak was his first.[14]

During VP-11's absence, experimentation was under way at Kaneohe to apply alternative camouflage to the PBYs of Lt. Cdr. Argyll E. Buckley's VP-24 (which had not yet changed its designation to VP-12). PatWing 1 began the experiments during the first two weeks of October, with the darker colors officially prescribed later by Rear Adm. John S. McCain, ComAirScoFor. An aerial photograph of the base dated 10 October shows six aircraft—almost surely the PBY-1s of VP-24—painted in such a manner. It is also certain that six of the PBYs from VP-11 were painted in similar manner, either in San Diego or after their arrival at Kaneohe.[15]

During VP-11's month-long absence, preparations went forward among Lt. Cdr. Buckley's VP-24 crews to exchange the last PBY-1s of PatWing 1 at San Diego. Leaving VP-14 as the air station's sole squadron tenant for twenty-three hours, the thirteen PBY-1s took off

Vertical view of the warm-up and parking aprons near Hangar 1 at Kaneohe on 10 October 1941, which shows the change in the livery for six PBYs. In this photo, with VP-14's parking area out of the picture at left and with VP-11 in San Diego on 10 October, it is certain that these aircraft are PBY-1s from then VP-24, occupying space on the aprons that was assigned to VP-11 on the day of the Japanese attack. Judging from the date of the image, it is almost certain that experimentation occurred with the new camouflage (applied to aircraft from VP-24) prior to the ComAirScoFor directive from 13 October. VP-24 turned over these aircraft in San Diego on 28 October. Meanwhile, six of the new aircraft from VP-11 received similar applications of the new camouflage. On 26 November, the camouflage was pronounced a success by Rear Adm. McCain, indicating "marked superiority over [the] standard method of painting." (NARA II, 80-G-279381, cropped)

A PBY-5 at NAS San Diego on 7 October 1941, painted in a multicolor camouflage scheme. (Cressman)

and arrived in San Diego early on 28 October. Effective that date, the squadron's designation was changed to VP-12. Turning in their planes at San Diego, the crews from VP-12 remained there, performed flight tests, and departed on an overnight flight that put them on the waters of Kāne'ohe Bay at 0840 on 8 November. At that juncture, PatWing 1 became the first of Rear Adm. Bellinger's two wings to be fully equipped with PBY-5s.[16]

With the first week of November drawing to a close, improvement of equipment for Hawai'i's patrol squadrons involved two units, one each from PatWings 1 and 2. During 5–7 November, VP-14 lay in upkeep at NAS Kaneohe Bay, intent on exchanging its early production PBY-5s, acquired in January and February, for a dozen newer aircraft. At NAS Pearl Harbor, meanwhile, VP-23 likewise made ready for the flight stateside to replace its PBY-2s.[17]

The two squadrons departed O'ahu on 8 November, arriving at NAS San Diego the next morning. There the crews rested while changing out their old planes. After the completion of rigorous flight tests, the two Hawai'i-based squadrons judged the aircraft fit for service. With the small seaplane tender (ex-minesweeper) *Pelican* (AVP-6) and seaplane tender (destroyer) *Thornton* (AVD-11) plane guarding, VP-14 and VP-23 departed San Diego on 22 November, arriving in Hawai'i the next day.[18]

By late 1941, NAS Kaneohe Bay stood as a critical component of the Hawaiian defenses. As the squadrons basing there broke in their new PBYs, the air station still looked brand new. Its open, spacious, and undeveloped character invited comparison to the undulating grasslands of the American Southwest. SK2c Jamie R. Murphy observed that, "Acreage-wise . . . [Kaneohe] would make a good-sized Texas ranch." Despite constant development at the station during 1940 and 1941, the men still regarded the facility as small and quite beautiful.[19]

Blessed by beautiful surroundings and a relaxed work schedule, the morale of the men remained uniformly high into the late months of 1941, with the vast majority of the men enjoying the environment and their jobs.

Notable exceptions occurred in the months just before the war with the arrival of a number of reservists, whose sentiment differed from the prevailing mood at the base. Many of the men were not financially able to bring their families out to the islands and thus were not enthusiastic about the calls to return to active service.[20]

Having the money for a night out in Waikīkī or anywhere else proved always an issue. Accordingly, most of the men depended on the familiar red buses of "Windward Transit" to provide economical conveyance to Oʻahu's hot spots—twenty-five cents for a one-way trip into Honolulu. An inexpensive though lengthy conveyance, the wooden vehicles took about an hour to negotiate the serpentine thoroughfare that traversed the Nuʻuanu Pali, winding their way down into Honolulu on the south side of the Koʻolaus. The buses invariably disgorged their eager passengers onto the busy streets of Honolulu at the YMCA at 250 South Hotel Street, a location that fronted the Black Cat Café.

Sometimes the long ride into the city provided a thrill a minute, with the "Red Rocket" scraping against volcanic outcroppings and guard rails on either side of the road. But nothing seemed to faze the determined bus drivers, who were apparently hell-bent on maintaining the schedules.[21]

In the latter months of 1941, however, the skies darkened over "Mōkapu, the beautiful peninsula." The situation in the Far East grew increasingly critical in the wake of Japan's occupation of Indo-China that prompted an American embargo of oil and scrap iron on 26 July.[22] In mid-October, the collapse of the Konoe government further elevated the sense of crisis in Washington. By the end of November 1941, based on intelligence derived from Japanese diplomatic message traffic, it was apparent to the United States that relations with Japan had reached a breaking point, as the "negotiations . . . looking toward stabilization of conditions in the Pacific [had] ceased." On 28 November, OpNav sent a "war warning" message to Adm. Husband E. Kimmel (CinCPac) that outlined the grave circumstances and warned that "an aggressive move by Japan [was] expected in the next few days."[23]

A city bus (not the "Red Rocket") stands at the drop-off point near the familiar "Army and Navy Y.M.C.A" sign at 250 South Hotel Street. View circa 1930s. (Wenger)

The Black Cat Café—across Hotel Street from the Army and Navy YMCA—was among the first eating establishments that servicemen encountered when coming into Honolulu on the bus lines. The principal hallmark of the locale was the multitude of men crowding the nearby streets and sidewalks. Note the red triangle of the YMCA sign just below and right of the café sign. (USAR 1592)

On 29 November, in light of the threat of sabotage and the tense international situation, Cdr. Martin addressed his men on the parade ground. Martin sternly admonished those who stood before him, re-emphasizing the importance of the standing orders that had been issued and of maintaining readiness in light of current conditions.[24]

During the first week in December, Kaneohe's PBY squadrons practiced locating, shadowing, and attacking an "invading" force at night. Daytime drills incorporated torpedo and high-altitude bombing assaults during the morning hours. Similarly, the supporting seaplane tenders simulated detection of inbound air strikes, conducted evasive maneuvers and practiced damage control and the refueling and towing of disabled ships. These exercises capped the intensive training after Adm. Kimmel assumed command as CinCUS on 1 February.

Cdr. Harold Montgomery "Beauty" Martin, command-ing officer, NAS Kaneohe Bay, shown here seated in his second-floor office in the Administration Building on 27 November 1941. Note Pu'u Hawai'iloa in the background. (NHHC, NH 96661)

For men assigned to the station, Cdr. Martin tended to dispense with Saturday inspections, feeling that his men needed to accord priority to maintaining the sta-tion in top operating trim. On that weekend, however, late developments on Friday, 5 December, caused Mar-tin to order just such an inspection for the following morning, as he had received a warning regarding the "possibilities of sabotage which were unusually immi-nent." Accordingly, in the plan for the day for Saturday, 6 December, Martin mustered the station's comple-ment on the parade ground in front of the Adminis-tration Building.

In an unusual move, however, rather than conduct-ing the inspection, for the second time in two weeks Martin ordered the division officers to bring the sail-ors in close for an announcement. Drawn up almost directly in front of his commanding officer, AMM3c Guy C. Avery saw that the skipper seemed "intensely nervous." Echoing his admonition of 29 November, Martin said, "Men, I have called you together here this morning to tell you to keep your eyes and ears open and be on the alert every moment. You are probably the nearest [to] war that you will ever be without actually being in it." With that, he instructed the division offi-cers to take charge, dismiss, and clear the field.[25]

After a quiet Saturday evening, daybreak on O'ahu's windward shore on 7 December 1941, and the serenity indigenous to "Mōkapu, the beautiful peninsula" and its reef-encrusted waters and shores, reflected tranquil-ity for the 303 Navy men, 31 officers, and 95 Marines assigned to the station and three patrol squadrons bil-leted at Kaneohe, enticing some to grab a few extra hours of rest. The men who had returned from liberty

NAS Kaneohe Bay and "Mōkapu, the beautiful peninsula" viewed from ten thousand feet looking southwest on 24 November 1941, two weeks prior to the Japanese attack and three days prior to the "war warning" from Washington. Note the large runway at right still under construction. Preparations are well under way for additional hangar facilities with footings poured for a third structure on the west end of the warm-up platform and utility excavation in progress for yet another hangar destined to replace the small Maintenance Hangar midway between the two large existing hangars. That the base is a "work in progress" is plainly evident, although the principal buildings that house the officers and men are nearing completion, such as the enlisted barracks northeast of the hangars, the married enlisted housing east of the extinct volcano Pu'u Hawai'iloa, and the officers' housing along the north shore of the peninsula. Of particular interest is Pu'u Hawai'iloa itself at left center, with the station's control tower perched atop the hill's summit. (NARA II, 80-G-418995, cropped)

the previous night used those pleasant morning hours to sleep off the effects of revelry in Honolulu and elsewhere.[26]

In view of the international tensions that had prompted the "war warning" and had animated Cdr. Martin's remarks of the previous day, Sunday, 7 December, proved a normal workday—not a day of rest—for several PBY crews. PatWing 1 drew the responsibility for the morning security patrols and for the "daily search of operating areas as directed" prescribed in Pacific Fleet Confidential Letter 2CL-41 (Revised).[27]

That morning, the burden of the early-morning search mission lay upon VP-14. Accordingly, crews readied three aircraft for the flights. An hour after the end of the mid-watch, AOM3c Jackson L. Harris, on duty in the Bombsight workshop, installed bombsights in each of the PBY-5s waiting on the apron close to Hangar 2. With all preparations complete, at 0630, three PBYs, equipped with depth charges, machine guns, and ammunition, skimmed across the waters of Kāne'ohe Bay and lifted away. The three flying boats had orders to fan out for searches of a roughly 145-degree quadrant

Ens. William P. Tanner Jr., A-V(N), circa 18 August 1941, while assigned to VP-14 at NAS Kaneohe Bay. (NPRC, St. Louis)

Ens. Thomas W. Hillis, A-V(N), circa 30 November 1940, while assigned to VP-14 at NAS San Diego. (NPRC, St. Louis)

Ens. Otto F. Meyer Jr., A-V(N), circa 30 November 1940, while assigned to VP-14 at NAS San Diego. (NPRC, St. Louis)

that covered operating areas southeast, south, and west of Oʻahu.[28]

The lead crew under Ens. William P. "Bill" Tanner Jr. A-V(N), in 14-P-1 (BuNo 2419) had orders to patrol the naval defensive sea area and the approaches immediately south of Pearl Harbor's entrance channel. Tanner then fanned out far to the west and southwest of the island. Ens. Otto F. "Freddie" Meyer Jr.'s crew in 14-P-2 (BuNo 2418) flew due south of Oʻahu and searched the operating areas that lay south and southwest of the island, flying two large out-and-back tracks, south and north. Ens. Thomas W. "Tommie" Hillis, A-V(N), in 14-P-3 (BuNo 2420) shaped courses that produced a near-mirror-image of Meyer's pattern, first flying southeast from Kaneohe with the emerging sun in his windshield. The crew then conducted two large out-and-back searches over the channels separating Oʻahu and Molokaʻi and Lānaʻi to the southeast, and then patrolled the operating areas south of Oʻahu.[29]

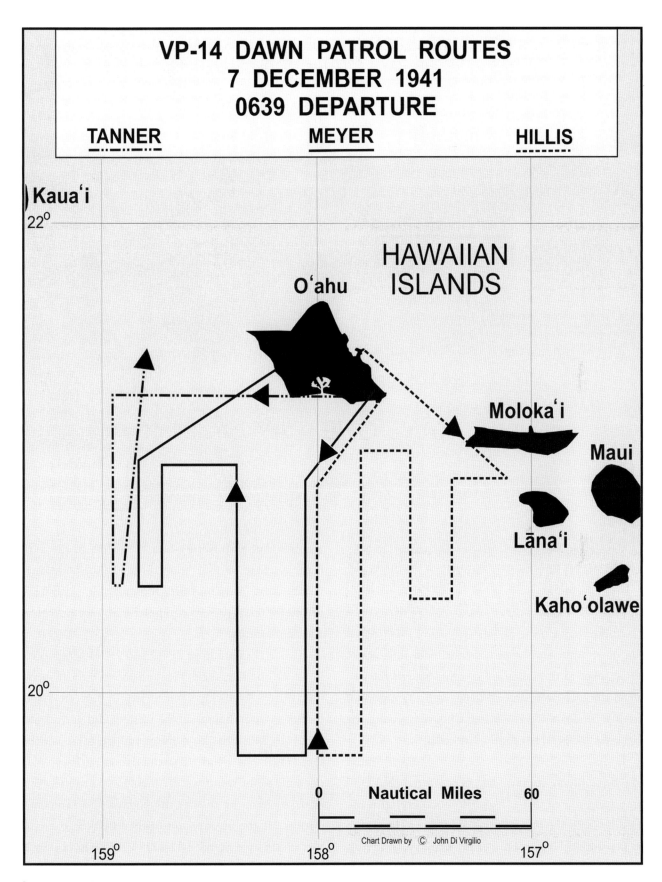

Search patterns flown by Tanner, Meyer, and Hillis during the morning security patrols on 7 December 1941. (Di Virgilio)

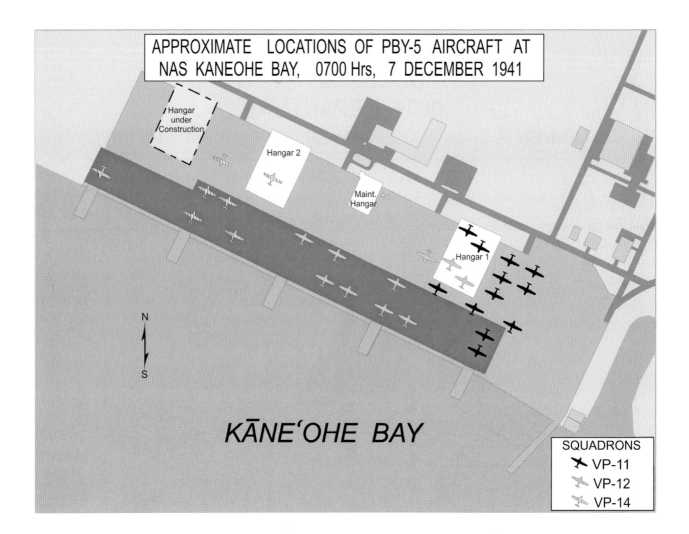

APPROXIMATE LOCATIONS OF PBY-5 AIRCRAFT AT
NAS KANEOHE BAY, 0700 Hrs, 7 DECEMBER 1941

Hangar
under
Construction

Hangar 2

Maint.
Hangar

Hangar 1

N

S

KĀNEʻOHE BAY

SQUADRONS
✈ VP-11
✈ VP-12
✈ VP-14

The hangar line, aprons, and seaplane ramps at NAS Kaneohe Bay, showing aircraft present on the morning of 7 December 1941. Note that the moored PBYs are at left and off the map below. (Di Virgilio)

As the engine noise of the dawn patrol faded, peace and quiet again enveloped Kaneohe, with little activity apparent to the untrained eye. Sunday was the day when the men were able to sleep, with the mess hall serving breakfast for a few extra hours, allowing for extra rest and breakfast for the late risers.[30]

Looks, however, were deceiving. Rear Adm. Claude C. Bloch, commandant of the 14th Naval District, had ordered that a "Baker 5" condition of readiness be maintained at all times, which mandated that 50 percent of the patrol planes in Hawaiʻi be ready on four hours' notice. NAS Kaneohe Bay exceeded that

requirement, with twenty-one of its PBY-5s (58 percent) available on four hours' notice. Nine additional Catalinas sat ready on thirty minutes' notice, all thirty-three aircraft present equipped with machine guns and ammunition.[31]

Two PBYs each from VP-12 and VP-14 lay moored in Kaⁿeʻohe Bay, likely on a line between the "Coconut Grove"—a thickly wooded area of palm trees and former vacation houses on the western end of Mōkapu Peninsula between the runway and the west end of the hangar line—and "Coconut Island" (Mokuoloʻe) one mile to the southwest.[32] An engineer manned each plane, standing by to start the engines at a moment's notice. Of the twenty-nine other PBY-5s present, two aircraft each from VP-11 and VP-12 sat in Hangar 1 undergoing maintenance (having armor and self-sealing

A portion of the PBY mooring area south of the station in Ka̅ne'ohe Bay, 16 October 1941. Note the "Coconut Grove" at lower right and Coconut Island (Mokuolo'e) at upper center. Seven PBYs (probably from VP-14) are present. The smaller plane at lower right is an F4F from the *Enterprise*, with wheels down at low altitude. (NARA II, 80-G-418994)

fuel tanks installed, among other things), while one VP-14 machine sat in the nearly completed Hangar 2 for an engine check. Five machines from VP-11 sat on the apron east of Hangar 1, with the remaining nineteen flying boats from all three squadrons arrayed at various positions along the east-west axis of the warmup platform.[33]

Kaneohe, however, lacked heavy antiaircraft defenses, as earlier in the weekend the Army had withdrawn elements of the 98th Coast Artillery (AA), placed there during the Hawaiian Department's No. 1 Alert status.[34] Standing down from the weeklong alert, the Army ordered all such units to their home bases from their dispersed positions. That circumstance notwithstanding, at dawn on 7 December, NAS Kaneohe Bay stood prepared to meet the day, following to the letter its directive regarding the required state of readiness.[35]

# TWO

# "THIS IS THE FIRST TIME I'VE EVER SEEN THE ARMY WORKING ON SUNDAY"

While the sun crept over the horizon and cast long shadows reaching to the northwest, noteworthy coded message traffic found its way into the radio logs in Kaneohe's communications office on the second floor of the Administration Building at 0706. While conducting the morning security patrol south of Oʻahu, a PBY from PatWing 1 (Ens. Tanner's 14-P-1) had "Sunk an enemy submarine one mile south [of] Pearl Harbor."[1]

Ultimately, the communications duty officer called over to Hangar 2 and contacted Lt. Murray Hanson.[2] Hanson was the VP-14 division commander, squadron communications officer, and a Perrysville, Ohio, native who was then "killing time in [the] hangar, reading the morning paper."[3] Hanson learned that one of his squadron's planes had just informed Adm. Kimmel's headquarters that it had sighted and bombed a submarine one mile south of Ford Island. CinCPac "had sent . . . a Jig on it," that is, requesting that Ens. Tanner's radioman verify and repeat the message. The time was 0730.

Hanson proceeded straightaway to the Administration Building. Once there, he waited upstairs in the communications office for the message to be repeated, making small talk and looking out the windows at the beautiful Hawaiian morning and the sunlit Koʻolaus.

It occurred to no one that "the message was anything but spurious." Tanner's radioman had simply picked the wrong code group and changed the message's meaning. Nonetheless, despite this "obvious error," efforts to verify the sinking went forward.[4]

Meanwhile, from officers down to the newest "boots," Kaneohe's servicemen and dependents immersed themselves in the beauty and tranquility of a typical winter morning in Hawaiʻi, with the sunlight just strong enough for warmth and with just enough of a northeasterly breeze for comfort. Cdr. Martin, in his quarters, closest of all officer billets to the sea, relaxed over a cup of coffee in his blue silk pajamas and prepared to make cocoa for David, his thirteen-year-old son, who was then reading the morning paper in front of a big window.[5]

Three-quarters of a mile to the southwest in Kaneohe's dispensary, Lt. Cdr. Herman P. McCrimmon—one of the station's senior surgeons and a burly east Texas native—sat in his office dressed in whites with feet propped on the desk, waiting for the paperboy. After attending medical school to escape a life of "picking cotton and watermelons," "Mac" McCrimmon landed an idyllic billet in Hawaiʻi, satisfied that he and his family were perfectly safe, as far from the European war as they could be. With great delight, he looked forward to being picked up by his redheaded wife, Adelaide, during the forenoon watch at 1000 and to the late morning and afternoon he would spend with her and their two sons, "Jerry" and "Packy."[6]

The café in the Enlisted Recreation Building seemed unusually busy for a Sunday morning. AOM3c Cecil I. Hollingshead, a twenty-one-year-old Texan, appeared from Barracks 4, adjacent to the recreation building. Hollingshead slept late after a day off and missed early breakfast, but got up at 0700 and decided on a nice sit-

down meal. Similarly, Raleigh, North Carolina, native EM3c Herman W. Barber arose late, preferring the quieter atmosphere of the restaurant, where he ordered ham and eggs. Oklahoman AMM2c Arthur R. Grace Jr. of VP-11 finished breakfast and stepped outside. He spotted planes over the station, which was not unusual, particularly as the men were accustomed to simulated strafing runs on the PBYs by Army Air Force pursuit pilots, both in the water and on the aprons.[7]

Some devout souls made their way to divine services, among them AMM1c (NAP) Joseph C. Engel of VP-12, his wife Angie, and their fourteen-month-old son Joseph Jr. Leaving for church, which was just outside the main gate, Engel turned and waved to AMM1c (NAP) Dale S. "Chubby" Lyons, a fellow NAP and squadron-mate with eight years of service. Lyons headed in the opposite direction from his base residence at 409-D Jarros Drive toward Hangar 1, where he intended to paint a bicycle for his son, John Robert, who was two months short of his third birthday.[8]

Working from a platform atop a wheeled scaffold, a maintenance crew from VP-11 services 11-P-4 (BuNo 2423) in Hangar 1 at NAS Kaneohe Bay. One particular feature of the aircraft—the air scoops of the downdraft carburetors, positioned at top center inside the cowlings and above the Pratt & Whitney R-1830-82 engines— identify the aircraft as a PBY-5 and thus date the photo from November or December 1941. Note the station's J2F-1 Duck in the background at left. (Dohrmann)

In contrast to the relative peace and quiet of the quarters and café, the two large hangars hummed with activity, with scheduled modifications moving forward, including installation of armor, self-sealing fuel tanks, and the emergency replacement of cracked nose sections on the engines for several PBYs. In Hangar 1, Ens. Rodney S. Foss, D-V(G), of VP-11, Arkansas native and a May 1941 graduate of the Naval Reserve Midshipmen's School at Northwestern University, supervised a work crew that had been toiling all night installing armor and self-sealing tanks in 11-P-4 (BuNo 2423), the first PBY-5 in the squadron to benefit from such improvements. By 0700, Foss had allowed some of the men to return to their barracks, while others had just secured from breakfast. While the sailors sipped their coffee and looked out at the "mirror slick" bay there was hardly a breeze blowing.[9]

On the station's far western edge at the southwest corner of the runway, in the bungalow that served as billet for the seamen and ratings who maintained Kaneohe's two utility planes, AMM3c Avery and AMM2c Lester Morris dozed in their bunks upstairs on the bungalow's sun porch, with all the other men away at breakfast. Avery then arose, dressed, and gazed out to sea, impressed by the utter tranquility of the scene, the light breeze, bright sun, and "dream-inducing quietness. All was well with the world."[10]

All was not well, however, in the early morning hours of 7 December. After traversing the stormy north Pacific, a powerful Japanese naval task force of six aircraft carriers—with supporting battleships, cruisers, destroyers, and submarines—steamed two hundred miles north of O'ahu. From that position, the carriers had already put aloft 183 fighters, carrier bombers, and carrier attack planes. Their plans called for eleven Type 0 carrier fighters from the 5th Carrier Division—five under Lt. Kaneko Tadashi of the *Shōkaku* and six under Lt. Satō Masao of the *Zuikaku*, with Lt. Kaneko in command—to strafe NAS Kaneohe Bay.

Prior to landfall during the approach to O'ahu, overall fighter commander Lt. Cdr. Itaya Shigeru antic-ipated enemy opposition and ordered his force to begin a general climb to six thousand meters to maintain an altitude advantage over any American fighters that may have been vectored north of O'ahu. Accordingly, the *kansen* pilots donned their oxygen masks and gained altitude. If they found themselves opposed by U.S. fighters, Lt. Kaneko's brood was to provide top cover over the harbor at six thousand meters. To the utter amazement of the Japanese, however, no American planes contested their approach.[11]

Just then, the northern tip of O'ahu came into view, followed soon by Cdr. Fuchida Mitsuo's deployment order and "surprise" flare, which prompted most of Itaya's pilots to abandon their plans to concentrate over Pearl Harbor and to proceed instead with attacks on the island's airfields. Lt. Kaneko's instructions were to speed toward the installations on eastern O'ahu at an altitude of 4,500 meters. Although his top priority was now NAS Kaneohe Bay, if there were insufficient targets present there he was to shift farther southeast and attack Bellows Field, ten miles down the coast.[12]

Hence from a position generally northeast of Kahuku Point, the *Shōkaku* and *Zuikaku* fighter units formed up, peeled away to the southeast at 0745, and sped down the northeast side of the Ko'olau Range, skirting the windward shore of O'ahu at the designated altitude. Kaneko's fighters—the first to charge down toward their objective—made ready to seize control of the air and attack their primary target, the PBYs at NAS Kaneohe Bay.

Everything went smoothly until the Japanese encountered a civilian plane just north of the Mormon Temple five miles down the northeast shore and about ten miles from the point of deployment. An Aeronca 65TC Tandem (NC-38838), rented from Marguerite Gambo by the Hui Lele Flying Club, droned at an altitude of one thousand feet just offshore, heading southwest toward Laie.[13] Instructor Nathan G. "Tommy" Tomberlin had arisen early at his 4458 Kahala Avenue residence for a lesson with student James "Jimmy" Duncan, a civilian shipfitter from Honolulu. Apparently, with or without orders, several of Kaneko's subordinates dove to the attack and squeezed off a few short bursts.

Fortunately for Tomberlin and Duncan, the Aeronca sustained nonfatal, though significant, damage and the "Zeros" roared past, making no effort to follow up their initial runs. The encounter was noteworthy, however, as it represented the Japanese naval air arm's first shots of the war, albeit directed at defenseless civilians. Perhaps a case of the jitters had prompted the fighters to engage in such an indiscriminate and wasteful attack. WO Abe Yasujirō, Lt. Kaneko's wingman, later admitted to being nervous over meeting American fighter pilots for the first time. Nonetheless, despite any jitters and with their appetite for action whetted, Kaneko's aggressive brood

sped away from the Mormon Temple on a southeasterly course toward Kāne'ohe Bay.[14]

When Lt. Kaneko's fighter unit resumed its southeasterly track, the pilots caught a glimpse of their objective through the diminishing cloud cover and verified two critical pieces of intelligence. First, many PBY flying boats sat on the aprons, while others lay moored in the bay south of the runway, thus requiring no advance toward the secondary target at Bellows Field. Second, the skies ahead looked devoid of any American defenders. Accordingly, Kaneko gave his men the green light for the attack on Kaneohe. From 4,500 meters, the eleven fighters dove to the attack. Approaching the north coast of the Mōkapu Peninsula, Kaneko led his men into an eastward turn to set up their initial runs from upwind, about ten clicks of the compass north of east.[15] On the ground, at about 0750, American sailors and Marines observed a group of aircraft speeding across the station at low altitude from the west.[16]

Meanwhile, engine noise attracted the attention of Commander Martin and his son. Even after going to the

The Mormon Temple complex two miles south of the hamlet of Kahuku and the site of the encounter between Marguerite Gambo's Aeronca from the Hui Lele Flying Club and fighters from the 5th Carrier Division. View taken on 16 February 1939. (USAHI, RG36S, Photo Album, Denver Gray Collection)

Commanding Officer's Quarters, the house of Cdr. Harold M. "Beauty" Martin, showing the front elevation, looking northeast on 2 September 1941. (NARA II, 71-CA-156B-14541)

NAS Kaneohe Bay's Administration Building, looking southwest on 9 April 1941, and Cdr. Martin's destination on the morning of 7 December. His office was on the second floor, above the OOD office and just to the right of the apse at center, behind the saluting gun at far right. (NARA II, 71-CA-156B-14233)

window of his quarters, Martin thought nothing of it because he assumed that the aircraft were from the carrier *Enterprise* (CV-6), returning to Oʻahu after a mysterious absence of over a week. Shortly thereafter, however, the planes executed a right-hand turn, a violation of the station's flight rules. Approaching nearly head-on at about eight hundred feet of altitude, the aircraft proved difficult to identify positively, but when they banked and exposed their fuselages, David, who now had his nose pressed against the window glass, noted quite correctly that "they had red circles on them."

The elder Martin recognized instantly the identity of the planes. He hurried to the bedroom, grabbed a pair of trousers and a shirt, pulled them on over his pajamas, and ran to his car for the mile-long drive south toward the flight line and his office on the second floor of the Administration Building. Just as he sat behind the wheel, the firing started. Martin cranked the ignition and raced away at breakneck speed toward his post in clear violation of the 15 mph speed limit he himself had imposed. Martin estimated that he was doing about 50 mph, with tires squealing at every turn. The noise sent people running to their windows, and even venturing outside, to identify the scofflaw. At that moment, the group of Japanese aircraft—hidden for the moment by Puʻu Hawaiʻiloa, the large hill that separated the officer housing on the Mōkapu Peninsula's north shore from the hangar line and buildings to the south—reappeared at rooftop level, one of them strafing the control tower atop the hill.[17]

Racing around Puʻu Hawaiʻiloa to the east, Martin made a hard left turn into the station proper, screeching by Kaneohe's post office (formerly the gate house). By the time he reached his destination, the "firing had become quite heavy and the first plane in the water began to burn." Running inside, he placed an immediate telephone call to the 14th Naval District Headquarters, informing duty officer Lt. Cdr. Harold Kaminski, D-V(G), that Kaneohe was under attack. At that juncture, the headquarters passed to Martin news of the action over Pearl Harbor, which laid to rest any supposition that the raid on Kaneohe was an isolated incident.

As Martin turned to the tasks at hand, the response of those in the building, both military and civilian workers alike, impressed him. "There was no panic. Everyone went right to work battling back and doing his job."[18]

Elsewhere in the Administration Building, while still awaiting confirmation of the submarine incident south of Oʻahu, Lt. Hanson and the communications duty officer looked out of the second-floor windows and heard low-flying planes. One remarked, "This is the first time I've ever seen the Army working on Sunday." Just as one of the aircraft "passed low over the seaplane operating area," a PBY-5 riding at anchor in the bay burst into flames. "Almost simultaneously," Hanson observed, "the low flying aircraft did a chandelle, and as he rolled away from us I saw the 'meatball,' the rising sun insignia of the Japanese naval arm on the underside of the Zero's wing." It was 0752. At that moment, Hanson thought of his pregnant wife, Margot, and whether or not he would live to see her again.[19]

"With realization came action." Hanson ran downstairs to the officer of the day's office in the apse, just below Cdr. Martin's office, shouting that the station was under air attack by the Japanese and that the OOD should sound the alarm and notify his commanding officer. The OOD had come to the same conclusion independently, but when he and Hanson went to sound the alarm, they found that none existed. Makeshift arrangements called for the civilian workmen's steam whistle on the timekeeper's shack to be used for such a purpose, but since there was no key for the padlock and no steam, there was no alarm. Hanson then called VP-14 skipper, Lt. Thurston B. Clark, then with his wife Jane, daughter Fairfax, and son Arthur at their residence in Quarters "V."[20] Clark was already aware of events and arrived soon after, strafed while en route. After breaking out .45-caliber automatic pistols from the OOD Armory, both men crouched behind a corner of the Administration Building, squeezing off shots at the Japanese fighters as they roared by.[21]

In all likelihood it was a civilian, Samuel K. "Sam" Aweau Sr., who first passed word of the attack up the line. Born and reared on the windward shore at Kaʻaʻawa, Aweau was a general labor foreman and heavy equipment supervisor at

Lt. (jg) Murray Hanson, circa June 1937, upon completion of flight training at NAS Pensacola, just prior to his transfer to VS-42 on board the aircraft carrier *Ranger* (CV-4). Note the "aviator tan line" on Hanson's forehead. (NPRC, St. Louis)

Lt. (jg) Thurston B. Clark, circa 15 July 1934, while undergoing flight training at NAS Pensacola. (NPRC, St. Louis)

Kaneohe, employed there by Contractors, Pacific Naval Air Bases since September 1939. Realizing the true nature of events, he rushed to a telephone and called Bellows Field. "Kaneohe," he yelled into the receiver, "is being bombed by Japanese planes!" The message recipient proved disbelieving, however, and advised Aweau to "Go read the funny papers!" Frustrated but undeterred, Aweau telephoned his foreman at Hickam Field, pleading with him to pass the word along, again to no avail. "Drunk again?" retorted the supervisor. Aweau, determined to verify his original observations once and for all, went back to the hangar line and confirmed his suspicions when he found himself on the receiving end of a strafing run; Aweau leapt from his car and scrambled into the bushes.[22]

At the restaurant in the Enlisted Recreation Building, after EM3c Herman W. Barber had just ordered his ham and eggs, some of the other men said, "Well, the Army's

putting on a show for us." The restaurant was in the first-floor apse, with windows on all sides. The dozen or so sailors, along with the four waitresses and cooks, dropped what they were doing and ran to the booths along the west windows to watch the spectacle. AMM2c Grace had just stepped outside moments earlier and had spied numerous aircraft over the station, which was not unusual.[23]

Barber remained seated, patiently waiting to be served. With the arrival of his ham and eggs, he was all set to begin eating when he heard another sailor exclaim, "There's smoke coming up from the hangars!" Everyone ran back to the windows to look, but their view was blocked by the Administration Building to the southwest. Barber got up from the counter and ran south to the barracks where he was to report in case of fire. Upon arriving, he received the word, "We're under attack! You guys take off and go to the armory to get a weapon!" Simultaneously, someone back in the restaurant commented, "Why, hell, you can't

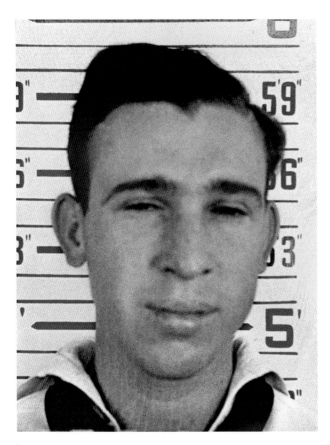

Sea2c Arthur R. Grace, circa 1940. (NARA, St. Louis)

fire blanks in a machine gun!" One of the fighters made a half roll, revealing the *hinomaru*. At that point, AMM2c Grace started for Hangar 1, running the entire mile that separated the restaurant from the hangar line to the southwest. By the time he arrived, the fighters had circled the station and had begun their second pass.[24]

Under the upward gaze of the men in Hangar 1, then drinking coffee in the south side shops, fighters appeared suddenly, dove out of the wind, and machine-gunned the PBYs in the bay. On one hand, it was quite normal for pursuit pilots from Wheeler Field to try and scare the pants off the men at Kaneohe with mock attacks, even with airborne PBYs. Just then, however, one of the aircraft burst into flames. Seeing from an office window the flying boat catch fire, AMM2c Otto V. Horky of Staunton, Illinois, pitied the poor U.S. Army pilot: "Oh boy, he had too much to drink last night. Will he get court-martialed?!"[25]

Almost all the men in the hangar's engineering office then ran the 175 yards to the shore even though there was no boat there and thus no way to rescue AMM2c Walter S. Brown, a Nebraskan and former schoolteacher, and AMM1c (NAP) Daniel T. Griffin, a pilot with almost four years' experience, the engineer plane guards standing watch in the pair of PBYs from VP-12. Then another fighter appeared, opened fire, and set yet another anchored PBY ablaze. Still not fully aware of the reality, the men gaped in astonishment at the "crazy Army pilots." Then the aircraft banked, revealing the *hinomaru*, and to a man the entire group raced pell-mell back to the hangar, led by Horky.[26]

Chased back into Hangar 1 by gunfire, Horky and other sailors saw fire beneath one of the Catalinas on the apron between the hangar and the water. Horky instinctively jumped on a Case ramp tractor, shouting for assistance with a tow bar so that he might pull the PBY away from the flames. Just as the tractor emerged from the hangar, however, a bullet or explosive shell struck the engine, stopping the vehicle. Jumping off, Horky ran to the squadron's armory small arms locker to begin breaking out pistols and rifles.[27]

After going off duty at 0200, VP-12's AOM3c Robertus M. "Bert" Richmond, hailing from Hannibal, Missouri, had retired earlier to catch some sleep in the ready room under Hangar 1's north mezzanine.[28] Just before 0800, the "rattle of machine gun fire and the roar of fighter planes coming low over the hangar" proved a rude reveille. Richmond struggled into his pants and shoes, only to be greeted by the zing and rattle of Japanese bullets ricocheting inside the hangar, augmented by a cacophony of curses and orders cutting through the morning air.[29]

Hearing machine-gun fire, Sea2c Robert W. Ballou of VP-11, a Wyoming native and former CCC worker, thought that the Army was staging a mock attack on the hangar. Ballou then encountered Ens. Rodney S. Foss, D-V(G), the squadron duty officer, who ordered all men to their battle stations. Ballou and the other sailors could not resist running outside Hangar 1 to view the developing attack for themselves, a reckless act that at the time seemed to be a "very natural thing" to do. Sadly, inside the hangar, Foss fell mortally wounded, among the first American casualties of the Pacific War, as one of the initial Japanese strafing runs struck him down at the foot of one of the stairways to the mezzanine on the south end of the building.[30]

Elsewhere, bullets crashing through the glass of Hangar 1's bayside mezzanine second-floor offices startled Sea2c Dale E. Speelman, who had just concluded his watch. Rushing for cover, Speelman saw Foss lying unconscious at the foot of stairway leading down into the hangar. Meanwhile, Ens. Joseph G. Smartt, A-V(N), an Austin, Texas, native and Foss's relief, arrived and hurried to the office area in the hangar's mezzanine, secured VP-11's records, and called his superiors. It was at about that time that the radioman on duty in Hangar 1 received a teletype from Pearl Harbor saying that the harbor was under attack, to which the radioman replied, "What the hell do you think they are doing here?"[31]

The attacks on NAS Kaneohe Bay occurred prior to those elsewhere on Oʻahu.[32] Thus, at first, official notification going out from Kaneohe received little credence. In the opening seconds of the attack, someone from VP-14 in Hangar 2 thought to notify the authorities at NAS Pearl Harbor about the havoc unfolding on the windward shore. Accordingly, a teletype went out at about 0755, just as Japanese *kanbaku*s from the carrier *Shōkaku* were pushing over into their initial dives over Ford Island. The authorities at Pearl Harbor, however, proved as unbelieving as Sam Aweau's foreman and requested that the message be repeated.[33]

Walking toward Hangar 2, AOM1c Alfred D. Perucci, a three-and-a-half-year veteran of patrol aviation, heard aircraft noise and noticed three *kansen*s, probably Lt. Kaneko's lead section, flying in a westerly direction toward the Pali. In a matter of seconds they reversed course, heading back toward the hangars and PBYs on the apron. Seeing the *hinomaru*s, Perucci thought, "Those are Japanese planes." In a matter of seconds the aircraft opened fire.[34]

At approximately 0755 Lt. Kaneko led his consolidated fighter unit from the *Shōkaku* and the *Zuikaku* in

Ens. Rodney S. Foss, D-V(G), circa 12 June 1941. (MCB Hawaii)

a blistering strafing attack over NAS Kaneohe Bay that lasted until about 0810.[35] Initially, some of Kaneko's fighters appear to have targeted the control tower before all six quickly shifted over to assist Satō's five Zeros then roaring toward the four PBY-5s moored at thousand-yard intervals in Kāneʻohe Bay, south or southwest of the station's seaplane ramps.[36]

After the *kansen*s set fire to the Catalinas on the water, they turned their attention to the hangar line and to the PBY-5s parked on the aprons and warm-up platform. It took only a minimum of effort for the eleven Japanese pilots to seek out targets of opportunity. Incendiary 7.7-millimeter ammunition set aircraft afire almost immediately. Detonations of the 20-millimeter explosive ammunition sent jagged hot fragments ripping through aluminum fuel tanks. The gasoline drained into the PBYs' interiors and onto the pavement, setting off frightful conflagrations.[37]

Lt. Kaneko Tadashi, leader, *Shōkaku* fighter unit. (Prange)

WO Abe Yasujirō, no. 1 wingman to Lt. Kaneko, *Shōkaku* fighter unit. (Izawa)

## TABLE 1

### First-Wave Attack on NAS Kaneohe Bay

Lt. Kaneko Tadashi

*Shōkaku* Fighter Unit

| 11th *Shōtai* | 12th *Shōtai* |
|---|---|
| Lt. Kaneko Tadashi | Lt. Hoashi Takumi |
| WO Abe Yasujirō | PO1c Matsuda Jirō |
| PO1c Nishide Korenobu | |

Lt. Satō Masao

*Zuikaku* Fighter Unit

| 1st *Shōtai* | 2nd *Shōtai* | 3rd *Shōtai* |
|---|---|---|
| Lt. Satō Masao | Lt. Makino Masatoshi | WO Kodama Yoshimi |
| PO1c Kamei Tomio | PO1c Shimizu Ginji | PO2c Komiyama Kenta |

PO1c Nishide Korenobu, no. 2 wingman to Lt. Kaneko, *Shōkaku* fighter unit. (Izawa)

Lt. Hoashi Takumi, section leader, *Shōkaku* fighter unit. (Izawa)

PO1c Matsuda Jirō, wingman to Lt. Hoashi, *Shōkaku* fighter unit. (Izawa)

Lt. Satō Masao, leader, *Zuikaku* fighter unit. (Prange)

PO1c Kamei Tomio, wingman to Lt. Satō, *Zuikaku* fighter unit. (Prange)

Lt. Makino Masatoshi, section leader, *Zuikaku* fighter unit. (Prange)

PO1c Shimizu Ginji, wingman to Lt. Makino, *Zuikaku* fighter unit. (Prange)

WO Kodama Yoshimi, section leader, *Zuikaku* fighter unit. (Prange)

PO2c Komiyama Kenta, wingman to WO Kodama, *Zuikaku* fighter unit. (Prange)

AOM3c Moreno J. Caparrelli on 28 May 1938, while undergoing flight training at NAS Pensacola. (NARA, St. Louis)

Sea2c Armand "Pete" Petriccione of VP-11 lay in his bunk in Barracks 4 when he heard firing from the Marine watchtower. Running to the window, he saw aircraft with Japanese markings flying over the station. Although the young Newark, New Jersey, native needed no further confirmation, a terse and pointed announcement that Petriccione would never forget blared over the barracks' public address system, "All hands report to the hangar decks. We are under attack by the Japanese."[38]

Although the sound of gunfire awakened many of the men in the barracks, it failed to immediately alert all of them to the situation outside. When everyone rushed to the windows near the bunk of RM3c Richard R. J. Moser, someone witnessed an explosion in the distance just as a plane zoomed by the windows. Almost in unison, all the men yelled, "Japs!" Even the distinctive markings of the Japanese carrier fighters did not convince all the men as to the nature of the attack. VP-12 shipmate AMM2c Cecil S. Malmin, who like Moser was from the

Pacific Northwest, was absolutely convinced that Army fighters had arrived to carry out some sort of exercise and had gone to extraordinary lengths of painting red balls on the wings for realism.[39] But after observing tracers striking the ground in the vicinity of the aprons and hangars, Malmin knew otherwise.[40]

The friends of AOM3c Henry M. Popko, a Worcester, Massachusetts, native, proved difficult to rouse. After arriving breathless from a two-hundred-yard sprint from the Administration Building, Popko ran into Barracks 5 to awaken as many VP-12 shipmates as he could. Lying in adjacent bunks, AOM1c Earnest Eubanks and AOM1c (NAP) Moreno J. Caparrelli thought their friend had been drinking. Just at that moment, however, a Zero roared past the window. Caparrelli, one of the squadron's experienced enlisted pilots, exclaimed, "Jesus Christ! He ain't shittin'!" With that, Eubanks and Caparrelli sprang from their bunks, pulled on clothing, and raced outside, getting a substantial jump on most of their comrades.[41]

After waking up late in Barracks 7 after a big night in Honolulu, Sea2c Robert U. Hanna, who had reported to the NTS San Diego exactly one year before, thought there was a fight outside. Listening to the shouts, he decided to "let that fight go" and go back to sleep. At that juncture, a boatswain's mate burst into the room with a .45-caliber pistol pointed at the ceiling, yelling "I got him! I got him!" Hanna jumped out of the bed, dressed quickly, and ran outside, and at that moment he recognized that a strafing attack was under way. Seeing the Japanese plane, Hanna knew he had to get to the fire hall, worrying that he would be court-martialed for being late. Running down the covered walkways, he headed toward the Mess Hall and crossed the open expanse separating that place from the Administration Building where the fire engine sat parked.[42]

Marine Barracks, NAS Kaneohe Bay, nearing completion on 26 August 1940. View looking northeast from the Mess Hall lanai. (NARA II, 71-CA-156A-13870)

At the Marine Barracks in Building 8, Pfc. Joe M. Trest, a veteran forest fire fighter in the CCC, was up early and heard the roar of aircraft engines. Even after seeing the *hinomaru* on the bottom of the wings, Trest and the other Marines stood fast for a time, wondering whether the Army was on maneuvers. Incredibly, at that juncture, there were still a few disbelieving Marines who did not retrieve their rifles, still thinking that some mock attack was under way. Even with a few sergeants present, neither orders nor directions came forth. "We were pretty hard to handle ourself [*sic*], because everything was just utter confusion."[43]

Other Marines, including Pfc. James L. Evans, who had lied about his age to join the Marine Corps in June 1940 at age sixteen, heard explosions and low-flying planes but thought nothing of the commotion until someone ran into the building and screamed, "We're being attacked by the Japs!" In the "general panic" that ensued, the men scrambled for their rifles although ammunition was at a premium because of the locked storage area adjacent to the recreation room in the barracks' west wing. It took a

few frantic minutes to locate the supply sergeant, and even more time to convince the bureaucratic NCO that he should issue the ammunition without "proper authority."[44]

For most at the station, the struggle to "shake off the haze of unconsciousness" did not take long. At approximately 0740, Sea2c Doyle A. Bell—attached to the Ordnance Department and one of the many enlisted men who had arrived from San Diego during the past five months—heard a voice blare over the loudspeakers sounding the muster call for Section Three. Bell gave some passing thought to ignoring the call as he knew that his section was not scheduled for duty that day, but, knowing he was better off checking out the situation, dressed and stepped outside Barracks 7, exited from the lanai west to the muster area outside, intent on taking up the issue with BM2c George W. Lunn, the master-at-arms and a true "old-timer," with Army service in the Meuse-Argonne offensive during the World War. Meanwhile, following their inspection of the Brig, SK2c Jamie R. Murphy and Lunn passed through the Marine Barracks and headed up the covered walkway leading to the station personnel barracks. Sea2c Bell noticed Lunn and Murphy and approached them to ask whether he was indeed on duty. Just at that moment, Lunn noticed a lone fighter flying up the channel at Kāne'ohe Bay. The aircraft banked steeply over the Boathouse, apparently headed for Lunn and Murphy. Instantly aware of the plane's unfriendly character—and armed with a .45—Lunn drew his sidearm and squeezed off an entire magazine at the aircraft. Just as RM3c Moser bounded down the stairwell and out the doors of Barracks 5, BM2c Lunn was still banging away with his .45-caliber Colt automatic pistol. The Japanese aircraft proceeded out to sea. Immediately, Lunn and Murphy left a stunned Sea2c Bell and set out at a dead run for the Administration Building to notify the officer of the day. For Bell, at least, the incident solved the issue as to who was on duty. Prior to Lunn and Murphy's arrival, however, the officer of the day heard the firing and was attempting to notify other commands of the attack, including the authorities at Pearl Harbor.[45]

Sea2c Doyle A. Bell, circa April 1941, shortly before his arrival at NAS Kaneohe Bay on 4 August 1941. (NARA, St. Louis)

Meanwhile, more and more sailors made their way south from the barracks via the questionable safety of covered walkways that connected the five buildings to the Enlisted Mess Hall. Many of the men held fast, forgoing the footrace to the hangar line and Armory. The bluejackets in the Mess Hall stood "stunned by the suddenness of the shooting." With no other cover available, most of the men considered it suicidal to proceed farther south until a break in the action. Among them was Sea2c Warren G. Kearns, a Nebraskan from VP-12, whose determination to seek protection was matched only by the swiftness of those who did so first. Kearns raced frantically about the hall and succeeded in locating an empty space underneath one of the forty-six mess tables, but only after finding all other spots fully occupied.[46]

Enlisted Mess Hall interior on 26 August 1940, prior to installation of the mess tables. The cafeteria line lay in the opening at the left. (NARA II, 71-CA-156B-13868)

American accounts noted a momentary lull at this juncture, perhaps lieutenants Kaneko and Satō reversing course between runs. Following the announcements over the barracks' public address system, AOM3c Popko and many others waiting in the relative safety at the Mess Hall and barracks decided that the time for action had come, and "It was like a wave leaving the barracks." But after circling to starboard toward the sea, the fighters again careened into the station from upwind, zooming past the barracks and firing bursts at the buildings north of the hangars, catching Popko and others perhaps halfway to their destination. To their credit, none of the men turned back despite the great peril. To Popko, it appeared as though one of the Zeros chased AMM1c (NAP) James K. "Squash" Marshall all the way to the hangar line, and for years afterward his friends made an overstated claim that Marshall, another of VP-12's experienced enlisted pilots, outran the pur-

suing Japanese. However exaggerated the later stories were, all the men cheered lustily when they saw that Marshall successfully negotiated a path to safety.[47]

West of Kaneohe's runway, the station's pair of utility planes sat in the vicinity of the maintenance crew's bungalow, one of them an OS2U-1 Kingfisher (BuNo 1713) assigned to ComPatWing 1, Cdr. Knefler "Stuffy" McGinnis, and the other a J2F-1 Duck (BuNo 0190) assigned to Commander, NAS Kaneohe Bay.[48] Five of the men billeted at the bungalow had returned from breakfast and, together with another group of men on the apron, were preparing Cdr. McGinnis' OS2U-1 for an early-morning flight.[49]

The Kingfisher was among the first aircraft at Kaneohe to sustain damage.[50] At that moment, the floatplane lay ready for warm-up with a group of men, including a boatswain and mostly aviation machinist mates, milling about nearby. One of the petty officers had just pulled the prop through by hand when the Japanese began their attacks.[51] Within moments, the aging Kingfisher lay "thoroughly riddled," with its wings looking "like a sieve." Next, the J2F-1 sustained hits

View of the southern end of Kaneohe's runway on 4 September 1941, showing the station's Grumman J2F-1, bracketed by two SBD-2s, a Navy aircraft (left) from a carrier air group and a Marine aircraft (right) from MAG-21. Note the bungalow at far left, home to the maintenance crew for the station commander's Duck. (NARA II, 80-G-279361, cropped)

to the gas tank, oil tank, gas line, ignition system, and wing fabric. With bullets flying all around, the attending brood of sailors scattered, with most taking refuge in the bungalow, some repairing to the adjacent weeds. With a solitary .45-caliber pistol among them, there was little else to do.[52]

Down at the waterfront at the other end of the station, approximately twenty-five men assigned to the Boathouse had no firearms available apart from two .45-caliber automatic pistols assigned to the petty officers in the duty section. After seeing aircraft firing and

flying low over the station, the defenseless men scattered to find cover. Returning from morning mess to his duty station with the boats, Sea2c Francis F. "Frank" Davis, a Hilliard, Florida, native with six days short of a year in service, recalled later, "We didn't know what to do." Running to the Boathouse, Davis found that other shipmates had already sought protection there. Instinctively, Davis went for the armored bomb target boat, squeezing down between the two massive Hall-Scott V-12 engines.[53]

A similar situation developed in Building 21— Bombsight Workshop and Storage—where a number of men fleeing the hangar line sought refuge. With Japanese fighters making firing passes on VP-11's PBYs nearby, stray bullets struck the building in several places, sending glass shards from shot-out windows flying throughout the interior of the shop. Among those hiding out in the building was Fresno, California, native

AM3c Francis F. Davis at NAS Kaneohe Bay on 21 January 1942. (NARA, St. Louis)

View of the recently completed Boathouse at the eastern end of the warm-up platform at NAS Kaneohe Bay, looking east on 9 April 1941. (NARA II, 71-CA-156F-14241)

Lt. (jg) Wallace L. Kennedy, ChC-V(G), the base chaplain, who had been at Kaneohe for less than three weeks. After one firing pass by the Zeros, Kennedy blurted out, "We had better get out of here! It is better for one man [the man on duty] to get killed than all of us!" The chaplain's words, however true they might have been, proved to be little comfort for that one man on duty. An incensed AOM3 Jackson L. Harris was still standing watch, waiting for his 0800 relief that never came.[54]

At the Dispensary, three hundred yards northeast of the hangars, the "terrific noise of low flying planes" attracted Lt. Cdr. McCrimmon's attention. From the north window of his office—room 230, on the second floor between the dental and physical exam rooms—McCrimmon saw "three planes in close formation at about tree top height shooting tracer bullets." Someone nearby remarked that the Army was putting on maneuvers, so the doctor strode to the window to get a better look. Three times, the aircraft circled and returned to the hangar two blocks away, firing tracers each time. Although McCrimmon wondered about the situation, he was not particularly alarmed and continued to watch.[55]

Building 21, Bombsight Workshop and Storage, at the corner of Second Street and Avenue C, NAS Kaneohe Bay, seen looking northwest on the morning of 9 September 1941. (NARA II, 71-CA-156B-14561)

After returning from the Mess Hall to his quarters in the Dispensary, Texan HA1c Robert E. Hoffman heard machine-gun fire outside, and he and the other men there ran to the front and side windows. It occurred to Hoffman that the Army Air Force was at practice, so the men stood there and watched "a good show," listening to the whine of the aircraft. But when the strafing kicked up dust from the ground, and particularly when the planes banked, showing their insignia, Hoffman realized that "this was the time to get scared . . . the hair stood up on the back of my head. I could not believe it! It was a complete surprise." The chief pharmacist's mate on duty shouted at the sailors, "All men on duty!" but Hoffman and the others found it difficult to concentrate on their work while being drawn to the windows to watch the low-flying Japanese aircraft fish-tailing their way across the station.[56] Hoffman thought the distinctive sound of the 20-millimeter cannon fire was very much out of the ordinary.[57]

Not all the men in the Dispensary could see the events transpiring outside, but at least one guessed that something was amiss. Patient Sea2c John S. Kennedy, a young Washington state native, was intimately familiar with the sound of .30- and .50-caliber machine-gun fire and knew there was trouble outside when he heard the slower, low-pitched jackhammering of the Japanese 20-millimeter guns. A few of the patients could not resist the temptation to go outside to watch the events to the south. All received stern orders to remain indoors, with Sea2c Kennedy instructed to herd the patients back inside. No sooner had the doors closed than a Zero flew by, hosing down the Dispensary with machine-gun fire.[58]

Almost simultaneously, Lt. Cdr. McCrimmon—having crossed the hall from his second-floor office to the windows facing south—still watched events unfold across the way. Alarmed when smoke belched from behind the buildings in the distance, he dispatched an ambulance manned by HA1c Hoffman and another corpsman to investigate the cause of the fire near the hangars, standard procedure in the case of any fire.

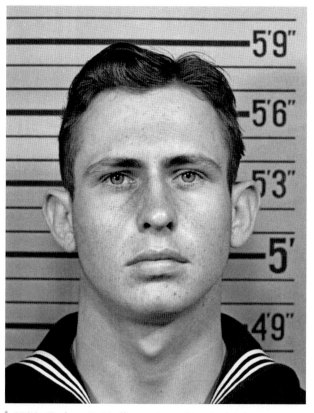

HA2c Robert E. Hoffman, circa 1941. (NARA, St. Louis)

At that point a lone plane, reversing course and circling after completing a strafing run, flew in from the direction of Pearl Harbor. It sped directly over the Dispensary, and at that moment McCrimmon saw the Japanese markings and exclaimed, "That was a Jap plane and they are attacking us!" Instantly, the doctor rushed to the telephone, called the authorities at Pearl Harbor, and asked for help. The man who answered replied that "all hell had broken loose" over the harbor and that there would be no help forthcoming. Setting down the receiver, McCrimmon's next thought was to call his wife Adelaide, whom he expected to arrive from Kailua at about 1000 when he was scheduled to go off duty. She answered the phone and the doctor declared in a rush, "Don't come near this place! The Japs are giving us hell!" Mrs. McCrimmon answered nonchalantly, "Oh—come on home, all is forgiven." A bit perturbed at his wife's flippant response, McCrimmon replied, "This is no joke! This is the real McCoy!" He held out the phone, hoping his wife could hear

the background noise. A mortified Adelaide McCrimmon then understood, and her "knees turned to water." The doctor hung up after instructing her to stay put with their two sons, aged five and ten. Billeted in a house three miles or so down the beach in Kailua, Mrs. McCrimmon peered northwest toward Kaneohe. The scene reminded her of "wasps flying around a nest."[59]

Meanwhile, ordered by Lt. Cdr. McCrimmon to get under way in one of the two Packard ambulances, HA1c Hoffman and a pharmacist's mate departed to make a circuit around the base and render assistance where necessary. Driving over curbs and dodging fire hydrants, the pair headed for the hangar line with Hoffman in the passenger seat. The pharmacist's mate drove "in an erratic fashion" while Hoffman craned his neck out the right side window, keeping a lookout for Japanese aircraft. In time, Hoffman grew more fearful of his comrade's wild driving than of the enemy. After

Lt. Cdr. Herman P. McCrimmon (MC) and wife Adelaide wait for an evening meal to be served at a dinner party, circa 1941. (McCrimmon)

AMM1c Daniel T. Griffin. (NARA, St. Louis)

Lt. (jg) William W. Gardner receives the Air Medal on 5 February 1944. On the morning of 7 December, AMM1c (NAP) Gardner traded places with AMM1c Daniel T. Griffin, who perished in one of VP-12's PBYs. Gardner felt guilty for the rest of his days. (NARA II, 80-G-454384, cropped)

several circuits, the ambulance had picked up enough wounded to justify a return to the Dispensary.[60]

Simultaneously with the strike on the utility planes, the four PBY-5s in Kāneʻohe Bay caught fire following the Zeros' strafing attacks over the water south of the seaplane ramps. The *kansen*s had destroyed all four PBYs from VP-12 and VP-14, leaving burning wreckage in the water to mark the spots where the aircraft had been anchored. The two crewmen from VP-12— Nebraskan AMM2c Walter S. Brown and AMM1c Daniel T. Griffin—both perished with their planes and were among the first casualties of the morning. The nature and location of their wounds indicated clearly that both sailors were looking up at the sky, searching for the attacking aircraft, when gunfire struck them in the head. Griffin's family—wife Lucile, daughter Danell, and son Donald—lived in Kaneohe's base housing at 451-D Minteer Street. Earlier, Griffin had taken the duty watch of AMM1c (NAP) William W. Gardner.[61]

RM3c George C. Wilson of VP-14—Philadelphia-born but reared across the river in Oaklyn, New Jersey— and AMM3c Paul B. "Van" Van Nostrand both survived the attacks by Lt. Satō's fighters and escaped from the two blazing PBY-5s. Van Nostrand had attempted to go forward to the bow turret to defend his aircraft, but as a precaution, the crew had wired the .30-caliber Browning down to prevent it from coming adrift during rough take-offs. Try as he might, Van Nostrand could not unship the Browning and put the turret in action.[62]

In the ensuing moments, Japanese gunfire struck the PBY and set the aircraft afire. Van Nostrand exited the plane, dove into the water, and began swimming to shore. As he approached the shore, Japanese fighters strafed the water nearby, prompting him to dive toward the bottom of Kāneʻohe Bay, where he encountered a

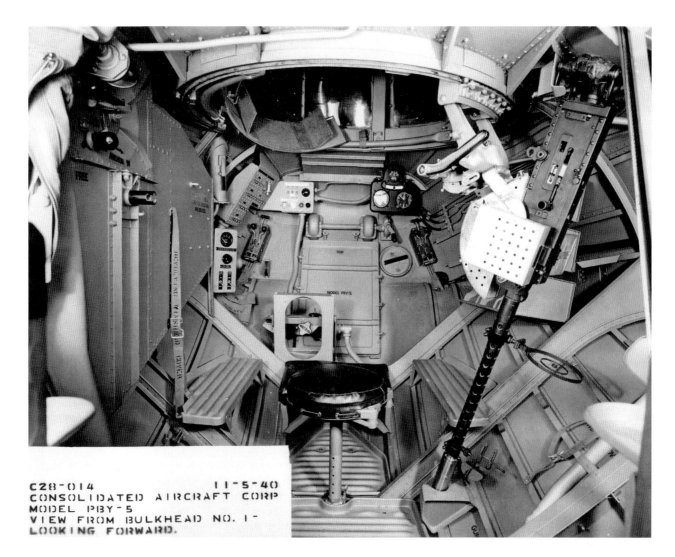

C28-014                    11-5-40
CONSOLIDATED AIRCRAFT CORP
MODEL PBY-5
VIEW FROM BULKHEAD NO. 1-
LOOKING FORWARD.

Bow turret of a PBY-5, looking forward. Note the Browning .30-caliber machine gun suspended at right. Although Van Nostrand did not specify the gun position to which he reported, the configuration of the turret conforms to his description of a loose gun swinging about during rough takeoffs. (NARA II, 72-CA-57D-15)

large drain pipe emptying from the shore. The sailor crawled into the pipe and took cover for as long as his breath allowed. After surfacing for air, he retreated to the pipe once again, forced down by Japanese gunfire. When Van Nostrand came up for the second time, he saw chaos erupting on the seaplane ramps beyond the Coconut Grove, treaded water for a time, and then proceeded toward shore.[63]

That morning, on the six-month "anniversary" of his induction into the Marine Corps, Pvt. John F.

Nichols Jr. was up as usual in the Marine Barracks at 0515 to bring the horse patrol to breakfast. Driving down closer to the hangar line, Nichols thought he saw bullets striking the water. Riding with Nichols, Pfc. Lucius C. "Red" Melton, a lean, red-haired Mississippian and "plank-owner" of Kaneohe's Marine Detachment, said, "No, they wouldn't be shooting real bullets. It'd hurt somebody."

Back at the horse patrol's billet, meanwhile, while policing the grounds of the trash from the party of the previous evening, the men saw fighters making firing passes and flying at crazy angles over the station. Assuming the planes to be friendly, they said, "the Marines are sure out early this morning" complete with "smoke and sound effects." Increasingly concerned, however, someone called the main gate and inquired, and guards

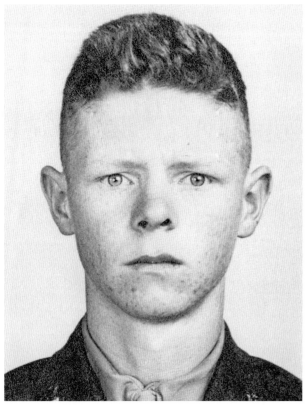

Pvt. Lucius M. Melton, USMC, 16 August 1940. (NARA, St. Louis)

Pvt. John F. Nichols Jr., USMC, 29 March 1941, one week after his enlistment. (NARA, St. Louis)

Pvt. Gordon Poling, USMC, 6 February 1940. (NPRC, St. Louis)

Pvt. Kenneth A. Little, USMC, 23 August 1940. (NARA, St. Louis)

Pvt. David H. Thomas, USMC, 11 July 1940. (NARA, St. Louis)

confirmed that the planes were Japanese. Finally, Pvt. Nichols pulled up to the old residence, got out, and looked up as an aircraft passed overhead. One of the men nearby said, "there's a rising sun on that," and instantly all the men in the vicinity knew the Japanese were attacking.[64]

Sgt. Gordon Poling, the NCO in charge of the horse patrol, bellowed, "Get your rifles!" All obeyed promptly except Pfc. Kenneth A. Little, an avid motorcyclist and hunter, known to be a heavy sleeper, who incredibly still slumbered in his bunk. Pvt. Nichols did not bother to disturb him, but simply took Little's rifle and opened fire. The Marines lay in the sand dunes, squeezing off shots from their Springfields, while others opened fire from the cover of the house at the Japanese aircraft turning overhead and reversing course back over the base, where towering columns of dark smoke boiled up from the hangar area. Poling pulled out his .45 after passing his rifle to SC2c Harry C. Chilton of VP-14, a

recent transfer from the seaplane tender *Curtiss*, who just happened to be visiting.[65]

Moments later, Pfc. David H. Thomas—born in Tarkio in northwest Missouri—and several other men ran across the road but sought cover as they were strafed. Thomas jumped into the ditch, breaking his wrist, although at that time he did not realize the injury was serious. His pain grew progressively worse, and he decided to report to the Dispensary, but when he arrived there, the long line of wounded men convinced him to bear the pain and return to his position.[66]

Officers who lived in Kailua received word of the attack, although the messages were sometimes delayed. At 0815, the telephone rang at 5 Kalaheo Drive, the residence of Lt. Edward E. "Ed" Colestock, Kaneohe's operations officer.[67] His ten-year-old daughter Jane, known as "Tory," answered, since both Ed and his wife were sleeping in after a late-night dinner party in Honolulu the night before.[68] Jane, Colestock's wife, groggily instructed her daughter to ask the identity of the caller and say that her husband would return the call later. After a short interval, Tory soon returned and blurted out "The man says, 'My God, get him up! It's a matter of life and death!'" It took the caller about five minutes to convince Colestock of the veracity of his tidings, but Colestock had to call a former shipmate from the *Lexington* just to make sure. At that juncture, the Colestocks looked out the window and saw the Japanese planes over Kaneohe.[69]

"Ed got dressed, gave me a peck, and went," Jane Colestock recalled. "Oh Ed," she said, "I don't want you to go over there," something she later classed as a "clever remark." Before he left, Ed Colestock said soothingly, "I guess there'll be a lot of things you don't want from now on." After Colestock got into his car and drove off toward the station, Jane, Tory, and Jane's little brother Dick, who had just gotten a new sailor suit for his birthday that was coming up a fortnight away, stood out by the fence and watched him go as Japanese planes attacked the air station.[70] Jane "did a little praying." Her husband reached the station unharmed, although a strafer holed the rear window and shot off one of the rear tires.[71]

Captivated but clueless civilians near Kailua point out aircraft south of Kaneohe. The man at right is using a pair of binoculars. (Lord)

Elsewhere in Kailua and vicinity, civilians did not receive any official word of the attack, and they awoke to the sound of gunfire and engine noise and wondered what was transpiring on the peninsula. Although they were thoroughly accustomed to low-flying aircraft, the prolonged racket at Kaneohe seemed unusual, particularly for a Sunday. Some residents gathered on their lanais to scan the horizon and the early-morning sky with binoculars, while others took the events in stride and sat back to watch the "air show" unfolding to the north.

One mile northeast of the hangars, in the Bachelor Officers Quarters, the cooks and mess attendants were preparing breakfast. MAtt1c Walter W. Simmons—a native of Everett, Washington, and a steward in the officers' mess—set tables and made last-minute preparations in the dining area. Earlier, he heard what he thought to be simulated machine-gun fire. Knowing that the Navy generally did not fly that early in the morning on Sundays, he attributed the disturbance to Army war games. With a few minutes left before breakfast, Simmons ambled out onto the BOQ's south galley platform to "watch the show." Upon noticing tracers, he thought, "Damn, the Army is playing rough!" When one of the circling aircraft exposed its *hinomaru* in the bright morning sunshine, however, the reality of what was happening struck him like a bolt of lightning.[72]

Simmons ran back into the galley and asked the cooks to confirm what he had just witnessed, but they

Type 0 carrier fighters from the 5th Carrier Division (circled at upper right and lower left) bear down on the naval air station, while a PBY-5 burns alongside a dredge in Kāne'ohe Bay. (Lord)

snorted disdainfully that he had gone "nuts." Quickly returning to the platform once again, it was clear that either planes or buildings were burning far to the southwest. Simmons dashed into the wardroom, meeting Ens. Norris A. Johnson, A-V(N), VP-11's assistant material and engineering officer, who had just reported for breakfast. When Johnson viewed the events transpiring near the hangar line, he needed no further prompting. Both men tore out of the wardroom on a mission to wake all the other officers, no small task with four wings and three decks to cover, going door to door. By then, however, the other cooks and mess attendants joined in.[73]

AvCdt. Norris A. Johnson, circa December 1938, while undergoing flight training at NAS Pensacola. (NPRC, St. Louis)

Elsewhere in the BOQ, 1st Lt. Randolph S. D. Lockwood, the Marine Detachment's company officer in charge of drills and instruction—after resting up from a late-night date with Ann Sherman,[74] Cdr. Martin's niece—turned off his alarm and heard what sounded like handfuls of gravel thrown against a window. Glancing quickly out of his second-floor window that faced north toward the ocean, Lockwood saw nothing. He went down the passageway to get to a window where he could see something, but Pu'u Hawai'iloa blocked his view. Then he saw aircraft disappearing around the hill. Standing with Lockwood was an ensign who remarked, "This is the Army Air Corps [sic] out performing on Sunday." A Navy messman, however, standing below on a lower level, had a better vantage point. Seeing tracer bullets that the officers could not, he turned to a buddy and said, "My God! Those are real bullets!" Startled, the ensign alongside Lockwood exclaimed, "I'm going to get down to the hangar." Lockwood responded, "I'm going to get down to the Administration Building." Dressing quickly, Lockwood ran to his car and drove down the hill toward the hangar line.[75]

Ens. William K. "Doc" Spry, D-V(G), PatWing 1's assistant personnel officer, lay asleep in his bunk in the BOQ until awakened by noise outside. From across the hall, Lt. (jg) Wilfred N. "Bill" More, SC-V(S), the wing's supply officer, burst into the room shouting, "They are here, Doc! They are here!" For a few moments, More and Spry argued over whether the Japanese were actually attacking the station. Then Spry finally arose and ran across the hall to More's room. Sure enough, there was plenty of smoke down by the hangars, but the former did not make the connection until one of Lt. Kaneko's Zeros roared past the window. At last galvanized into action, Spry dressed frantically while mess attendants raced up and down the hall, hollering, "Everyone up!" The sailors yelled, "The Japanese are here!" as they pounded on the doors.[76]

Meanwhile, strafing planes had the BOQ under attack by the time Spry reached the lobby. With bullets "stinging the concrete building," he decided to take the south exit and run back across the circular drive to his car in the parking lot east of the BOQ. Spry sprinted to his automobile, joined by Lt. (jg) More and Pharm. Edgar J. Maddox (HC) who asked whether he could tag along and be let out at the Dispensary. The trio discovered that a Japanese bullet had jammed the driver-side door. The damage to the latch forced all three to pile in on the passenger side, with Spry swearing at the delay. With that, the three men were ready to be off, though awaiting one more passenger. After awakening many of the officers, MAtt1c Simmons decided this was one adventure he was not going to miss. He hopped in with Spry and the others for the ride, joining an impromptu caravan of vehicles transporting other officers and men to the hangars.[77]

Capt. Randolph S. D. Lockwood, USMCR, 27 May 1942. (NPRC, St. Louis)

Midn. William K. "Doc" Spry, USNR, circa 1941. (NPRC, St. Louis)

Wilfred N. "Bill" More, circa 10 June 1938, upon his application for a commission in the U.S. Naval Reserve as a lieutenant (junior grade), Supply Corps, Special Service. (NPRC, St. Louis)

Lt. Cdr. Edgar J. Maddox (MC), 17 September 1954, while the executive officer of the Naval Hospital Corps School at NTC Great Lakes. (NPRC, St. Louis)

Bachelor Officers Quarters, NAS Kaneohe Bay, nearing completion on 9 April 1941. The wing at center that contained the dining room (1) and galley/dormitory (r). It was from the first-floor deck on the right that Matt1c Walter W. Simmons watched the attack unfold. View looking northeast. (NARA II, 71-CA-156E-14246)

A similar situation developed among the pilots of VP-11 residing on the BOQ's upper deck. In his ocean view, third-floor suite, Ens. Muckenthaler—who had reported to NAS Kaneohe Bay in company with Pensacola classmate Ens. Joe Smartt—had just arisen to prepare for the day's work, as he and his squadron-mates were to relieve Ens. "Bill" Tanner's patrol later in the morning. That duty notwithstanding, the young ensign had ample time for a leisurely breakfast and morning mass prior to reporting to the squadron offices in the south mezzanine of Hangar 1. Muckenthaler was shaving when, from directly across the hall, fellow pilot Ens. George S. Clute, A-V(N), burst excitedly into the suite, having just come the from the room of Ens. Hubert K. Reese Jr., A-V(N). With a still-warm bullet in hand,

he exclaimed, "Some crazy Army pilot is strafing the BOQ." Both men looked out the oceanside windows and saw a Japanese fighter headed straight toward them, firing as at it came. The aircraft banked, pulled up, and revealed a "meatball," spurring both men to action. Muckenthaler dressed hurriedly amidst increasing commotion in the hallway. Hearing someone yell, "Our planes are burning," he quickened his pace. Without pausing to look at the PBYs aflame to the south, he raced to the stairwell leading to the lobby on the first deck.[78]

As more officers prepared to leave, the biggest question seemed to be which route to the hangar line might be the safest. As soon as the men gathered the gumption to venture outside, another flight of aircraft zoomed past, firing at the barracks on the way to the hangars. Finally, Ens. Albert L. "Al" Dodson, A-V(N) of VP-14, on the second anniversary of accepting his appointment as an aviation cadet, made his way with several others out the back door of the BOQ and proceeded in their car along unpaved Kapilikea Road that ran around the north side of Pu'u

Ens. Albert L. Dodson, A–V(N), circa 18 August 1941. (NPRC, St. Louis)

Ens. John L. Genta, A–V(N), circa 6 September 1941. (NPRC, St. Louis)

East lobby of the BOQ at NAS Kaneohe Bay, looking southwest on 9 April 1941. (NARA II, 71–CA–156E–14245, cropped)

(right) Ens. Charles P. Muckenthaler in San Diego with his two-tone 1941 Oldsmobile sedan, prior to his departure for Hawai'i in 1941. (Muckenthaler)

(bottom) The situation east of Hangar 1 late in the first attack wave or after the Japanese departure. Fires rage out of control among five PBYs parked on the apron beside the hangar, with no firefighting efforts yet in evidence, although a group of sailors are walking toward a partially burned Catalina at right center. Note the sailor at far right, who has probably just left the Armory (out of view behind the photographer), crossing Second Street at its intersection with Avenue B carrying a BAR (see inset), encouraged to speed up his pace by the approaching two-tone 1941 Oldsmobile speeding west. The car's driver was Ens. Charles P. Muckenthaler of VP-11, with another officer visible on the passenger side seat. Muckenthaler purchased the car in Pensacola just before going to Hawai'i. Note the reflection of the Torpedo Workshop (Building 20) on the car's doors. Much, if not all, of the attack photography at Kaneohe is the work of VP-11 photographer P3c Leland R. Kofoed. See Kennedy, *Forgotten Warriors*, 49. (NARA II, 80-G-32828)

Hawai'iloa on a path that took them west, away from the flight pattern of the Zeros. The relative safety of the drive ended, though, when the officers converged onto D Street at the former gatehouse and approached the hangar line, which was still under heavy and sustained strafing.[79]

Frantic officers thronged the BOQ lobby, all determined to report to their duty stations but nonetheless hesitant to expose themselves needlessly to the strafing. Muckenthaler burst from the stairwell, intent on making the short dash to his two-tone 1941 Oldsmobile four-door sedan that lay in the parking lot just outside the lobby entrance. A mad rush for the doors ensued, although a number of officers turned back, repelled by another strafing attack. The men scattered "like chickens," but miraculously the incoming fire injured only Ens. John L. "Johnny" Genta of VP-11, A-V(N), who sustained a cut on his arm, either from a bullet or a masonry fragment. Exhibiting the quickness noted by the Naval Reserve Flight Selection Board, Genta retreated, temporarily, into the safety of the lobby. The men sprinted outside once again, however, and reached the parking lot unmolested. Muckenthaler and his passengers sped south toward the hangar line, arriving at Hangar 1 shortly before the departure of the Japanese.[80]

East of Pu'u Hawai'iloa among the two-story, four-family flats in the enlisted married housing area, sailors heard the commotion and gunfire and responded accordingly. RM1c (F-4-C) Daucy B. Goza of VP-14 sat sipping a morning cup of coffee with his wife, Edith, when he noted a "sham attack" under way to the south. Seeing the "rising sun" insignia, Goza, along with many other married men, set off running for the hangar line.[81]

Squadron-mate AMM1c (NAP) Walter J. Curylo was with his wife in the middle of breakfast in his duplex at 417-C Jaros Sttreet. As Cecelia Curylo was in the last stages of a pregnancy, the couple decided to stay close to the base during the weekend.[82] Disturbed by the noise outside, the couple stepped out to the porch to investigate. The first thing he saw was an aircraft attacking the control tower on Pu'u Hawai'iloa. A veteran of service in the U.S. Asiatic Fleet, Curylo recognized the insignia

on the aircraft immediately, but simply could not believe what he saw. But when the PBYs began to burn, he jumped into his car, picked up shipmate EM1c Frank J. Brown, and commenced the frantic drive to Hangar 2. Strafing attacks forced the pair to abandon their car, whereupon they joined the throng of servicemen proceeding on foot to the hangars.[83]

AMM2c (NAP) Walter J. Curylo, 4 February 1941. (Curylo)

ACOM (PA) John W. Finn, one of VP-14's chiefs, was engaged in a good-natured debate with wife Alice about who was going to make coffee. It took not only the sound of machine-gun fire, but also the banging on their door by a neighbor to fully alert Finn. Like many others, he found himself "driving like mad" the mile or so to his hangar in his 1938 Chevrolet. At first, Finn instinctively observed the 20 mph speed limit, but then heard an aircraft roaring in from astern. "As I glanced up, the guy made a wing-over, and I saw that big old red meatball, the rising sun insignia, on the underside of the wing. Well, I threw it into second and it's a wonder I didn't run over every sailor in the air station." Disregarding danger, Finn floored the accelerator.[84]

Waking up at about 0800, the newly married Y1c Kenton Nash heard the roar of aircraft engines and wondered what was happening. Still in her nightgown, Minnie, his wife of three weeks, went to the back window facing the BOQ, with her husband chiding, "Why are you standing by the window? Those people going down the roadway can see you!" Looking to the left, there was smoke, and she told her husband that there was fire in the hangar area. Nash went to the window and announced, "Well that isn't the hangar. That's the PBYs on the bay." At that point someone ran by the house and said, "We're at war!" but Nash did not believe him. Seeing a Japanese plane speeding past, Nash blurted, "They're really going all out. They've even painted the rising sun on that plane." Yet another neighbor came by repeating the previous alarm and showing off the holes in his car. This last evidence convinced Nash, who told his wife that he was going down to the hangar and that he would be back shortly. Not fully realizing the gravity of the situation, Minnie Nash started making coffee and mixing pancake batter.[85]

Marine Sgt. Charles H. Roberts was up early because he was to go on duty at 0800 at the main gate only fifty to seventy-five yards away from his second-floor apartment in Quarters 447. At exactly 0750, he noticed smoke rising from the bay, and then saw strange aircraft turning nearby. Seeing the "red balls" on the bottom of their wings, Roberts knew instantly that Kaneohe was under attack. He shook his slumbering wife, Romania, and exclaimed, "Come on and get up! Let's go! We're being attacked by Japanese!" Still half asleep, his helpmate mumbled groggily, "Huh?" Roberts repeated his announcement and ran outside. Finally awake, his wife went to the window to see what was going on. While running to the guardhouse, Roberts met the wife of Sudetenland-born CCStd (PA) Anthony "Tony" Lorenz, who supervised the Mess Hall.[86] "Gerty" Lorenz raced down the street with her two small children—John, eight, and Geraldine, six—and queried, "What the hell is going on?" Roberts answered, "We're being attacked by the Japanese!" "No shit?" "No shit!" Roberts kept running.[87]

When Roberts arrived at the gate, the guard truck was just set to depart and relieve the other sentries about the post. Roberts ordered the driver to leave immediately and to double the sentries rather than relieve them. Then, with Sgt. Roberts on board, the truck accelerated down the Territorial Highway in anticipation of the hard left turn at the intersection with Avenue D to pick up another load of Marines at their barracks adjacent to the Mess Hall. Simultaneously, Maj. John C. Donehoo came toward the intersection from the opposite direction with his four year-old daughter, Eleanor, on board. Though wanting to take the child to church, he decided she was too young for the service without the rest of the family present, and thus intended to drop by the Quarters "L" just north of the BOQ and pick up wife Marie and his other two daughters, Christine and Elizabeth. Meanwhile, Sgt. Roberts' driver, recognizing the major's car, courteously slowed down to allow his commander to pass in front, but Roberts told the driver (still woozy from partying the night before), "Don't wait for him! Go on!" Undeterred, or suffering from a hangover-induced slow reaction time, the driver slowed down anyway, allowing Donehoo to turn down Avenue D.[88]

The truck sped south down the avenue where, just past the Mess Hall, the road curved to the right and merged with Avenue C, which led to the flight line. A Japanese fighter came up the road strafing and caught Maj. Donehoo's car in a burst of fire that raked the automobile, front to rear. Projectiles struck the front fenders and punctured the left front tire, forcing Donehoo off of the road into a ditch. Seeing a woman standing nearby, he entrusted his daughter to her and continued toward the Administration Building. The same fighter strafed Roberts' truck. The aircraft was so close that the gunfire no longer converged, striking the ground on either side of the vehicle. Looking behind, Roberts saw the *kansen* strafe the "tower" on Pu'u Hawai'iloa and then reverse course for another pass on the station. Roberts thought it best for the men not to be in a moving vehicle, so the driver turned immediately to the right, returning to the Marine Barracks, where the leathernecks disembarked and ran inside the barracks.[89]

Sgt. Charles H. Roberts, USMC, 8 April 1941. (NPRC, St. Louis)

Maj. John C. Donehoo Jr., USMC, 8 December 1941. (NARA II, 80-G-32856, cropped)

Meanwhile, north of the base, while coming out of an early church service with his wife and son, Bronx, New York, native AMM1c Joseph C. Engel could see the strafing and smoke in the distance. Nonetheless, the entire family hopped into the car for the short drive back into the station, where the trio found their progress blocked by an incredulous Marine guard at the main gate. "You're NOT going to bring your family back in here. Can't you see we're under attack?" Engel argued his point with the guard, saying that he had to go to the hangar line and that his wife and son would stay north of the base at the beach. With that, wife Angie entered the fray. "I will have to have a blanket and some food." At last, the conscientious Marine relented and allowed the sailor's family to return to their first-floor flat at 409-A Jaros Street, from which point Engel proceeded hurriedly toward Hangar 1. On the way there, however, he received an order to head for the station's Armory instead.[90]

On the far north shore, on the ocean side of the base, noise and "a lot of shooting" awakened the family of Texas native Lt. Oliver L. Billingsley, D-V(S), who, after two years at the U.S. Naval Academy, had left the service in 1919. Serving in a number of administrative occupations and as a company commander in the Civilian Conservation Corps, Billingsley applied for a commission in the U.S. Naval Reserve in May 1935. Called to active duty in 1941, he reported to NAS Kaneohe Bay as ship's service officer on 17 March.

At about 0800, his wife Mynila remarked, "A lotta noise going on this morning." Her husband replied, "Yes, I guess it's maneuvers, or practice, or something." Mynila hopped out of bed and donned a housecoat. Coming back in after retrieving the morning paper, she observed casually, "There's smoke coming up from the hangars." Being close to the beach, the view to the south was obstructed and nothing but the smoke was visible. Her husband

AMM1c Joseph E. Engel with son Joseph Jr. and wife Angie, circa late 1940. (Engel)

dismissed the comment, thinking that a smoke screen was part of a practice. No urgency attended their conversation, and the pair simply sat, absorbed in their newspaper. After a minute or so, Mrs. Billingsley got up and looked outside once again. "Listen," she reported, alarmed that time, "if they threw up a smoke screen down there, it's out of control, because I can see the blaze now." Her husband declared that there seemed to be something happening and that it was a shame to miss out. At his behest, the family got in the car and drove at a leisurely pace across the station to investigate, Mynila in a zipped up house coat, her husband in a pair of pants with no shirt, and ten-year-old Betty Ann bouncing in the back seat.[91]

Under normal circumstances, the Marine color guard raised the national ensign in front of the Administration Building. Just as Maj. Donehoo had run to the building from his stricken automobile, he observed the ongoing efforts to make colors. Two men near the flagpole—Cpl.

Walter E. Soboleski and Pfc. Frank "Abie" Mindel—strove mightily to accomplish the task, albeit in fits and starts. Soboleski, a one-time upholsterer at the Hupmobile auto plant in Detroit, had but one thought . . . get the colors up! Every time the flag rose, however, Mindel pulled it down, fearful of attracting unwanted attention by strafing Zeros, shouting, "Pull it down! Pull it down! They'll come down and kill us all!" During the last hoist, Soboleski—very much the larger man, besting his Russian-born comrade by five inches and thirty pounds—hoisted Mindel as well before the latter finally dropped off. Also present at the pole was Tar Heel native Bug1c (V-6) Theodore J. Moss. In light in the prevailing chaos, Moss dispensed with sounding the call for morning colors and blew "Flight Quarters" and "Fire Call" instead.[92]

When 1st Lt. Lockwood arrived at the Administration Building from the BOQ, the halls seemed strangely quiet, with no Marines present. After sprinting to the desk where he stored his helmet, .45-caliber pistol, and web belt, he ran out of the office and encountered Cdr. Martin, who grabbed Lockwood. "For God's sakes!" Martin exclaimed,

Pfc. Walter E. Soboleski, USMC, circa early 1939, while serving in the Marine Detachment on board the heavy cruiser *Minneapolis* (CA–36). (NARA, St. Louis)

Pvt. Frank "Abie" Mindel, USMC, 30 November 1939, with the Recruit Depot Detachment at Parris Island, South Carolina. (NARA, St. Louis)

## FLIGHT QUARTERS
### (Boots and saddles)

The Navy bugle call for "flight quarters." (USN)

## FIRE CALL

The Navy bugle call for "fire call." (USN)

Sea2c Robert U. Hanna, circa 1941. (NPRC, St. Louis)

Sea2c Herschel H. Blackwell, on 12 January 1942. (NARA, St. Louis)

"Get the Marines!" Lockwood made straight for the Marine Barracks, taking a shortcut that led him diagonally across the parade ground. Endeavoring to get into the barracks as quickly as possible, he ran to the lanai between the barracks and the Mess Hall, forgetting that the lanai at that location had no point of entry. Lockwood attempted to hop the wall along the breezeway connecting the Mess Hall to the barracks but could not get over the six-foot-high ledge. Several "pairs of friendly hands" appeared and helped the lieutenant over the edge of the lanai.[93]

By this time, Sea2c Robert U. Hanna and several other sailors assigned to the Kaneohe Fire Department likewise converged on the Administration Building, where the Seagrave pumper lay parked. With perhaps eight men hanging on for dear life, the engine driver took off cross-country, bouncing over curbs on a direct line to the fires on the parking aprons. Strafed, Hanna abandoned the fire truck, running instead for the station

Armory. Sea2c Herschel H. Blackwell of Houston, Texas, also hopped on board, reasoning that being on a moving vehicle was better than standing still waiting to be strafed. Eventually, he jumped off the truck just as it came to a stop near Hangar 1.[94]

Back in the Marine Barracks, 1st Lt. Lockwood found men already bounding down the steps with M1917 steel helmets, Springfield rifles, and two bandoliers of ammunition each. Platoon Sgt. Theodore L. Franks had corralled about forty-five men, to whom Lockwood gestured "follow me" and, together with Franks, double-timed the group across the parade ground toward the Administration Building. Once there, Lockwood deployed the men into four squads of skirmishers, one on each side of the building, with instructions to open fire and lead the attacking planes by three lengths.[95]

Soon after, as the enemy fighters whizzed past, the Marines opened up as ordered. As Racine, Wisconsin,

Pvt. Wesley H. Bott, USMC, 26 July 1940. (NARA, St. Louis)

native Pfc. Wesley H. Bott did so, the aircraft screamed in at incredibly low altitude, seemingly no more than seventy-five feet off the ground. Not knowing how effective their shooting was, the Marines kept it up, with the heat from their rifles burning their hands. Despite the discomfort, it was gratifying to know they had something to do rather than huddle for cover. While firing from his position outside the Administration Building, Bott felt bullets whizzing by his head. Looking to the rear, there was a man shooting from the cover of a steel door that led under the building. Bott bellowed disdainfully, "Get your tail out here! Let's stand up here! Be a man!"[96]

Back at the Marine Barracks, the men who had not departed with Lockwood and Franks awaited direction or orders regarding what to do next. Just as Sgt. Charles H. Roberts arrived, he overheard someone call out, "These people are using real bullets. What am I supposed to do?" Roberts gave immediate orders to open

fire, although some of the Marines had already done so through the windows in Barracks 8. In the meantime, Roberts ran to his locker and retrieved his helmet, rifle, and cartridge belt, and for some reason stripped his bunk, pushing the contents into the locker. In the barracks storeroom, Roberts retrieved two machine guns, used formerly for training purposes only, with the web belts loaded with dummy ammunition. The men reloaded the belts with live rounds and, shortly after 0800, set up the guns atop the lanais running from either side of the barracks via the exterior second-story doors to provide cover for the barracks and headquarters. Coming back outside, he encountered a large liberty party of sailors dressed in whites outside the Marine Barracks. The men had run from the transportation pickup point near the foot of Pu'u Hawai'iloa and seemed frantic to obtain a Marine uniform to make themselves less conspicuous.[97]

In the company of several other Marines, Pfc. James Evans took one of the available Browning .30-caliber water-cooled machine guns up to the second deck with the intent of mounting the weapon on the roof that afforded an excellent field of fire against the Japanese fighters then circling over and near the barracks. Boosted up the ladder, Evans opened the hatch and emerged just as a Japanese fighter roared over at rooftop level.[98] After setting up the machine gun, Evans and the others discovered there was no live ammunition available, so he and rest of the men commenced firing with their .30-caliber Springfield rifles. Taking advantage of the cover afforded by the hatch, Evans moved part way down the ladder, braced his elbows on the roof, and fired. From his perch, he had a superb view of the chaos near the hangars, where everything seemed to be burning. There were, however, signs of the bluejackets mounting a defense, as red tracers stabbed at the sky from the apron, even from the PBYs on the aprons and ramps. After squeezing off five rounds and realizing that a lone rifleman would hit nothing, Evans backed down the ladder and joined a group of Marines firing through the windows on the second deck, where a more concentrated fire might have a more telling effect.[99]

The Marine Barracks (Barracks 8) at NAS Kaneohe Bay, seen during construction on 29 August 1940, looking east. The hatch by which Pfc. James Evans gained access to the roof and deployed his .30-caliber machine gun is visible atop the roof at left-center. The covered walkways (referred to incorrectly by the men as lanais) connected the barracks to the buildings on either side. Note the lack of an opening in the walkway at right that impeded 1st Lt. Lockwood's reaching the building. (NARA II, 71-CA-156A-13879, cropped)

Despite Evans' decision that the roof was not the place to be, perhaps a dozen or so men on the second deck of the barracks ascended the ladder to the roof. Eventually, though, there was a feeling among the men of "Let's go back down; this is not getting it." The Marines ran down to the first floor and then outside in front of the Mess Hall and opened fire once again. Shortly thereafter, some automatic weapons showed up in the vicinity: a water-cooled machine gun, several BARs, and Thompson sub-machine guns. Moments later, and still with no orders, Pfc. Joe M. Trest—who had worked as an upholsterer

Pvt. James L. Evans, USMC, circa 15 February 1941. (NPRC, St. Louis)

in Milwaukee, Wisconsin, prior to enlisting—and several other men ran over to the Administration Building and stood in the inside corner formed by one of the wings that projected from the building so that their backs would be secure, and then opened fire. There, a bullet from one of the strafing fighters (or from friendly fire) pierced the leg of Trest's trousers.[100]

With men converging by the hundreds on the chaotic hangar line and aprons, the demand for any weapon was instantaneous, frantic, and disorderly, with scores of sailors hurrying to the station's main Armory east of the hangar line in the Utilities Shop and Parachute

Loft, Building 19.[101] The men also reported to the rifle racks, or ordnance sheds in the two large hangars, and to at least one other subsidiary armory. Enlisting the aid of several other sailors, Sea2c Doyle A. Bell (assigned to the station's Ordnance Department) opened the main Armory, whereupon they commenced passing out weapons to their eager comrades. Naturally, belted ammunition and the Browning and Lewis machine guns disappeared first.[102]

Bell and others displayed astonishing coolness when, with the building full of men, one of the Zero pilots squeezed off a quick burst of fire, sending bullets and explosive shells through the Armory's large window. Although no one fell, the 20-millimeter rounds blew holes through the ammo locker's quarter-inch steel doors. The unflappable armorers continued their work amid smoke and the acrid fumes of burning powder.[103]

Kaneohe's Armory, designated in the original base plans as the Parachute Loft and Utilities Shop. The Armory served as a principal gathering point during the attack. Note the Koʻolau Range in the background at left. Photo dated 2 September 1941. (NARA II, 71-CA-156F-14566)

Lt. Oliver L. Billingsley, D V(S), circa 1941. (Billingsley)

Betty Ann (l) and Mynila Billingsley (r), circa 1941, taking in the sights at the overlook near the Nu'uana Pali. (Billingsley)

Incredibly, as the attack reached its height, Lt. Billingsley's family, after leaving their beach house to see the sights, was still unaware that anything was wrong, even with the Japanese planes "zipping around" and firing. When their car reached the hangar line, Billingsley stopped the vehicle, got out, and encountered an incredulous young sailor who ran up and blurted, "Those are Japanese planes up there! Get your family back to their quarters!" With that, Billingsley jumped back in, turned the car around, and raced back to the cottage, with Mrs. Billingsley noting later that the drive back was "a little faster than we went over." However fast, though, the drive was a quiet one with not much said, even as a Japanese fighter strafed the vehicle. The pilot scored no hits but kicked up dust within about twenty feet of the car. Upon his arrival at the cottage, Lt. Billingsley dressed hurriedly, instructed his family to stay inside, and then departed immediately for his battle station. The family did not stay inside, however. The extended distance from the center of action drew Mynila and Betty Ann to the yard outside to watch.[104]

Simultaneously, men assigned to the squadron duty sections in or near the hangars took immediate action, breaking out machine guns and ammunition from the ready aircraft within a few minutes. Among the first to get a .50-caliber machine gun into action was AOM1c Moreno J. Caparrelli, who had earlier been so disbelieving that an attack was under way. Men rushed straight to the platform amidst the parked planes where they commenced firing from the side blisters of the PBYs, securing only when the planes caught fire and literally burned from beneath them. Others served the .30- and .50-caliber machine guns from all manner of improvised hardware such as tail wheel mountings and water pipes driven into the ground with sledgehammers. Some even discharged their weapons with barrels resting on the shoulders of their comrades. VP-12's AOM3c Henry M. Popko donated his skivvie shirt to the cause, giving it to a squadron-mate who wrapped it around the barrel of a .50-caliber machine gun.[105]

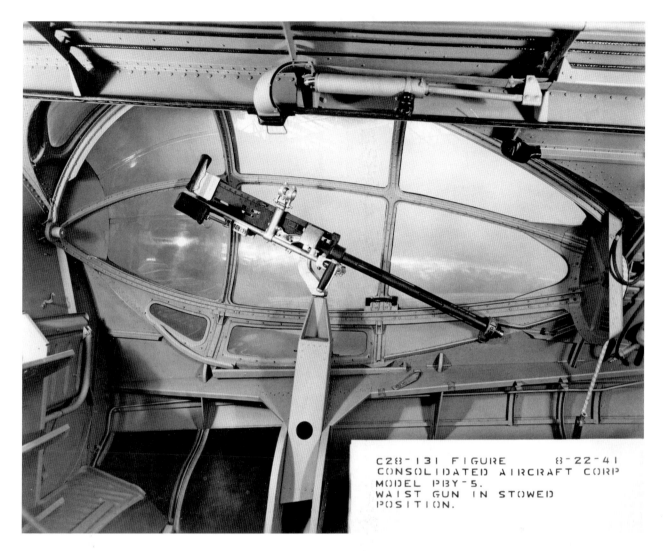

C28-131 FIGURE          8-22-41
CONSOLIDATED AIRCRAFT CORP
MODEL PBY-5.
WAIST GUN IN STOWED
POSITION.

The side waist blister on a PBY-5 showing a Browning .50-caliber machine gun in a stowed position. These guns were among the first (and easiest) to be fired or passed down to sailors on the ground. (NARA II, 72-AC-57B-131)

In Hangar 1, the men waited for no clerk or ordnanceman or for permission to fire. VP-12's AMM1c Ragnar N. "Scotty" Nilssen—born in Trondheim, Norway, though not proficient in the language—was standing in front of the hangar, making arrangements to be taken out to one of the PBYs at anchor in the bay when the attack unfolded, literally at his feet. Realizing the gravity of the situation, Nilssen ran back into the hangar and, finding the recently installed rifle case locked, kicked out the glass and grabbed a Springfield and as much ammunition as he could carry. With three years of ROTC training and time as captain of the rifle team (not to mention naval training with the .50-caliber machine gun), Nilssen sprinted outside and commenced firing immediately. At that point he heard no other rifle fire, but soon shipmate AMM1c Raphael A. "Ralph" Watson joined in alongside with a .30-caliber machine gun, cradling the Browning in his arms with yet another sailor feeding ammunition.[106]

Sea2c John R. Bacon from VP-11—a recent enlistee from California and native of Victorville in the Mojave Desert—with less than two months at Kaneohe, took a rifle from the case in Hangar 1 almost at the same moment as did Nilssen. Faster than most of his comrades, Bacon was among the first men from his squadron to emerge onto the apron south of the hangar and open fire. Meanwhile, while firing at the attacking aircraft, Nilssen happened to

Sea2c John R. Bacon, circa late 1941. (NARA, St. Louis)

AvCdt William L. Pack, circa 4 December 1940, while undergoing flight training at NAS Pensacola. (NPRC, St. Louis)

hold the barrel of his Springfield too close to Ens. William L. Pack, A-V(N), a pilot from VP-12, who had driven into the base earlier, leaving wife Lois in their off-base housing near Kailua. "Don't fire that gun with the barrel so close to my head," Pack yelled. "You almost blew my head off!" Moments later, Nilssen fired again but was still too close. "You almost did it again!" Pack shouted. "You're worse than the Japs!" Pack soon found relief, however, as Nilssen ran out of ammunition.[107]

The warm-up platform and aprons afforded little or no protection, and the recklessness with which the men counterattacked unquestionably contributed to the sailors' steadily mounting casualties. The exertions of VP-11's Sea2c Robert W. Ballou—a lanky, sandy-haired twenty-year-old who enlisted in Salt Lake City just nine months before—proved typical. After being ordered to his battle station by Ens. Rodney S. Foss, Ballou sprinted to the rifle case in Hangar 1, where he grabbed the next available Springfield rifle

and "ran out the backside onto the ramp." Lt. Kaneko's carrier fighters cut him down immediately, with machine-gun fire striking him in the left arm and leg. At least one other companion fell likewise. Two "buddies" placed Ballou on a canvas cot and rushed him toward an ammunition truck that had been pressed into service as an ambulance. Another fighter appeared, however, and commenced firing, which prompted the stretcher bearers to set Ballou's cot on the pavement and head for cover. Engrossed by the spectacle of tracers coming his direction, the stricken Ballou realized suddenly that his rescuers had abandoned him. Despite the searing pain from his leg wound, he hopped up and reportedly outran several acquaintances for the safety of a concrete-encased latrine.[108]

AOM3c Cecil I. Hollingshead arrived during a brief lull in the strafing attacks and charged to one of the hangar's ordnance shacks—in a storeroom along the centerline of the hangar below the waterside mezzanine—and broke

Sea2c Robert W. Ballou, circa 1941. (NARA, St. Louis)

ACOM Robert L. Schnexnayder, circa 1942. (O'Conner)

out weapons and ammunition. Just then, another section of Japanese fighters attacked the hangar. In response, Hollingshead and several shipmates gathered machine guns and ammunition and rushed to the construction area west of Hangar 1, where contract laborers had excavated footings for the expansion of the Maintenance Hangar. The men used a foundation of concrete blocks upon which to mount a half dozen or so Brownings. Using the blocks for cover, the men were able to serve the machine guns and even fire several rounds at the attackers. They deemed the larger .50-caliber weapons impractical at that juncture, however, as they proved too difficult to handle without a proper mounting. When firing, one man would hold the gun or brace it on the concrete blocks while his shipmate fired.[109]

Although Hollingshead laid down fire with one of the Brownings, he soon became preoccupied with helping other sailors who experienced trouble with their weapons. Quite a bit of time went into clearing

jams for the men, most of whom had had little ordnance training. Particularly annoying was that some of the impromptu crews had machine guns that were set, for example, with a right-hand feed, and thus unable to accept a left-hand magazine. Hollingshead thus spent a great deal of time matching magazines to weapons, an unnerving task considering his unprotected position and proximity to the ordnance. All the while, Hollingshead could only wonder: Where were the Army fighters from Bellows Field?[110]

After the initial rush for rifles in Hangars 1 and 2, those issuing arms managed to maintain a surprising degree of order. Amid great confusion and vociferous demands for anything that would shoot, VP-11's reservist AOM1c Robert L. Schnexnayder proceeded calmly with his work in Hangar 1, his cool demeanor preventing the scramble for weapons from turning into a riot. Thus armed, the men rushed out to the warm-up apron, where they received instructions to disperse and fire at will.[111]

The thin walls of the hangars afforded more psychological comfort than cover. Sailors seeking sanctuary from strafing aircraft proved quite dismayed afterward by the large number of bullet holes in the hangar doors, and even in the girders. One of the men cut down was ACOM (PA) Lester A. "Skinny" Grisham—AOM3c "Bert" Richmond's chief—who had taken charge of the men then attempting to roll two of the squadron's PBY-5s out from the southern end of the hangar. As the strafing Zeros roared past, Richmond glanced down. Chief Grisham lay writhing in agony on the hangar floor, holding a shattered left thigh but still bellowing orders at his subordinates, using the very best of his "Good Old Navy Vocabulary, and mad as hell for being knocked out of the fighting on the first day of the war."[112]

With Herculean exertions, officers and enlisted men alike braved enemy fire in attempts to save PBYs that had been set on fire. Like the men firing on the platform, they threw themselves into the task with total disregard for danger. Two VP-11 men—RM1c Joseph T. Crownover and VP-11's leading chief, ACMM (PA) Harry G. "Duke" Byron—typified the irrepressible "hot-blooded fighting spirit" prevalent among those engaged in fighting fires.

Early in the attack, Crownover manned a .30-caliber machine gun outside Hangar 1 on the platform about eighty feet from the ramp. As one of Lt. Kaneko's fighters flew low overhead, he saw his ammunition strike the *kansen* and noticed gasoline streaming from the passing Zero. Meanwhile, Byron—unable to find a weapon—could only shake his fist in rage at the aircraft overhead. Crownover and Byron both turned to the task of battling numerous blazes on the platform, even as the Mitsubishis pressed their attacks. While engaged in pulling Catalinas to safety and extinguishing fires, both men sustained serious wounds, with Crownover receiving multiple gunshot wounds in the head and left eye and Byron suffering multiple gunshot wounds, including a 20-millimeter round that ripped open his abdomen. Incredibly, both men continued their work despite their ghastly wounds, ceasing only when forced by their comrades to seek treatment.[113]

RM1c Joseph T. Crownover, convalescing from his injuries, circa 1942. (Crownover)

At length, despite his iron will to continue, Byron, "a tough man," was on the verge of collapse, holding onto one of the sprinkler system pipes. AMM2c Otto V. Horky rushed to his chief's aid and pushed the intestines back in, as "they looked like hell." Although Byron's breathing was shallow, he gasped his gratitude, "Thanks, Horky, thanks." Amazingly, he was able to walk, so with Horky and shipmate AMM2c Ronald W. Jackson supporting him, the trio walked outside Hangar 1. There they laid Byron down behind a pile of old engine stands for cover to await transportation to the Dispensary. Deeply moved at having to leave his friend, Horky regarded Byron as the best friend a man could have if he did his duty, but "hell on earth" if he did not. Telling their shipmate they would get an ambulance for him, Horky and Jackson then ran back into the hangar to resume their efforts to secure weapons.[114]

| AMM2c Otto V. Horky. (Horky) | AMM2c Ronald W. Jackson, circa 1942. (Dohrmann) |

With the intensity of the attacks beginning to wane, Horky found Ens. Foss unconscious and motionless on the hangar floor with a .45-caliber pistol alongside on the concrete just before sailors bore away the dying officer to the Dispensary. Horky picked up the weapon and found that it had no magazine. After a search high and low for a magazine without success, he found a generous supply of .45-caliber ammunition and grabbed all he could stuff into the front pockets of his shirt, which only caused the shirt to dig into the back of his neck. Although the lack of a magazine was still an issue, he discovered that one could still fire the weapon . . . pull back and lock the slide, insert one round into the chamber, release the slide, and fire.[115]

Elsewhere on the ramp, AMM1c Cecil S. Malmin set to work immediately holding down a bore sight mount from which other sailors fired back at the fighters overhead. He next moved to a group of men that teamed up with a ramp tractor and, assisted by VP-12 pilot Ens. Wilber J.

Wehmeyer, A-V(N), and others, attempted to move a still intact PBY-5 away from the area that seemed to be the object of concentrated strafing. But their activity only attracted the attention of the vigilant *kansen* pilots, and soon the aircraft and the party attempting to save it came under attack. Miraculously, all the men escaped unhurt, but not the PBY, as Japanese incendiary ammunition set fire to the fabric on the wing.[116]

Back in the south mezzanine of Hangar 1, efforts to safeguard Kaneohe's communications were under way. Duty officer Ens. Smartt and RM3c Charles E. Day, "aware of the dire necessity of uninterrupted communications," hovered like protective hens over their teletype machines in total disregard for personal safety. Although as a practical matter the ability to maintain communication made little difference in how events unfolded, the zeal displayed by Smartt, Day, and so many others proved an inspiration and provided a much-needed morale boost under the grimmest circumstances imaginable.[117]

Ens. Wilbur J. Wehmeyer, circa 5 December 1940. (NPRC, St. Louis)

When the attack began, VP-14's duty section leader AOM1c Alfred D. Perucci, who hailed from Salem, Massachusetts, ran immediately to the duty barracks close to Hangar 2 and alerted the duty section crew. Then, running to the subsidiary armory adjacent to the barracks, he opened the compartment and began issuing rifles, machine guns, and machine-gun mounts. Having no keys for the ready ammunition lockers, Perucci shot away the lock with his pistol.[118]

Like their fellow sailors in Hangar 1, the men in Hangar 2 got into action immediately. The efforts of VP-14's AOM1c Thomas E. Kerr—just shy of two years into his second enlistment—proved typical. After setting up two machine-gun positions on his own initiative during the opening moments of the battle, Kerr rushed to retrieve ammunition belts, only to find the ready locker in Hangar 2 secured with a padlock. Kerr pulled his pistol, shot away the lock, and issued all available arms and ammunition so the guns could keep firing, at least for the time

being. Demand outstripped the supply and exhausted the ready ammunition all too quickly. To remedy the shortage, AOM1c Perucci, who had exhausted the ordnance at the nearby subsidiary armory, directed the men to start belting loose ammunition. Soon the sailors thus engaged found themselves locked in a frantic race to keep up with what must have seemed an insatiable demand.[119]

A winded Sea2c Lyle A. Jackson, just eleven days short of his nineteenth birthday, arrived at Hangar 2 following a three-quarter-mile cross-country sprint from the parade ground and ran to the PBYs that sat on the parking apron. Suddenly someone in a waist blister in one of the Catalinas called down and demanded assistance. The sailor inside lowered a .50-caliber Browning machine gun, prompting the confused Jackson to yell over the din, "What do I do with it?" The impatient reply came quickly: "Mount it and shoot it!" Jackson then ran west to the construction site where, in recent weeks, the framework of the future Hangar 4 had just been erected. Among the materials, he uncovered some steel tubing on which to mount the Browning, but then realized that he had no ammunition. A return to Hangar 2 revealed that no belted ammunition was yet available, and with others under the tutelage of AOM1c Perucci, Jackson set to work on the manual belting machine that lay on the hangar floor.[120]

In addition to the nonstop work of the belting crews, the men of VP-14 did everything in their power to bring weapons to bear against the Japanese. Among many others in Hangar 2, Y2c James L. Beasley, AOM3c James E. Walters, and AOM3c Delbert C. Jones ensured that a supply of ammunition was passed to the men just beginning to fire outside. Then, enlisting the aid of two men in VP-14's duty section, including AMM3c Frank A. "Wop" Tucci and AMM2c Glenn L. Cummings, the sailors collected .50- and .30-caliber machine guns recently removed from the PBYs on the apron. As a reward for their energetic exertions, each of the three men commandeered one of the Brownings, Perucci and Tucci two .50-calibers and Cummings a .30-caliber. Shipmates AOM3c Robert F. Weston and AOM1c Morton N. Frey joined in, hammering away at

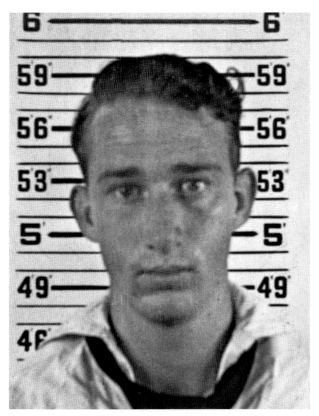

Sea2c Lyle A. Jackson, circa 1941. (NARA, St. Louis)

the aircraft overhead. Meanwhile, sailors shuttled back and forth to keep their comrades supplied with ammunition. At length, Perucci felt compelled to resume his supervisory activity in Hangar 2 and, after firing for a short time, gave his machine gun to another man in the duty section and reported to the hangar.[121]

Following a frantic drive from the enlisted married housing, ACOM John W. Finn arrived at Hangar 2 only to find that the duty section under AOM1c Perucci had already issued all available arms. Satisfied that proper defensive measures were under way, Finn turned his attention to certain safety concerns, particularly the dangerous cache of depth charges stowed on bomb trailers in the hangar. He issued instructions that they be moved immediately, along with machine-gun ammunition that had been emptied from the ready locker and piled onto the floor. Perucci and AOM1c Edward J. Sullivan carried out the necessary move. Finn next recognized the acute shortage of mountings for the machine guns that had been removed from many of the PBYs. Hurriedly,

Finn scrounged the only three mounts available; others had to be improvised with angle iron and scrap metal. Under Finn's direction, metalsmiths and welders turned out thirty-two mounts by the end of the attack.[122]

Meanwhile, Lt. Kaneko's eleven fighters departed as suddenly as they appeared, leaving behind a wrecked NAS Kaneohe Bay. The kansens formed up, drew off to the north, and headed in a westerly course across the island at low altitude en route to the rendezvous area off Ka'ena Point, O'ahu's westernmost tip. The cramped coveys of ponderous PBYs—in many places wingtip to wingtip—must surely have seemed a dream target to the Japanese pilots, whose exuberant claims totaled fifty-six aircraft destroyed plus five set ablaze at their moorings, nearly twice the number of aircraft actually present. However inflated the claims were, however, they reflected the confusion and chaos that now beset the stunned bluejackets. Though it is difficult to arrive at completely accurate numbers, by the time of Lt. Kaneko's departure at about 0830, fully half of Patrol Wing 1's strength lay destroyed or disabled on the aprons.[123]

The fight was not completely one-sided, however, as gunners on the ground noticed that a number of the attacking fighters trailed thin plumes of smoke or fuel, and they all hoped that at least a few of the fighters might not complete their return flight. Such expectations were not to be realized, however, as all the Zeros from the 5th Carrier Division returned safely, although four kansens—one from the Shōkaku (Lt. Kaneko's) and three from the Zuikaku—sustained damage, including one aircraft that suffered the detonation of a 20-millimeter round inside one of its Oerlikon wing guns. The Japanese, for their part, had expended most of their 20-millimeter rounds—more than a thousand rounds—and almost seven thousand rounds of 7.7 millimeter.[124] For the Japanese fighter pilots who had been so nervous and apprehensive over their prospective encounter with the Americans, it all seemed too easy. "Without any opposition," WO Abe Yasujirō, Lt. Kaneko's number one wingman, later recounted, "the strafing runs were like target practice."[125]

Seen from the housing south of the air station near Kailua, fires from the aircraft moored in Kāneʻohe Bay appear to have burned out but still rage on the aprons to the north. A section of three *kansen*s has appeared, possibly Lt. Kaneko Tadashi's lead section from the *Shōkaku*. The other four sections had only two aircraft each. (Lord)

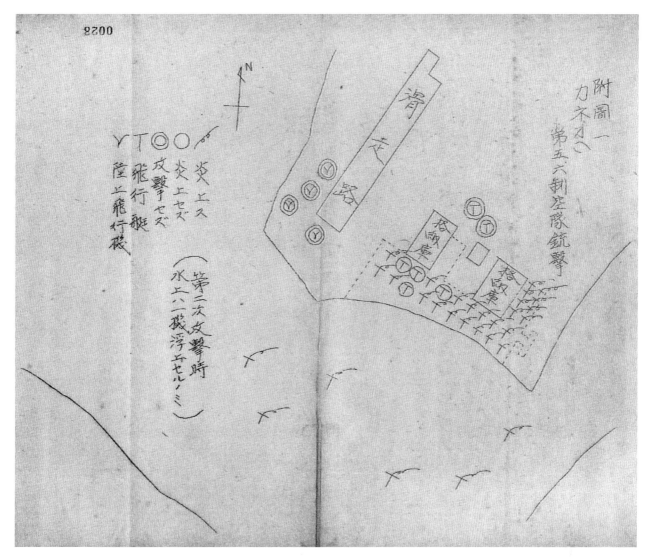

Chart from the *Shōkaku*'s action report shows the collective impressions of Lt. Kaneko's fighter pilots regarding the first attack wave on NAS Kaneohe Bay. Note the six PBYs (designated by a "T") claimed to have been set afire in the water, although the Americans moored most of the four ready aircraft much farther northwest than this diagram shows. Some few of the aircraft (within a single circle) came under attack but survived, while two flying boats (within a double circle) north of the hangar line were not attacked. Note also the four land planes (designated by gull wings) Kaneko's men found in the vicinity of the nearly completed runway west of the hangars. Aided by their attack photography, the Japanese compiled a surprisingly faithful rendition of the base. (*Shōkaku* Report, BKS)

Meanwhile, back on the ground at NAS Kaneohe Bay, an eerie stillness descended on the station. Reflecting on his walk back from the Armory to the hangar line, Sea2c Bell later recorded: "As I got back to the flight line near the armory, everything became quiet—no planes, no gunfire—just the smoke, the fire, the dead and a terrible lingering confusion. I was eighteen and had never imagined that I would see war, or that this would be what it was like. In my naiveté, I thought, 'No one will believe this happened.'"[126]

Similarly, AOM3c "Bert" Richmond could scarcely believe the scene that lay before him and summed up the results of the attack, declaring that, "when the fighters quit us they left us a sad sight."[127]

All three squadrons at Kaneohe sustained terrible blows, though VP-14's situation left the unit a bit better

A PBY-5 from VP-14 lies upended on the parking apron south of Hangar 2 with gasoline tanks ablaze following the strafing attack by Japanese fighters from the 5th Carrier Division. (NARA II, 80-G-32831)

off than its two sister squadrons, as the three PBYs still out on patrol had escaped the attack. Although both ready aircraft moored in Kāneʻohe Bay were lost, the plane guards were safe. Gunfire and flames gutted three of the six Catalinas on the platform, but the solitary PBY parked in Hangar 2, 14-P-9 (BuNo 2369), still sat intact.[128]

Meanwhile, after reaching the shore following the sinking of his PBY in the bay, plane guard AMM3c Van Nostrand was particularly incensed at having to leave behind a brand-new pair of shoes on board his aircraft. Looking about, he realized immediately that VP-14's other plane guard, RM3c Wilson, had not come ashore. Simultaneously, as soon as the Japanese departed, AOM1c Perucci—after getting ammunition

belting under way in Hangar 2—hailed the coxswain of a passing boat to rescue RM3c Wilson and to retrieve machine guns and ammunition from the aircraft wreckage in the bay. Together, Perucci and Van Nostrand went out to the sinking PBY, located RM3c Wilson nearby, helped him in, and salvaged some equipment from the Catalina before returning to shore near Hangar 2.[129]

VP-12 suffered aircraft losses comparable to their sister units, with perhaps half of the squadron's twelve PBY-5s being destroyed or badly damaged during the strafing. Among the machines either operational or salvageable were 12-P-7 (BuNo 2441), which lay south of the Maintenance Hangar, and the holed but otherwise intact 12-P-1 (BuNo 2424). Two other Catalinas close to the seaplane ramps near the water lost wing fabric to fires but seemed otherwise salvageable. The two ready aircraft in the bay, however, had burned and sunk. Most of the squadron's other PBYs burned, with their places on the apron marked by ashes and upended wreckage.[130]

The boat likely used by AMM3c Paul B. Van Nostrand and AOM1c Alfred D. Perucci to recover RM3c George C. Wilson lies at upper left, along the edge of shoreline in front of Hangar 2. Beyond the boat are the trees of the "Coconut Grove," converted into a defensive strongpoint during the lull. Note the incinerated empennage and wing of a PBY at upper right. (NARA II, 80-G-32858, cropped)

Sea1c Alfred D. Perucci, circa 1937. (Perucci)

AMM3c Paul B. Van Nostrand. (Van Nostrand)

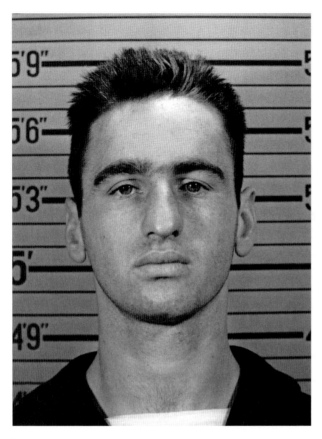

RM3c George C. Wilson, circa late 1941. (NARA, St. Louis)

With PBYs burning at every point along the platform, there were few options available to would-be salvagers. The sight of their beloved Catalinas in such dire straits caused a number of men to weep openly. Others seethed with rage. Often, all that could be done was to pull individual aircraft away from the towering columns of burning aluminum and aviation fuel, an action that, ironically, made the surviving planes (now unconcealed) more accessible targets.

Perhaps one of the more optimistic attempts at "concealment" centered on 12-P-1, assigned to VP-12's commanding officer, Lt. Cdr. Argyll E. Buckley. Caught in Lt. Kaneko's strafing attacks on the apron between Hangars 1 and 2, the aircraft suffered numerous punctures and was leaking gasoline "like a yard sprinkler."

A PBY continues to burn in the far background, while 12-P-7 (BuNo 2421) rests on her beaching gear at left-center. Very early in the attack, AOM3c Jackson L. Harris thought that Lt. Kaneko's Zeros were Army P-40s making mock attacks on the dredge in the far background, at right. (NARA II, 80-G-77610)

Another VP-12 machine, 12-P-2 (BuNo 2425), lies smoldering in the foreground with 12-P-7 at right and a 1940 Dodge pickup truck passing at left. (NARA II, 80-G-77605)

Because the aircraft had not yet caught fire, however, the men moved the machine from VP-12's assigned area on the warming up platform, "secreting" the plane on 2nd Street north of the hangar line, between the Maintenance Hangar and the Squadron Office Building. During the move, RM3c Richard R. J. Moser clambered atop an adjacent shed in front of the building, straining upward against the starboard wingtip float to ensure that it cleared the shed as men rolled the Catalina north.[131]

Other enterprising individuals on the platform endeavored to perform a similar task with 12-P-3 (BuNo 2435). Thoroughly shot up and with its port wing afire, the PBY must have appeared to be a hopeless case. Nonetheless, sailors tried to move it into the water in hopes of extinguishing the flames there. After crews secured a line to the float of the burning wing on one end and to a ramp tractor on the other, the tractor driver stepped on the gas a bit too hard considering the aircraft's tender condition and promptly tore away the wing section outboard the port engine. The rupture of the fuel tank set off a blinding gasoline explosion that, momentarily at least, scattered the would-be salvagers. At a loss of knowing what to do with the wing section, the tractor driver pulled his amputated payload, scraping across the pavement, and released the line down at the edge of the water. Back on the apron, the flames soon subsided around 12-P-3, and, with a dozen or so officers and men holding onto a line attached to the hapless PBY's empennage, the aircraft descended Ramp 2 into Kāneʻohe Bay, where the men hoped to begin efforts to extinguish the fire.[132]

12-P-1 (BuNo 2424) rests in front of the Squadron Office Building after being moved by men of VP-12 following the first-wave strafing attacks. Note the shed at left on which RM3c Richard R. J. Moser stood to ensure that there was sufficient clearance for the starboard float to pass. In the foreground lies an improvised machine-gun position (.50-caliber Browning at left and .30-caliber Browning at right) erected in the utility footings excavated for the future Hangar 2. (NARA II, 80-G-77638)

It was probably VP-11 that sustained the most material damage as a result of Lt. Kaneko's attacks. Except for the two planes undergoing maintenance in Hangar 1, the squadron's entire complement of aircraft lay east and south of the hangar line bathed in the brilliant morning sunlight, unobstructed by the columns of smoke that arose from VP-12 and VP-14's parking aprons to the west.[133]

On the aprons east of Hangar 1, the firefighting equipment was in a better position to deal with the flames, and consequently the firemen and other sailors were able to save at least one of the lesser-damaged aircraft. Of the five VP-11 machines parked outside Hangar 1's eastern doors, Japanese strafers had set four afire almost immediately. The lone survivor, 11-P-3 (BuNo 2422), outboard and to the north of the other PBYs, lay perilously close to an inferno consuming a sister aircraft just to the south. A dozen or so men—working like ants dragging a moth through the grass—manhandled the huge plane north, away from the nearby conflagration. In a morning filled with fear, anger, and frustration, the sailors could count their labors well done, as 11-P-3 became the only VP-11 aircraft east of the hangar to make it through the attack intact, albeit seriously damaged.[134]

Shorn of her port wing, 12-P-3 (BuNo 2435) lies on the warm-up platform while sailors mill about. (NARA II, 80-G-77615)

Officers and men lower 12-P-3 into Kaneohe Bay from Ramp 2. Note the man atop the starboard wing and the dog near the water at left-center. Amid the three sailors in whites, Sea2c Earl L. Jones stands at center, facing the camera, identified in this photograph by his brother, Sea2c Gordon E. Jones, who (likewise in whites) stands just to the right of his sibling with his back to the camera. Both men enlisted on 2 April 1941 in Philadelphia and received consecutive service numbers. The pair reported to Kaneohe for duty in VP-14 on 2 December 1941, only five days prior to the attack. Sea2c Earl L. Jones sustained severe wounds from being struck in the right femur by bomb fragments shortly after this photo was taken. (NARA II, 80-G-32835)

VP-11 PBY (identifiable by the distinctive multitone camouflage scheme applied to the engine cowling) burns itself out on the apron south of Hangar 1. Two other VP-11 aircraft are visible through the smoke at right, the tail and burning wing section of one and an intact plane just visible along the photograph's right margin. (NARA II, 80-G-32839)

Smoke clears from the PBY empennage visible in the previous photograph, also revealing its proximity to Hangar 1. (NARA II, 80-G-77641)

On the outer row of aircraft east of Hangar 1, a VP-11 PBY lies with its fuselage consumed by flames just forward of 11-P-3 (BuNo 2422), whose bow protrudes into the picture at right. (NARA II, 80-G-32829)

Firefighting begins at last with a team of sailors directing a stream of water on the PBYs east of Hangar 1, albeit from a prudent distance. (NARA II, 80-G-77640)

Sailors manhandle 11-P-3 north, away from the fires. (NARA II, 80-G-32837)

The loss of many aircraft notwithstanding, perhaps the most organized and successful efforts at firefighting centered about the five PBYs parked on the apron east of Hangar 1. Three machines tied down adjacent to the hangar were total losses, but while they were beyond hope of saving, the fires and heat threatened men, materiel, and the hangar itself. Accordingly, with the arrival of the station's 1939 Seagrave pumper, the sole firefighting vehicle, crews gathered northeast of the hangar shortly after the first-wave strafing ceased and turned to the task of running out fire hoses and battling the blazes. Simultaneous with the repositioning of 11-P-3, sailors worked on extinguishing the fires consuming the northernmost PBY directly adjacent to the hangar. Then, as they brought those under control, they moved south down the apron to the next PBY. By

that time a second crew with hoses positioned itself on the hangar side. Further east, the outboard PBY on the south end of the line burned itself out with only minimal expenditure of labor and water, as saving Hangar 1 and its bombs, depth charges, and ammunition from nearby conflagrations took precedence.[135]

In addition to setting up machine guns near the hangar line, sailors consolidated a portion of the Brownings in construction excavations and "strong points" for the sake of concentrated fire and mutual protection. Men from VP-11 set up two such nests, one situated in the Coconut Grove, west of the hangars. The strongpoint boasted four Browning .50-caliber machine guns, a Browning Automatic Rifle, and one Lewis machine gun. Another nest with two machine guns lay in a semiprotected area nearby.[136]

Moving farther south, two teams work fire hoses on both sides of the northernmost PBY in line. (NARA II, 80-G-32834)

With fires extinguished sometime prior to 0900, a substantial proportion of VP-11 lies burned out close to Hangar 1. (NARA II, 80-G-77602)

Sailors watch the skies and man .30-caliber and .50-caliber Browning machine guns that rest atop a concrete footing. The excavation is for the extension of the small Maintenance Hangar, which would soon become the northwest corner of the new Hangar 2. (NARA II, 80-G-32840, cropped)

Civilian employees at Kaneohe also participated in the station's defense, placing themselves in harm's way alongside the sailors and Marines. One of the more notable was Alice Beckley Spencer, a civil service telephone operator, who, in concert with Cdr. Martin and many others, rushed to the Administration Building at the height of the attack. Taking over the telephone switchboard from the enlisted man then on duty, Spencer remained there for the entire day, oblivious to the dangers around her. Not only did her services prove indispensable during a time in which message traffic was inordinately high, but her very presence "in plain view of hundreds of officers and men passing through the building" exerted a decidedly calming and steadying influence upon those about her.[137]

The Japanese strafing attacks wounded a great many men at Kaneohe. The first order of business was to assist the wounded and set the dead aside for attention later. Many volunteers gathered the injured, administered first aid where possible, and provided transportation to the Dispensary that lay a half-mile to the northeast beyond the flight line. Men arrived for treatment by every conveyance, from private vehicles and pickup trucks to bomb trailers. While preparing for the rush of casualties, about ten minutes after the raid commenced, Lt. Cdr. McCrimmon rushed into the Dispensary's north wing to check the twenty beds in the first floor ward for vacancies. To his astonishment, not one bed was filled, although the former patients' belongings lay

The trees and cottages of the "Coconut Grove" at NAS Kaneohe Bay, seen on 20 April 1941. The dredge *Dillingham* lies at lower right. (NARA II, 80-G-339892, cropped)

strewn about the room as they had raced to report to the hangars. "In all my years of practice," McCrimmon mused later, "I have never seen every one [*sic*] get cured so fast."

With the arrival of the very first casualties by ambulance, McCrimmon and Lt. George M. Hutto (MC) reported immediately to the operating room located around the corner from the ward, and at the end of the corridor of the Dispensary's west wing. In addition to the doctors and corpsmen, ambulatory patients did everything possible to care for the stream of incoming casualties, although inevitably the wounded backed up almost immediately and the corridors became filled

with men needing medical treatment. Finally arriving to seek treatment for his leg, Sea2c Ballou found the station's doctors operating nonstop, according priority to multiple and extreme injuries.[138]

One of the most seriously wounded was Ens. Foss, from Hangar 1. Brought into the Dispensary barely alive, the young officer succumbed there at about 0830 as a surgeon attempted to extract a bullet from the right side of his neck. Foss was typical of a generation of Americans who joined the military during the buildup of 1940–41. A native of Monticello, Arkansas, he attended Louisiana State University and A. & M. College and, after enlisting in the reserves, attended the U.S. Naval Reserve Midshipmen's School at Northwestern University. Letters of recommendation characterized him as "industrious, trustworthy, and able." During Foss' term at Northwestern, he demonstrated

A stretcher bearer helps carry VP-14 casualty Sea2c Ray O. Schultz across Second Street in front of the Squadron Office building under the watchful eye of an officer at left. (NARA II, 80-G-77625)

these sterling traits when he rescued a man who fell off a seawall into Lake Michigan, an act for which the commanding officer at Northwestern recommended Foss for the Silver Life Saving Medal.[139]

NAS Kaneohe Bay suffered severely at the hands of Lt. Kaneko's fighters, taking heavy losses in people and planes. Its defenders had been in no position to resist the relentless onslaught with anything but sidearms, rifles, and machine guns. The men of NAS Kaneohe Bay, however, had defended themselves with ingenuity and guts, answering every demand made upon them. No one knew, however, whether or not the Japanese would be back.

The Dispensary at NAS Kaneohe Bay, seen looking north on 6 April 1941, shortly after its completion. Sailors assisting their comrades in reaching this building on 7 December saw this side of it on their trek north from the hangar line. Note the Dispensary's twenty-bed ward at right. (NARA II, 71-CA-156B-14236)

# THREE

# "I WOULD HIT THE TARGETS WITHOUT ANY MISSES FROM THIS ALTITUDE"

Meanwhile, the 167 aircraft of the 2nd Wave Strike Force under the command of Lt. Cdr. Shimazaki Shigekazu arrived northeast of O'ahu. As in the first wave, the 35 fighters gained altitude to ensure that no American interceptors would interfere with the attacks on the harbor and airfields, with the *Sōryū* and *Hiryū* units setting up over eastern O'ahu. While the dive-bombers and the majority of the attack units continued toward Hickam Field and Pearl Harbor, two *chūtai*s of nine aircraft each from the *Shōkaku*'s horizontal bomber group under Lt. Ichihara Tatsuo circled seaward to the east, separating from the formation after passing Mōkapu Peninsula.

Ichihara made a tactical assessment of the situation as soon as he could see Kaneohe clearly. In contrast to the scene that greeted the aircrews approaching Pearl Harbor, there were no antiaircraft bursts over the station, good news for the *Shōkaku* aviators. The bad news, however, was that a thick cloud bank extended north from the Ko'olau Range over the bay. Still worse, although the clouds broke apart over the bay and the station, they were still thick enough to interfere with sighting the target area during the approach and drop.

Lt. Ichihara's tactical orders directed him to climb from his 2,500-meter cruising altitude, to an attack altitude of 3,000 meters. Like the first attack wave's torpedo unit, which changed its approach to Pearl Harbor due to poor weather conditions, Ichihara broke with his planned deployment. As bombing through the clouds offered little chance of success, he decided instead to attack from underneath the patchy cumulus layer below. Accordingly, the eighteen bombers in his group began their descent, setting up their runs on Kaneohe from the southwest.[1]

Ichihara probably started his 2,000-meter descent while still well out to sea, continuing on a generally southerly course until he passed the coastal flats at Kailua and Lanikai.[2] Then banking to starboard, the eighteen *kankō*s flew past the He'eia fish ponds along the southern shore of Kāne'ohe Bay, ducking under the clouds as they passed along the shore. Setting up their downwind assault, the bombers turned hard to starboard, almost reversing their original inbound heading. Leveling out below the clouds at 500 meters the Japanese could see their objective clearly: Kaneohe's aprons and hangars.[3]

Ichihara's problem was that at 500 meters neither the bombsight nor the surface torpedo aiming sight could be used. Although the pilot of the lead aircraft could see the target ahead, he could hardly be expected to judge

84

the release point. On the other hand, the target would not come into view through the bombardier's aiming window until the very last second, making it impossible for the crews to correct their course late in the run. Thus a successful drop against the hangar line required more blind intuition and luck than careful calculations.[4]

Ichihara organized the attack by *chūtai*, with his own division leading and Lt. Hagiwara Tsutomu's trailing a kilometer or so behind, widening its turn to extend the interval.[5] Per established doctrine, upon entering the bombing course, the plane that carried the expert observer-bombardier for each division rotated into the lead, forward and to the right, from the formation's number two position, WO Ukita Tadaaki from the 1st *Chūtai* and PO1c Nakamura Kōjirō from the 2nd. Accordingly, all eyes in Ichihara's group shifted to the new lead aircraft and focused on PO3c Tozawa Hiroshi, Ukita's radioman, and awaited his signal to release. At the tip of the arrowhead, PO2c Okimura Satoru, Uki-

ta's pilot, observed that his line of advance paralleled perfectly Kaneohe's new runway that lay oriented with the prevailing northeasterly trade winds. Ichihara had set the course for the run flawlessly.[6]

Any fleeting Japanese hopes of catching Kaneohe unawares dissipated quickly, for the Americans noted the arrival of the second wave well before Ichihara and

Shortly after the arrival of the *Shōkaku* unit over Kāne'ohe Bay, a photographer pivots to the right and rear during the approach over the bay's southern shore, providing a view of the naval air station more than a mile below, looking south and seaward, beyond Mōkapu Peninsula. Close examination of the image reveals no smoke rolling skyward from the station, except for 12-P-3 burning just off the seaplane ramps, an indication that no bombing attacks have occurred. Note the thick patches of cumulus clouds over the bay, evidence that the Japanese have not yet descended to their attack altitude. It was this layer of clouds that prompted Lt. Ichihara Tatsuo to attack from the altitude of five hundred meters. (BKS, Nagai Collection)

During the descent and final deployment of the *Shōkaku*'s 1st *Chutai*, Nakajima Type 97 attack bombers under the command of Lt. Ichihara Tatsuo fly east just above the heavy cloud cover over the Heʻeia fish pond along the southern shore of Kāneʻohe Bay. Winter rains have inundated the area south of the fish pond. Note the armament of two 250-kg bombs under aircraft EI-325 at center and under EI-329 at right. (*Maru*)

*Right:* Lt. Ichihara Tatsuo, commander, *Shōkaku* horizontal bombing unit, and commander, 1st *Chutai*. (*Maru*)

company began their runs. Men at the station observed the bombers fifteen miles out to sea despite the cloud cover. Looking north from Mōkapu Peninsula, one had an unobstructed view, and it would have been difficult for any large formation of planes to arrive undetected. Cdr. Martin's perceptive wife, Elizabeth, recalled seeing the bombers "coming in directly from the seaward . . . slightly east of north." Martin himself later recalled that "the view up there [was] absolutely wide open."[7]

## TABLE 2

### Second-Wave Attack on Kaneohe Bay

Lt. Ichihara Tatsuo

*Shōkaku* Horizontal Bombing Unit

1st *Chūtai*—Lt. Ichihara Tatsuo

|  | Pilot | Observer/Bombardier | Radioman/Rear Gunner |
|---|---|---|---|
| 41st *Shōtai* | Lt. Ichihara Tatsuo | WO Isono Teiji | PO2c Munakata Yoshiaki |
|  | PO2c Okimura Satoru | WO Ukita Tadaaki | PO3c Tozawa Hiroshi |
|  | PO3c Origasa Yoshikazu | PO2c Matsuyama Yataka | PO3c Takada Tadakatsu |
| 42nd *Shōtai* | PO1c Saitō Yoshio | Lt. (jg) Yano Norio | PO3c Ibayashi Junpei |
|  | Sea1c Ōtani Shinji | PO2c Ōkubo Chūhei | PO2c Kodama Seizō |
|  | Sea1c Kawahara Takehiko | PO2c Yamanouchi Kazuo | Sea1c Gomi Shigeo |
| 43rd *Shōtai* | PO1c Ōkubo Masaru | PO1c Sugano Kenzō | PO3c Ishihara Yoshio |
|  | Sea1c Itō Tōgo | PO2c Shigeta Naoki | Sea1c Chūna Yoshimitsu |
|  | PO2c Ikakura Kōji | PO3c Satō Ichizō | PO2c Horie Isamu |

The appearance of Ichihara's bombers galvanized the Americans into action. The crew of the station's lone fire engine—including Sea1c Stanley D. Dosick—drove the red vehicle into Hangar 1. When the bombers appeared, unarmed sailors received orders to take cover, which, in the wide-open spaces of Kaneohe, "was sparse or non-existent." Some men jumped into ditches or under anything substantial. With the lack of suitable gun mounts still a problem, some sailors drove one-inch pipes into the ground, and those who were able took to their guns and opened fire at the approaching Type 97s.[8]

With the stage set for the low-altitude run on Kaneohe, on the starboard side and to the rear of Ichihara's nine-plane formation, PO2c Ōkubo Chūhei marveled at his commander's bravery and at his impromptu decision to charge in at five hundred meters. Ōkubo waxed confident: "I would hit the targets without any misses from this altitude." He then noticed automobiles speeding away from the station, where, despite the strafing attacks one hour previous, a number of PatWing 1's PBY-5s still sat parked in neat rows. The bombing approach, however, proved far less favorable than either Ichihara or Ōkubo anticipated or hoped, as the *kankōs* shook terribly in the strong, unpredictable, "tumbling" winds so typical of the Mōkapu Peninsula. Additionally, Ōkubo noted with alarm many tracers whizzing through his formation. Nonetheless, the Type 97s pressed forward, and at 0907, on the signal relayed by Ukita's radioman, Ichihara's nine bombardiers released eighteen 250 kg bombs. It was physically impossible for a bombardier to release both of his bombs at once, as he had to pull two release levers simultaneously for each of the two bombs, with the result that the aircraft traveled a considerable distance (perhaps one hundred meters or more) between pulls. Hence, the eighteen bombs fell in two separate, ragged patterns.[9]

Much of the fire directed at Ichihara's division came from a BAR, a Lewis gun, and four other machine guns set up east of the parking aprons in the Coconut Grove.

Regardless of their poor position relative to the Japanese inbound course, the American gunners rendered a good account of themselves, sending skyward a leaden hail at 90 degrees deflection that the low and relatively slow bombers could not evade entirely.[10]

Elsewhere, preoccupied with matters on the ground, VP-14's RM1c Daucy B. Goza, a nineteen-year naval veteran from Calhoun City, Mississippi, happened to look up and see nine aircraft headed directly for Hangar 2, with another nine in the far distance, all approaching quite low at about two thousand feet. Goza was positive that the incoming planes had the hangar in their bombsights, so he left the vicinity, first at a deliberate pace in a defiant show of bravery, then finally at a dead run in abject fear. With the *kankōs* at such a low altitude there would be little time to evade the missiles once they dropped. Keeping an eye on Ichihara's group, Goza, seeing the bombs fall, flung himself to the pavement in an instant.[11]

Lt. Cdr. Buck Buckley, skipper of VP-12, likewise realized too late the imminent danger approaching from the Koʻolaus. Wanting to put distance between himself and any explosions, he took cover in the bay, splashing out waist deep. He then thought better of it, however, and with seconds to spare splashed back out of the water and hid behind the blade of a bulldozer. Not far away, AMM2c Cecil S. Malmin of VP-12 stayed put, firing a .50-caliber machine gun from the side blister of one of the squadron's surviving PBYs, counting the bombs as they dropped.[12]

To VP-14's Lt. Murray Hanson, the plummeting Japanese bombs looked like "bunches of grapes." Fascinated as the dropping ordnance grew larger by the second, Hanson later recounted, "We were so mesmerized by the sight that only at the last minute did we snap out of it and realize that we were in imminent danger." All of the men scattered, with an eye to the sky trying to guess where the bombs might impact and thus judge the safest direction in which to run. One sailor ran frantically toward the water and, while looking up, tripped over a seawall and tumbled fifteen feet into the water, "wet and startled, but safe."[13]

Watching the bomb run from a greater distance and from an angle perpendicular to Ichihara's heading, AMM3c Guy C. Avery, a Georgian who re-enlisted in 1939 after fours years in the Fleet Reserve, thought the fresh northeasterly breeze pushed the first group of 250-kg bombs back to the southwest about fifty yards, out into the water. F3c Harry W. Haase of VP-11 agreed. It seemed like the Japanese failed to account for the strong Hawaiian trade winds. As far away as the explosions were on the aprons south of Hangar 2, the concussion from the detonations knocked AOM3c Richmond flat on his face. The worst was yet to come, however, as the next group of nine bombs detonated on the apron, with some fleeing and unfortunate sailors running directly toward the blasts. The explosions straddled the PBY where AMM2c Malmin manned his .50-caliber Browning. One of the flying fragments wounded him in the left elbow, and Malmin was aware that hot fragments might set the aircraft afire. Nonetheless, he remained inside, as he saw another group of bombers approaching fast from the southwest. Out on the apron, Lt. Cdr. Buckley barely escaped being crushed by the bulldozer heaved aside by the force of an adjacent explosion. Nearby, the portly Goza lay prostrate on the pavement, straining to make himself as flat as possible. After the planes flew off, Goza strode to one of the large bomb fragments that had buzzed overhead just seconds before and touched it—it was blazing hot.[14]

Nearby, meanwhile, Sea2c Lyle A. Jackson was still belting ammunition in Hangar 2 when heard someone shout, "Close the hangar doors! Here they come again!" Jackson ran to the doors, but found no one to assist and decided that the refuge afforded by a nearby ordnance truck was preferable to standing in the open. From underneath the vehicle, he heard the earsplitting detonations south of the hangar and the sound of breaking glass. It was not until the explosions stopped that he realized that he lay in a puddle of water, as the concussion from the nearby bomb detonations tripped the hangar's automatic sprinklers, drenching those who sought refuge there. Jackson then jumped to his feet and ran to the Hangar 4 construction site to the west to retrieve his machine gun, but it was gone. With nothing to fight back with and with little cover near the partly erected hangar, he next ran still farther west, seeking the safety of the Coconut Grove, where comrades were already firing from among the cottages and trees.[15]

Despite the high drama on the ground, the immediate results of the run proved disappointing for the Japanese. Due to miscalculation related to their extremely low altitude and an inability to use their bombsights, Ichihara's men dropped considerably short of their target—presumably Hangar 2—with half of the ordnance splashing into the water south of the aprons. As for the bombs that struck the parking apron, no one observed any direct hits on aircraft, although bits of concrete or fragments set at least one additional VP-12 aircraft afire (12-P-7) and possibly damaged three VP-14 machines parked near the construction site of the future Hangar 4 to the west.[16] The poorly executed bomb run notwithstanding, smoke, flames, and flying debris added to the terror and confusion near the hangar and hindered VP-14's efforts to launch the last three undamaged aircraft left on the platform.[17]

Back in the air, meanwhile, due to their proximity to the ground, Ichihara's aircraft trembled with the concussion from each explosion. Unaware of how little damage the unit had inflicted, however, PO2c Ōkubo exulted, "Yattazō! (We did it!)" Quickly retrieving his camera, he began photographing the scene. WO Isono Teiji, Ichihara's bombardier, recorded the dismal results of the 1st *Chūtai*'s attack with a motion picture camera. With the drop preserved for posterity, Ichihara rotated back into the lead.[18] Irrespective of the gains that the *Shōkaku* commander expected from the altitude tradeoff, the bombing run had paid paltry dividends. Moreover, the hoped for—though unrealized—increase in accuracy was accompanied by a blizzard of .30- and .50-caliber machine-gun fire, with the Japanese forced to fight their way through a storm of well-aimed tracers fired from a range of little more than a third of a mile.[19]

Although the 1st *Chūtai*'s attack concluded with all aircraft intact and with no injuries among the aircrews,

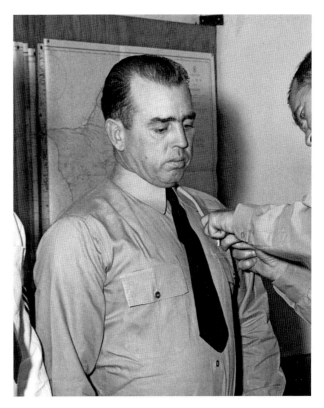

ACRM Daucy B. Goza receives the Purple Heart from Rear Adm. John W. Price on 24 May 1943. (NARA II, 80-G-70552, cropped)

Lt. (jg) Argyll E. Buckley, while assigned to VB-1B on board the aircraft carrier *Lexington* (CV-2), 1 July 1934. (NPRC, St. Louis)

it gave the Americans just enough time to get the range and prepare for Lt. Hagiwara's 2nd *Chūtai*, then approaching from the direction of the Ko'olaus. Emulating Ichihara, at 0910 Hagiwara entered his bombing run, roaring in at 130 knots. As the bombers approached the shore, however, the defenders at the Coconut Grove and many others opened fire and scored repeated hits on the incoming Type 97s, with much of the fire directed at the *kankōs* in the lead section. After rotating out of the lead into the number two position, Hagiwara's aircraft took hits on its electrical system, where bullets struck the secondary battery supply, knocked out the radio, and caused hydrochloric acid to spew into the cockpit. The acrid fumes ruined the voice tube and burned the eyes of pilot PO1c Ishikawa Satoki, who later found his bomber holed in eighteen places. Similarly, the section's number three aircraft commanded by PO2c Takahashi Hiroshi sustained serious damage, taking fire in the supplementary right fuel tank that caused the Type 97 to vent a plume of gasoline aft. Smoke from the pair of burning PBYs (12-P-3 and 12-P-7) and mist from Lt. Ichihara's previous botched drop into the bay mixed with the humid air, obscuring the station ahead. Unable to gain a clear view of the target during the awkward approach, and facing fierce and withering defensive fire from the bluejackets ahead and below, PO1c Nakamura Kōjirō—Hagiwara's lead bombardier—had seen enough. Deeming "the situation . . . unfavorable," he signaled an abort, and the formation circled east out to sea and reset for another run. Determined not to risk again the low-altitude gambit pursued by his commander, Hagiwara instructed Ishikawa to climb to 2,500 meters, from whence his *chūtai* would have to locate its target through a layer of broken clouds. At least from that safer altitude, the Japanese could expect relief from the American machine-gun and small arms fire.[20]

Meanwhile, Kaneohe's gritty defenders guessed correctly that something had gone awry with the attack, and they credited the station's antiaircraft fire and "strong point" machine-gun nests for driving off the Japanese and, perhaps, for wounding a lead bombardier. Sailors on the platform noted with satisfaction that several of the planes vented fuel to the rear as they retreated east. Apart from the nine bomb craters on the apron from Lt. Ichihara's drop and the loss of one additional PBY, the damage from the attack was not great. Had the Japanese acquired a clear view of the target, they would undoubtedly have pressed toward their objective. Nonetheless, their retreat, albeit temporary, led some American officers to opine that they "weren't too impressed by Japanese horizontal bombing."[21]

With the bombing attack turned aside, no one felt more relieved than the wounded AMM2c Malmin. During Hagiwara's aborted run, Malmin exited the aircraft from which he had fired earlier and took cover

WO Isono Teiji, Lt. Ichihara's observer and likely motion picture photographer on 7 December. (*Maru*)

Lt. Ichihara's observer, WO Isono Teiji, films the 1st *Chūtai*'s attack on NAS Kaneohe Bay. This collage of thirteen motion picture frames that covers the area from the new hangar under construction (the future Hangar 4) at left, Hangar 2 at center, to the small Maintenance Hangar just in the picture at upper right, then south to the apron and warm-up platform. The pattern of explosions moves across the image from left to right between the eight PBYs in the photo, with at least four of the 250-kg bombs dropping into Kāne'ohe Bay at lower right. The three bombs from Ichihara's lead section detonated in a tight pattern below Hangar 2's southeast corner. Those of the left section under Lt. (jg) Yano Norio bracketed the PBY-5s at center left, while those of the right section under PO1c Ōkubo Masaru detonated at center right, igniting the starboard wing tank of 12-P-7, parked about seventy-five yards north of the explosions. At lower right, 12-P-3 lies burning in the water just off the ramp. It is remarkable that despite their proximity, the explosions did not set fire immediately to the two PBYs from VP-14 that lie just below and to the left of Hangar 2. (NARA II, from Motion Picture Reel 242.290, Wenger Collection)

While Hagiwara reset for a second try, Ichihara likewise turned east, away from the station, led his division out to sea, and executed a clockwise turn into a full circle. Although Ichihara wanted to observe the damage inflicted during his bombing run, for the sake of safety he crossed well south and east of the hangar line. It was readily apparent that the attack had accomplished little, for there was no smoke boiling up from any of the hangars and he saw little evidence of additional damage to Kaneohe's complement of PBYs. Only one additional plume of smoke rolled skyward from 12-P-7 on the apron south of the Maintenance Hangar. Once again, WO Isono Teiji deployed his motion picture camera and filmed the scene. Then, just as Ichihara turned and shaped a westward course for the rendezvous off Ka'ena Point, PO2c Ōkubo peered to the southwest and noticed a tremendous amount of smoke across the Ko'olaus in the direction of Pearl Harbor.[23]

under a ramp tractor, accompanied by shipmates RM3c Perry V. Davis and AMM3c Gerald E. Coyle. After the bombers departed, Sea2c Wallace B. Richards, appeared suddenly with a bomb truck and told Malmin to hop in for the quick trip to the Dispensary.[22]

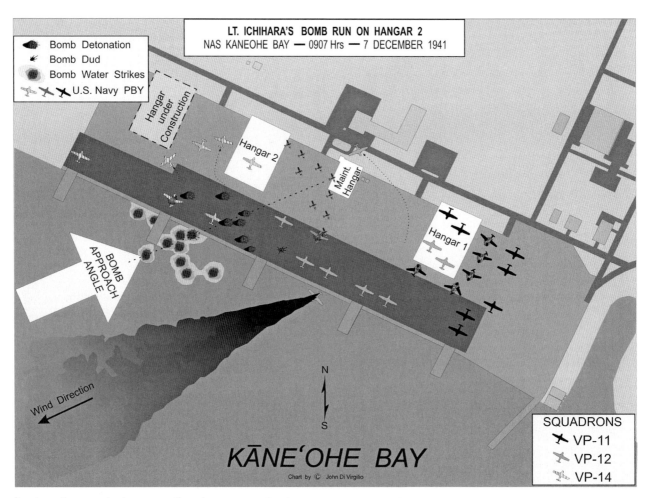

Chart showing the location of bomb craters south of Hangar 2 as a result of the strike by Lt. Ichihara's 1st *Chūtai*. Note that the diagram indicates that half of the eighteen bombs fell into Kāne'ohe Bay. (DiVirgilio, based on chart in "Naval Air Station Kaneohe Bay History," NHHC)

Set afire by fragments from the bombs of PO1c Sugano Kenzō's 43rd *Shōtai*, 12-P-7 lies broken and burning on the apron. (NARA II, 80-G-77623)

A bomb impact from the attack of Ichihara's 1st *Chūtai*, almost certainly the large crater opened on the apron south of Hangar 2, close to the water's edge. All the other bombs from this attack exploded with a much lower order of detonation. Based on the crater's position, the bomb came from Ichihara's number 6 aircraft, commanded by PO2c Yamanouchi Kazuo. Note the PBY-5 at upper left and the unfinished Hangar 4 in the far background. (NARA II, RG80, Formerly Security-Classified CNO Documents.)

Back on the ground, casualties continued to stream into the Dispensary, where McCrimmon had just started his third operation when the bombing began. Being preoccupied with his work, McCrimmon did not realize how frightened he was until the bombs started to fall. It was well that the operating room's two small windows opened to the north, so that the devastation on the hangar line to the southwest did not distract him further. With each bomb detonation, however, the door to the operating room swayed six inches in and out on its hinges. The swinging door became so annoying that McCrimmon posted a sailor to hold it fast so he could continue to operate.[24]

The distractions in the operating room were not without consequences. The third patient (then on the table) had sustained severe abdominal wounds that destroyed eighteen inches of small intestine. Flustered by interruptions and the swaying door, McCrimmon, with Lt. (jg) George M. Hutto—a 1936 graduate of George Washington University—assisting, decided upon a temporary colostomy. The procedure called for the surgeons to tie off the intestine temporarily and

During Lt. Ichihara's second fly-by at low altitude, observer Isono documents the destruction at Kaneohe with his motion picture camera just as another *kankō* (EI-329 with empty bomb crutches, commanded by WO Ukita Tadaaki) drifts into view from above. Interestingly, neither the 2nd Carrier Division fighters nor Lt. Hagiwara's bombers have attacked, as there are no fires visible except for 12-P-7 on the apron and 12-P-3 burning in the water. It is quite evident that the two PBYs from VP-14 near Hangar 2 did not catch fire as a result of the bombing attack. Note also that EI-329 is on a course inconsistent with executing a bomb release on the station, with the aircraft heading just north of east, rather than flying directly into the wind. A motion picture collage. (NARA II, from Motion Picture Reel 242.290, Wenger Collection)

attach the opening coming from the stomach to the abdominal wall, with the intent of reconnecting stomach and intestine after the flood of casualties ceased and the traumatized bowel had time to "rest." After concluding the operation and while scrubbing for the next patient, though, McCrimmon realized that he had sutured the intestine to the abdominal wall instead and simply dropped in the loose end from the stomach. "George, do you know what we did on that last patient? Get him back on the operating table!" The two surgeons quickly corrected their "plumbing error," and the patient (most likely ACMM "Duke" Byron) made a full recovery, demanding a steak dinner within ten days of the operation.[25]

Meanwhile, the reprieve that followed Lt. Hagiwara's abort proved short-lived because at 0915, seventeen Type 0 carrier fighters from the 2nd Carrier Division, under lieutenants Iida Fusata and Nōno Sumio arched in over Kaneohe from the northwest and renewed the

(above) View of NAS Kaneohe Bay during the second wave at approximately 0910, a strike photo taken from an aircraft of the *Shōkaku*'s *kankōtai* minutes after Lt. Ichihara's attack, but prior to that of Lt. Hagiwara. This presents the scene viewed by the fighters of the 2nd Carrier Division just prior to their strafing runs. At left, note the smoke columns rising from 12-P-3 still in the bay and from ill-fated 12-P-7 on the apron. Also an area of disturbed water is visible between the smoke columns, a result of the bomb detonations off shore, which churned up the shallow waters of Kāneʻohe Bay. All fires from the first-wave attack (except for 12-P-3) have been extinguished. (Makiel, via Ernest Arroyo)

(right) Lt. Cdr. Herman P. McCrimmon (MC), surgeon at NAS Kaneohe Bay's Dispensary, circa 1941. (Joseph P. McCrimmon)

Lt. George M. Hutto (MC), assistant surgeon at NAS Kaneohe Bay, circa January 1942. (NARA, St. Louis)

strafing attacks. The fighters had just concluded their combat air patrols high above, at six thousand meters, making two complete circuits over their assigned areas. Cleared for action by the empty skies above and below, Iida's *kansen*s tore into the parked PBYs with a vengeance, but the Americans, fully alerted, put up a blizzard of tracers so thick "that you could almost walk on it." Leading the 2nd *Shōtai* from Iida's *Sōryū* fighter unit, Lt. (jg) Fujita Iyozō, a bundle of nerves, shuddered at the sight below, breathing silent prayers that he might survive to fight another day. Well might he have prayed, for although at least five of the group claimed ground kills against six PBYs, American ground fire damaged many of Iida's group. The *Hiryū*'s fighters under Lt. Nōno Sumio entered the fray at 0915, but soon broke off their attacks after claiming only two PBYs set afire. Iida's *Sōryū* fighters had matters well in hand, and besides, Lt. Nōno had other fish to fry farther south, down the coast at Bellows Field.[26]

Despite the stiff resistance, Iida's men stayed the course over Kaneohe, executing two strafing runs near the hangar line, ferreting out targets there and in the water, including 12-P-3 just off Ramp 2, where the plane now lay burning to the waterline. The Zeros also strafed VP-14's machines launched into the bay during the lull, sinking both.[27]

The return of the *kansen*s proved a nasty surprise to sailors emerging from their cover following Ichihara's bombing attack on Hangar 2. Searching for cover in anticipation of the bombers' return, F3c Harry W. Haase, a Cleveland, Ohio, native, heard a VP-11 squadron-mate in the parking lot north of Hangar 1 call for help in setting up a .30-caliber machine gun retrieved from the nose turret of a nearby PBY. The Browning was of no use without ammunition, so the pair ran into the hangar and, joined by a third sailor, grabbed three cases of belted ordnance. No one followed the trio back to their position, opting for the comparative

Lt. Iida Fusata, second-wave fighter unit leader, *Sōryū.* (Prange)

**TABLE 3**

**Second-Wave Attack on NAS Kaneohe Bay**

Lt. Iida Fusata

*Sōryū* Fighter Unit

| 1st *Shōtai* | 2nd *Shōtai* | 3rd *Shōtai* |
|---|---|---|
| Lt. Iida Fusata | Lt. (jg) Fujita Iyozō | PO1c Oda Kiichi |
| PO1c Atsumi Takashi | PO1c Takahashi Sōzaburō | PO2c Tanaka Jirō |
| PO2c Ishii Saburō | PO2c Okamoto Takashi | PO3c Takashima Takeo |

safety of the hangar. Haase and company dashed out with their ammunition, prodded along by the strafing of Iida's Zeros. The incident burned itself into Haase's memory, as he recalled that "as we made our way back to the machine gun, we found ourselves dodging bullets like pedestrians trying to cross a street in heavy traffic." The spent bullets "spinning like a top" on the concrete mesmerized Sea2c Robert U. Hanna, who attempted, naively, to pick up one of the hot projectiles as a souvenir.[28]

During the previous strafing, many sailors found that the hangars' heavy rolling doors lacked armor and offered little protection, which seemed incredible to the sailors inside, who knew that it took a crew of ten to open and close them. When RM3c Richard R. J. Moser of VP-12 heard someone in Hangar 1 yell an order to take cover, he squeezed into the recess of one of the hangar's supporting I-beams, an arrangement that worked admirably, except that when the scenario repeated itself, Moser found every I-beam occupied and instead hid behind an ammunition truck that had pulled into the doorway of the hangar. Repeating the routine of the first wave, sailors in and near Hangar 1 returned fire, serving .30- and .50-caliber machine guns from the aprons and hangar windows, with the terrific jackhammer din reverberating through the cavernous building.[29]

For those manning the guns, firing at high-level bombers entailed less danger, but taking on fighters one-on-one seemed almost suicidal. At some point, an order came down that directed all the men to leave the aprons, but it is questionable whether the defenders would have obeyed, so great was their desire to defend the base. One of the men who stood his ground was VP-12's AOM1c Moreno J. Caparrelli. Matt1c Walter W. Simmons strove to keep the gunner supplied with ammunition and ran for safety when ordered, but only after securing two cans of .50-caliber ammunition for Caparrelli. Predictably, the casualties began to mount once again. The fallen near Hangar 1 included VP-12's AMM1c Raphael A. "Ralph" Watson, who had earlier served a machine gun on the warm-up platform so fearlessly. Everyone's friend, the amiable Watson lay critically injured with gunshot wounds in the chest and right shoulder.[30]

Meanwhile, after parking his car following the drive from the BOQ, Ens. Muckenthaler ran from his vehicle and, after frustrating delays, finally reported to Hangar 1 for duty amid the chaotic spectacle of attacking planes and determined defenders. Greeted by the desperate scene in and near the hangar, the young ensign was at a loss and wondered what to do next. Then he spied Ens. Joseph G. Smartt, VP-11's officer of the deck, who had taken over for the slain Ens. Foss early in the raid. Muckenthaler asked Smartt, "What are we supposed to do now?" While awaiting Smartt's reply, Muckenthaler noted the heroic efforts under way, with sailors doing everything possible to salvage aircraft, weapons, and ordnance. "The 'Old Man,'" Smartt replied, "wants us to meet in the ready room." Wanting to arrange patrol flights with the squadron's surviving planes, Lt. Cdr. Leon

Sea1c Raphael A. Watson, battleship *California* (BB-44) Aviation Unit, circa 1935. (Watson, cropped)

W. "Slim" Johnson had ordered a meeting of all available officers and aircrews. Soon joined by Ens. Robert J. "Bob" Waters, A-V(N)—a Brooklyn, New York, native and 1938 graduate of NYU—the ensigns hastened to the southwest stairwell leading to the ready room in the hangar's bayside mezzanine.[31]

Like Ens. Muckenthaler, Y1c Kenton Nash only just arrived in the vicinity of Hangar 1. By the time Nash started driving toward his objective in his 1940 Packard coupe, there was a break in the attack, but when Nash arrived, the second attack was under way, and sailors north of the hangar frantically admonished him to get out of his car. Close by, F3c Henry A. Haase of VP-11 and a civilian were struggling to get a machine gun into operation, laying the weapon atop a pile of reinforcing steel rods. Nash stood amongst some crated toilet seats trying to advise the two from which direction the enemy aircraft were coming. The assistance offered to Haase and the civilian distracted Nash—a newlywed Montanan

who joined the Navy to learn a trade—from his prime objective, to get to the hangar and pitch VP-11's personnel records onto the hangar floor where, in case of fire, they at least might be preserved by the sprinkler system.[32]

Back at Hangar 2, meanwhile, with his metalsmiths hard at work, ACOM John Finn, a veteran chief with fifteen years service, at last secured a .30-caliber machine gun from VP-14's painter, Ptr1c Alexander Drockton, and dashed out onto the platform under heavy fire. Assisted by squadron-mate and Coloradan RM2c Robert J. Peterson, Finn mounted the Browning "on an instruction stand in a completely exposed section of the parking ramp" on the bayside of Hangar 1, where the two sailors maintained their fire despite all opposition. Shortly thereafter, Finn switched over to a .50-caliber Browning and suffered wounds from gunfire or bomb fragments to his left arm and foot, and many lesser flesh wounds, but the pair persisted in their fierce resistance to the Japanese fighters.[33] Years later, Finn recalled: "I got shot in the left arm and shot in the left foot, broke the bone. I had shrapnel blows in my chest and belly and right elbow and right thumb. Some were just scratches. My scalp got cut, and everybody thought I was dying."[34]

Despite his horrific appearance, Finn was not dying, and until that juncture VP-14 had escaped with only several men wounded. It was probably during the strafing of the apron by the *Sōryū* fighters, however, that AMM3c Laxton G. Newman fell, the squadron's sole fatality that morning. Although the precise circumstances surrounding Newman's death are unknown, shipmates found him face down at the water's edge in the vicinity of Hangar 2 after the attack, a 20-millimeter round through his back. The twenty-five-year-old from Cravitz, Wisconsin, had wanted a career in the Navy and had earned advancement to AMM3c only a year and a week after his enlistment.[35]

Meanwhile, after climbing and circling downwind and emerging above the clouds over Kāneʻohe Bay, Lt. Hagiwara's division of nine *kankōs* approached from the southwest at 2,500 meters, re-entering its original bombing course on a bearing of 65 degrees. Subsequent

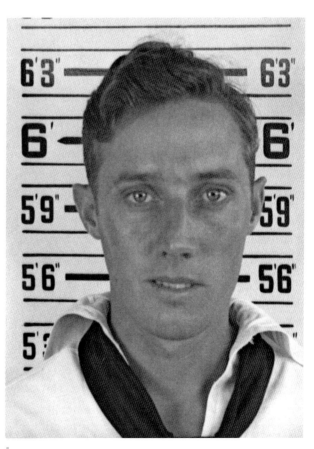

"Beyond the call of duty . . ." ACOM (PA) John W. Finn, wearing the Medal of Honor awarded for valor at NAS Kaneohe Bay on 7 December 1941. (USAR 2056)

AMM3c Laxton G. Newman, circa May 1941. (NARA, St. Louis)

VP-14's sole fatality, AMM3c Laxton G. Newman, lies at water's edge south of Hangar 2. At upper right, wreckage from two VP-14 PBYs litters the extreme western edge of the warm-up apron. (NARA II, 80-G-32858)

events are difficult to interpret, but evidence suggests the following.

Hagiwara's unit made two bombing runs, the first from the southwest. Unable to see the target area through the cloud cover during what was, in effect, a blind approach, Hagiwara signaled the crews to extend intervals to port and starboard, ensuring a wider coverage for the drop. He also instructed his men to let go of only half their ordnance in case of a ruined release. Expert bombardier PO1c Nakamura Kōjirō had only a few seconds to adjust his approach and drop the bombs and apparently misjudged the strong headwinds sweeping off Mōkapu Peninsula. Indeed, observers on the ground noted that, again, bombs fell off shore, well short of the aprons. Perhaps frustrated and reasoning that the clouds were thinner west of, and directly over, the station, Hagiwara circled yet again, setting up a run from the northwest, roughly parallel with Kaneohe's hangar line. This crosswind attack, though violating doctrine, would enable the lead bombardier to get a better view of the target.[36]

With Nakamura commanding the drop, radioman PO2c Fukushima Yoshio relayed the visual signal aft at 0920, and again nine 250-kg bombs plummeted toward the eastern aprons and Hangar 1, where a great many men were replenishing ammunition under the direction of Lt. Cdr. Buckley. The bombs fell in a looser "V" pattern this time, stretching to the north and south. With remarkable discernment, Sea2c Desmond V. Hatcher, despite his relative inexperience, astutely observed that "only the . . . leader had a bombsight and the others dropped in accordance with his verification."[37]

By the time the defenders comprehended the imminent attack, it was too late to evacuate Hangar 1. "Those of us on the outside," Ens. George F. Poulos of VP-11, a Manteca, California, native, remembered, "took shelter as best we could and watched the clusters of bombs drop toward the hangar." AMM2c Scotty Nilssen also noticed Hagiwara's drop, but accorded priority to reaching suitable cover over watching the bombs come down. Nilssen ran north frantically toward an open area when construction crews had stacked a supply of concrete reinforcing wire

mesh. Just as he crossed Second Street, the bombs began to explode.[38]

With perhaps some extra allowance for the "tumbling winds of Mōkapu," and with the 46th and 47th *Shōtai*s (Lt. (jg) Iwamura Katsuo and WO Suzuki Naoichirō) extending their intervals to port and starboard, respectively, the nine bombs fell on the platform, detonating on or near Hangar 1, and among the burned PBYs that lay on the parking apron south, and east of, the building. The red flashes and debris-filled clouds that mushroomed up from the hangar and adjoining aprons indicated a successful run to a much relieved Ichihara who—probably observing from some distance to the northeast—ordered radioman PO2c Munakata Yoshiaki to tap out a triumphant announcement to *Kidō Butai* at 0925[39] . . .

_ · · _ _    · · · ·    · · · · _    · · · · _    _ _ ·

"ユ-ヌ44リ" (yu-nu 44 ri), or,
"Results of our bombing on Kaneohe great."[40]

Lt. Hagiwara Tsutomu, commander, 2nd *Chūtai*, *Shōkaku* horizontal bombing unit. (*Maru*)

PO1c Ishikawa Satoki, Lt. Hagiwara's pilot. (Murakami)

WO Yonekura Hisato, pilot for lead bombardier PO1c Nakamura Kōjirō, 2nd *Chūtai*, *Shōkaku* horizontal bombing unit. (*Maru*)

Lt. (jg) Iwamura Katsuo, commander, 46th *Shōtai*, *Shōkaku* horizontal bombing unit. (*Maru*)

WO Suzuki Naoichirō, commander, 47th *Shōtai*, *Shōkaku* horizontal bombing unit. (*Maru*)

Lt. Hagiwara's nine Type 97 attack bombers (see inset at right) pass over NAS Kaneohe Bay while circling for altitude prior to their bombing attack. Note Hangar 2 at center with smoke rising from 12-P-3 in the bay and from 12-P-7 on the apron, indicating that Lt. Ichihara's attack has already taken place. (Lord)

Some seven thousand feet below, explosions rocked Hangar 1 inside and out, filling the air with smoke and debris that turned day into night. Three bombs scored direct hits, one exploding just inside the hangar doors a hundred feet from the north wall, bracketed by two others, both of which either failed to explode or did so with a low order of detonation. Two other bombs struck just outside the hangar among the PBY wreckage on the apron, opening up huge craters in the pavement. The concussion from the explosions proved so great that some men

thought that bombs had detonated depth charges inside the hangar. Blast concussion tore gaping holes in the roof, blew glass from the hangar doors, and carried away huge sections of fascia and siding from the outer walls, raining tons of debris onto the pavement in all directions. Making matters worse, one of the explosions northeast of the hangar ruptured a twelve-inch water main that disabled the sprinkler system in Hangar 1.[41]

North of the hangar, Y1c Kenton Nash of VP-11 was still about 150 feet from the building and 60 feet away from his car. Nash could only see a few strafing fighters and failed to notice Hagiwara's Type 97s high above. Suddenly, a 250-kg bomb exploded a short distance from his automobile, with the concussion breaking out the windows of the Packard and tipping it on its side. Nash remembered the glass breaking out "like

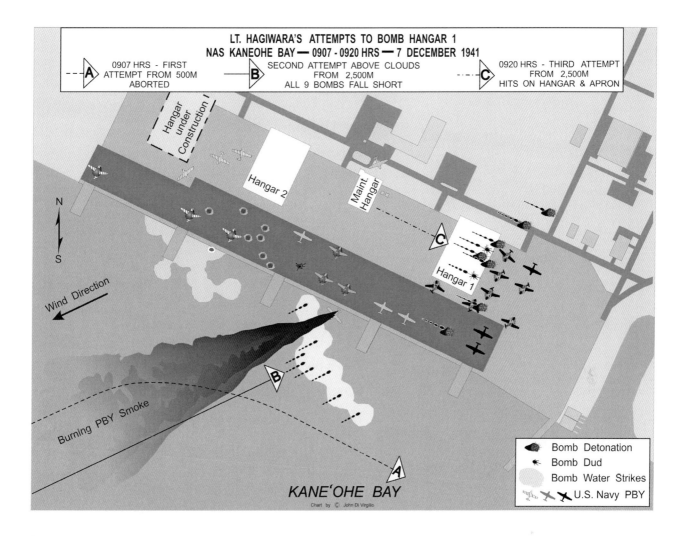

Chart showing the location of bomb craters in the vicinity of Hangar 1 as a result of the strike by Lt. Hagiwara's 2nd *Chūtai*. Once again, note that the diagram indicates that half of the eighteen bombs fell into Kāne'ohe Bay. (Di Virgilio, based on chart in "Naval Air Station Kaneohe Bay History," NHHC)

break-away windows in a movie." Then, while leaning up against the toilet seat crates, Nash realized that he had been hit by bomb fragments that carried away the humerus and triceps in his upper arm. With only the intact biceps keeping his lower arm in place, Nash walked over to a construction contractor's shack, passing the two nearby machine gunners knocked to the ground by the concussion. There was another sailor already in the shack, who took one look at the suffering Nash and tore up his shirt for a tourniquet up near the shoulder, an action that probably saved the yeoman's

life. One of his good friends drove by in an ambulance and stopped to pick him up. Nash got in, still fully conscious and with ears ringing, and the driver raced to get "out of there in pretty much of a hurry." Nash arrived at the Dispensary, where someone assisted him onto a mattress on the floor, where he was given something for shock, as he had also lost quite a bit of blood from the traumatic amputation of his arm.[42]

The dead, dying, and wounded lay scattered throughout Hangar 1, with stunned survivors shaken by the concussion. The explosions killed at least six men outright, and even one of the two duds that hit the hangar cut down a crew of sailors belting ammunition. The only survivor of that group was Lt. Cdr. Buck Buckley—VP-12's commanding officer—who less than fifteen minutes before had narrowly survived the bombing near Hangar 2. Miraculously, he escaped that second ordeal

# TABLE 4

## Second–Wave Attack on NAS Kaneohe Bay

Lt. Ichihara Tatsuo

*Shōkaku* Horizontal Bombing Unit

2nd *Chūtai*—Lt. Hagiwara Tsutomu

|  | Pilot | Observer/Bombardier | Radioman/Rear Gunner |
|---|---|---|---|
| 45th *Shōtai* | PO1c Ishikawa Satoki | Lt. Hagiwara Tsutomu | PO2c Sagara Eikichi |
|  | WO Yonekura Hisato | PO1c Nakamura Kōjirō | PO2c Fukushima Yoshio |
|  | Sea1c Murakami Nagato | PO2c Takahashi Hiroshi | Sea1c Kikuchi Shirō |
| 46th *Shōtai* | Lt. (jg) Iwamura Katsuo | WO Shibata Masanobu | PO3c Misumi Nobumatsu |
|  | Sea1c Hitomi Tatsuya | PO1c Shirai Fukujirō | PO2c Tomizu Giichi |
|  | Sea1c Satō Chōsaku | PO2c Ōta Rokunosuke | Sea1c Kobayashi Kazuo |
| 47th *Shōtai* | PO1c Satō Takashi | WO Suzuki Naoichirō | PO2c Miyanaga Eiji |
|  | PO2c Akao Akira | PO1c Ichijō Shinichi | Sea1c Etō Kinya |
|  | Sea1c Takei Kiyomi | PO3c Tanaka Tsunehiro | Sea1c Sakashita Kazuo |

View looking east from the water's edge on the warm-up platform south of Hangar 2, after Lt. Hagiwara's bombing attack. Smoke boiling up from Hangar 1 dominates the scene, while 12-P-7 still smolders at center. Wreckage litters the platform further down at right. 12-P-3 lies just off shore at far right, burned to the waterline. (NARA II, 80-G-77617)

Struck by three 250-kg bombs during Lt. Hagiwara's attack, Hangar 1 burns out of control as an automobile turns east on Second Street at the intersection with Avenue B. The worst of the fires were confined to the north face and office spaces. View taken in front of the Bombsight Workshop and Repair Building (just out of the photo at right), looking west. (NARA II, 80-G-32841)

Damage to the interior of VP-12's northern portion of Hangar 1. Note the enormous concrete slabs thrown up by the detonation of what was probably lead bombardier PO1c Nakamura Kōjirō's 250-kg bomb just inside the east doors. View looking south. A fire-damaged PBY is visible at far left. (USAR 1332)

View of Hangar 1 interior looking north, showing the extensive fire and blast damage sustained by the hangar roof. The Squadron Office Building is visible through the hangar doors at left, while a bomb crater and collapsed pavement is visible at lower right. Note the walled-in bay below the mezzanine on the lower level, just left of center, the probable location of the hangar's armory. (USAR 1331)

(above) Chunks of concrete litter the pavement near the crater opened up by a bomb detonation in Second Street, midway between Hangar 1 and the intersection of Second Street and Avenue B. Note the water-filled crater at right, presumably due to the twelve-inch main ruptured by the explosion. It was in this vicinity that AMM2c "Scotty" Nilssen took cover and Y1c Kenton Nash lost his left arm. (NARA II, 80-G-32842)

(right) Y1c Kenton Nash, circa 1941. (NARA, St. Louis)

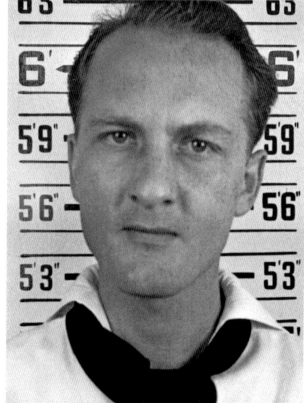

Ens. Lee Fox Jr., A-V(N), circa 5 August 1941, at the time of his assignment to the Fleet Air Detachment and VP-24 in San Diego. (NARA, St. Louis)

Ens. Robert W. Uhlmann, D-V(G), circa 12 June 1941. (NH 76372)

with only minor injuries. Two other officers from the squadron—Ens. Lee Fox Jr., A-V(N), and Ens. Robert W. Uhlmann, D-V(G)—were not as fortunate. Flying splinters or concrete shards struck Fox in the neck and chest and disemboweled Uhlmann. Both men were dead by the time would-be rescuers arrived. Fox—a member of the Intercollegiate Flying Club at the University of Pennsylvania—had received his commission as an ensign only four months before. Uhlmann, who studied at the University of Michigan's College of Engineering, had only two more months of service than Fox had.

Explosions also rocked the team watching over the teletype machine in the land line office up in Hangar 1's north seaside mezzanine. RM1c Thomas W. Helm III, who hailed from New Augustine, Florida, and RM3c Charles E. Day, a native of Beverly, Massachusetts, stayed at their post in the office safeguarding the teletype, where Helm stood fast despite losing the fourth and fifth fingers of his left hand. The pair abandoned their post only

RM3c Charles E. Day, circa late 1941. (NARA, St. Louis)

View looking east in Hangar 1's north mezzanine, gutted by explosions and fires resulting from Lt. Hagiwara's bombing attack. Note the effect of the intense heat on the windows, the stringers between the upright girders, and the office desks and filing cabinet. (USAR 1330)

after the machine seized and intense smoke and flames prompted an order for them to vacate the premises.[43]

When the bombs exploded, ensigns Smartt, Waters, and Muckenthaler were on their way up the stairs leading to VP-11's ready room in the south mezzanine. Even though the trio was on the opposite end of the hangar from the detonations, the terrific blasts threw all three men to the deck. Though stunned, Muckenthaler and Waters regained their footing and moved to assist Smartt, who lay motionless a few feet away, hit by multiple fragments in the neck and left rear shoulder. Muckenthaler tried to lift the tall, burly OOD, but the effort was futile; Smartt, the second watch officer from VP-11 to perish in as many hours,

lay dead. The sight of his gregarious Pensacola classmate and good friend moved Muckenthaler, a devout Roman Catholic, deeply, and he decided to administer last rites to his lifeless squadron-mate. Using saliva, he baptized Smartt "in the name of the Father, Son, and Holy Ghost," but then, regretfully, felt compelled to move on, as the needs of the wounded men in the hangar took precedence.[44]

Sea1c LeRoy G. Maltby of VP-11, a diminutive former resident of Yonkers, New York, belting ammunition in VP-12's Armory under the north mezzanine before the explosions, heard someone yell that the Japanese had returned and were bombing the airfield. Suddenly, a bomb detonated in the hangar doorway and the concussion knocked almost everyone flat. "The next thing I knew I was picking myself up off the deck," recounted Maltby, who was fortunate to have escaped with only cuts. The blast knocked out the wired glass in one of the walls of the Armory, and, looking out,

Ens. Joseph G. Smartt, A-V(N), circa 17 September 1941. (NARA, St. Louis)

AvCdt. Charles P. Muckenthaler, while in flight training at NAS Pensacola, 31 January 1941. (NNAM)

Ens. Robert J. Waters, A-V(N), circa 26 June 1941. (NARA, St. Louis)

Maltby saw several men knocked out and motionless, though apparently unwounded.[45] The wounded were there, however, as he next encountered AMM1c (NAP) Chubby Lyons with the heel blown off of one foot. Lyons, who had gone to the hangar that morning to paint his son's bicycle, just knew that with his right foot gone, his flying days were over.[46]

Elsewhere, RM3c Richard Moser sat stunned on the pavement with a "very dull feeling" and cognizant of little, apart from pieces of asbestos raining down from the shattered ceiling. Unable to walk but pulling himself along the hangar floor for a short distance with his arms, Moser realized he was injured only when seeing blood smeared on the concrete when he moved; he then passed out. Ens. Cyrenus L. Gillette, A-V(N), VP-12's assistant navigation officer, extracted Moser from the blazing hangar and transported the wounded radioman and three other sailors to the Dispensary in his Cadillac convertible. Gillette's leadership and initiative came

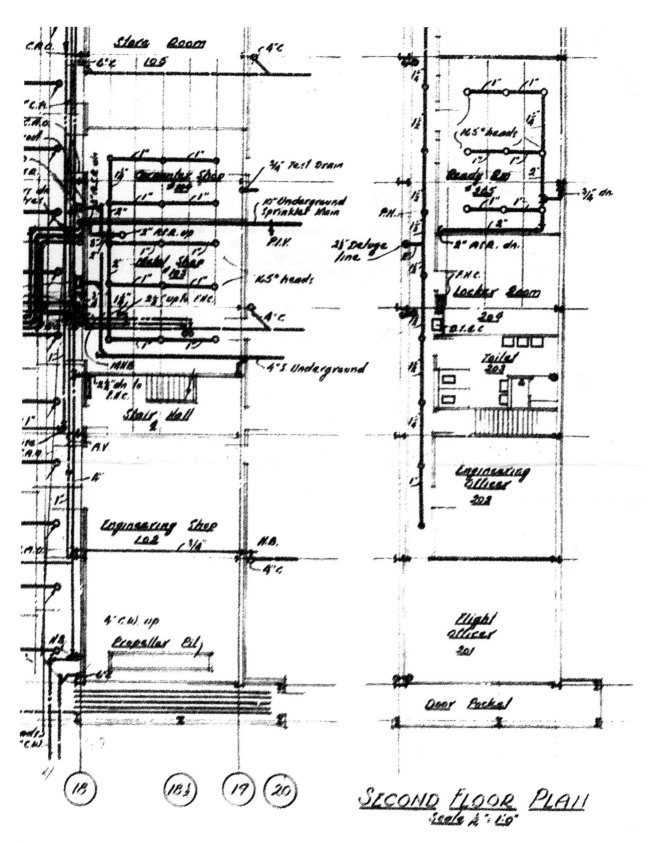

Portion of the architectural drawing for the hangars at NAS Kaneohe showing plans for the first (left) and second (right) floors of the mezzanine in the southeast corner of the hangar. Note the ready room (205) at upper right and the stairwell where fragments struck down Ens. Smartt. (NARA II, RG71A, Reel 1174)

Although the worst of the fires in Hangar 1 consumed the north end of the building, the south offices and shops also sustained blast and fire damage as a result of the bombing attack. Ens. Smartt was killed at far left. (NARA II, 80-G-77624)

naturally, as after completing a course of study at the General Motors Institute of Technology in 1935, he supervised one hundred men in the foundry at GM's Cadillac Motor Car Division and was remembered by management as "enthusiastic, ambitious, and capable."[47]

Other men soon joined Gillette in transporting the wounded. Although aircraft wreckage, bomb craters, fires, and smoke on the east side of the hangar prevented vehicles from gaining access to the building from that direction, the hangar's west doors were clear. Eager to assist,

Ens. Muckenthaler drove his 1941 Oldsmobile around to the west side of the hangar, following the 1941 Lincoln Zephyr driven by Ens. Carlton H. "Doltie" Clark, VP-11's navigation officer. Muckenthaler pulled up right behind Clark, bumper to bumper. Although *kansen*s reappeared and "strafed the hell" out of Clark's Zephyr, the Oldsmobile escaped without a scratch except for a broken light under the license plate. The two officers ran into the blazing hangar, searching for wounded sailors. As soon as Muckenthaler located several, he assisted the men into his Oldsmobile, backed away from the battered Zephyr parked ahead, and headed for the Dispensary.[48]

One of the sailors seeking cover in Hangar 1 before the bombing—Sea2c Armand "Pete" Petriccione—joined a group of comrades in a small room inside the

Of cinder block construction, the armory under the north mezzanine in Hangar 1 fared better than the thin-walled compartments on either side, but still suffered blown out windows and fragmentation damage to its exterior. Note the gutted office furnishings from the adjacent offices and shops. (USAR 1331, cropped)

building as soon as they saw Hagiwara's bombers passing over the hangar line. As a precaution, the men left the door open in anticipation of possible concussion. The bombs fell in short order, and though the open door may have lessened the dreadful shock of the explosions, fragments claimed Sea1c Luther D. Weaver, a machinist striker, a jolly "stringbean-type" and friend to all. Stunned, Petriccione went to his squadron-mate to lend aid, but Weaver was dead with chest wounds and his

back ripped open. Another VP-11 man commandeered a bomb rack truck and enlisted Petriccione's help and that of others to pick up the dead and wounded. Attempting to move Weaver, Petriccione's hand went clear through his friend's back. Somehow summoning the moral strength to continue his grisly task, he helped load and transport Weaver and others to the Dispensary. VP-12's AOM3c Donald McCoy assisted Petriccione in the grim business of preparing casualties for transport. After this duty, McCoy was so covered with blood that shipmate AOM3c Bert Richmond assumed that his friend numbered among the wounded.[49]

Meanwhile, with the main floor of the hangar now burning and filling with thick black smoke, Sea1c LeRoy Maltby searched for an escape route from the inferno,

(above) Prtr3c LeRoy G. Maltby receives the Purple Heart from Capt. Wallace M. Dillon at NAS Kaneohe Bay in early May 1943 for wounds received during the Japanese attack on 7 December 1941. Presumably the ceremony took place shortly before Dillon's departure on 18 May. (NARA II, 80-G-419190, cropped)

(right) Lt. (jg) Dale S. Lyons seated on the starboard wing of a Grumman F6F later in the war, holding his artificial lower leg at left. After nine months of hospitalization and rehabilitation, aided by the prosthesis, Lyons again qualified for flight duty, an extraordinary personal victory against the Japanese. (Engel)

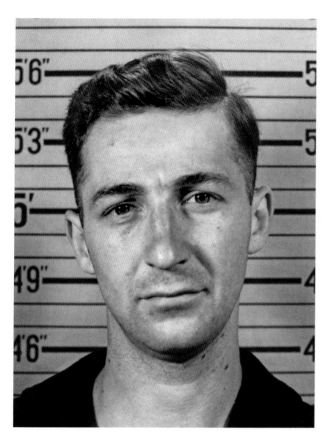

RM3c Richard R. J. Moser, circa late 1941, while assigned to VP-12. (NARA, St. Louis)

AvCdt Cyrenus L. Gillette, circa 1940, while in flight training at NAS Pensacola. (NPRC, St. Louis)

joined by others who had regained consciousness. The men picked up two unconscious shipmates and made their way through the office spaces on the north face of the hangar, passing through a window jarred loose by the explosions. After they emerged from the blazing building, a Zero roared down Second Street and chased them off the road, forcing the men to take cover between two paint lockers. Ultimately, a truck stopped, picked up Maltby and the wounded men, and took off for the Dispensary, although strafers forced the driver to forge a cross-country path to the northeast, weaving between buildings, through parking lots, and across the parade ground before reaching the Dispensary undamaged.[50]

Sailors from the station's fire department also fell victim to the bomb blasts. Staying with his engine until the

Sea2c Armand Petriccione of VP-11, who tended casualties after the bombing attack on Hangar 1. (Petriccione)

last, Sea1c Stanley D. Dosick—an aviation metalsmith striker and one of the Seagrave pumper's gallant crew—lay among the seriously wounded, with bomb fragments carrying away portions of his abdomen and right hip. Fellow sailors transported Dosick, barely alive, to the Dispensary, where he "expired shortly after admission."[51]

Quite apart from the dreadful carnage and the destruction of Hangar 1 itself, Kaneohe sustained significant material losses in Hagiwara's bombing attack; fire and blast damage destroyed not only the PBYs inside but also the station's Seagrave pumper that during the lull had rendered such admirable service among the PBYs east of the hangar. With sprinklers inoperable and firefighting impossible, flames gutted the office spaces on the hangar's north wall, claiming virtually all the files from VP-12 except for a few gunnery records.

Kaneohe's only fire truck, a 1939 Seagrave pumper, lies mangled and burned out east of Hangar 1. Lt. Hagiwara's bombing attack destroyed the vehicle—killing station fireman Sea1c Stanley D. Dosick at his post—inside the hangar. (NARA II, 80-G-32848)

Sea2c Stanley D. Dosick, between April and September 1941. (NARA, St. Louis)

The contents of VP-11's offices in the south mezzanine suffered similarly, except for the squadron's enlisted personnel files, flight logs, equipment logs, and various confidential data sheets that escaped only through the gallant action of Y2c Charles E. Williams, who, after earlier manning a machine gun near the hangar, ran alone into the blazing building to retrieve critical records. Loyal and conscientious throughout his thirteen years of service, like so many other sailors Williams rose to the occasion and deployed great courage while making the most of his talents and abilities.[52]

Meanwhile, after Hagiwara's bombing run, the *Sōryū* fighter unit continued its strafing against the American defenders. Unarmed men hunkered down and waited for the danger to pass, but those who had secured weapons stood firm and fired back. Because so many sailors had reported to their duty stations near the hangars, the shortage of arms was still very much in evidence. After acquiring weapons, some men held onto them tenaciously, although others found it within themselves to share. One such group of sailors clustered

AvCdt. George F. Poulos, while in flight training at NAS Pensacola, 5 December 1939. (NNAM)

Y1c Charles E. Williams, circa 1942. (Dohrmann)

about the Springfield rifle that VP-12's AOM3c Bert Richmond had acquired, with men patiently waiting their turn to fire several rounds before passing the rifle to the next man in line.[53]

Ens. Poulos of VP-11 put his .45-caliber automatic pistol into action from behind the protection of a tree trunk. After emptying all of his magazines at planes overhead, Poulos proceeded to the advance ordnance shack for additional ammunition, but instead discovered an ordnanceman inside who was badly wounded "in the left shoulder, chest, hip, and thigh."[54] Looking about for help, the ensign secured assistance and tore the shack's door off its frame. Within five minutes, the injured man was outside and ready for transport to the Dispensary.[55]

In the latter stages of their attack, after completing two runs on the hangars and aircraft, Lt. Iida's fighter unit shifted its strafing runs north, concentrating on the parked vehicles and buildings along Second Street, not because they were particularly worthy targets, but because they lay upwind from the great billows of smoke that rendered attacks on the aprons ineffective and impractical. Standing clear of the smoke plumes emanating from the flight line to the west, the station's Armory and nearby buildings became the focal point of several such attacks.[56]

After completing the return trip from the Dispensary, Ens. Muckenthaler parked his car and noticed that the doors of the station Armory were open. Despite the high probability that the lockers had been emptied, Muckenthaler ran in and requested a weapon. To his surprise, he received a .45-caliber Colt automatic pistol, holster, and magazine pouch suspended from a heavy web belt. Two sailors in whites were inside, armed with Springfield rifles and apparently awaiting the lead of some higher authority. Seeing ensign's bars, the pair followed Muckenthaler as he exited the Armory, though the latter felt somewhat inadequate to the challenge of providing leadership. As he confessed later, "I didn't know where the hell to go." Seeking shelter, the trio headed two doors up the street to the Bombsight Workshop and Repair Building, as Japanese fighters were over or near the station. Suddenly, the *kansens* reappeared and strafed the building. Much to Muckenthaler's surprise, the two sailors (whom he did not know) shouted his name, prompting the young ensign to hit the ground just as bullets shattered windows above them. They all ducked for cover.[57]

Private automobiles smolder following the Japanese strafing attack late in the morning of 7 December. The gutted north face of Hangar 1 is clearly visible in the background at left. (NARA II, 80-G-77626)

Meanwhile, a short distance down Second Street, stunned by the exploding bombs north of Hangar 1, Sea2c Herschel W. Blackwell Jr. picked himself off the ground and stumbled to his duty station at Hangar 2, although still stunned and bleeding from his nose and ears. Arriving at his destination, he found that conditions there hardly inspired confidence, as "everything was in turmoil. Nobody seemed to know what to do." A number of officers had shown up at that juncture, including Lt. George K. Huff, VP-14's executive officer. To Blackwell, it seemed it was "the chiefs who were really in charge of things."[58]

Back at the naval air station's Armory, meanwhile, AOM2c Richard L. Sands, one particularly burly sailor attached to the Ordnance Department, exited from the side door of the building just as a Japanese fighter approached. A six-foot, 180-pound Iowa native who re-enlisted in Des Moines shortly before his arrival at Kaneohe on 13 March 1941, Sands engendered strong feelings of both affinity and hearty dislike. While some regarded him as "an arrogant extrovert"—with at least one shipmate not wishing "to cultivate his acquaintance"—Sands nonetheless had a large circle of admiring friends who took his fondness for the bottle in stride. His nose—presumably broken in some past altercation—healed crookedly, reinforcing a rough-and-tumble image. Friend and fellow ordnanceman Bert Richmond declared that Sands was "a rugged citizen, but a darned good person to be around."[59]

Cradling a commandeered BAR, Sands emerged from the Armory just in time to squeeze off a short burst at one of the passing *Sōryū* fighters. Irritated that his fire had achieved no visible effect, Sands bellowed, "Hand me another BAR. Hurry up! I swear I'll hit that yellow bastard!" Noticing either the defiant Sands or, more likely, the tracers flying skyward, the Japanese pilot circled, reversed course, and strafed both the Armory and Sands, who somehow escaped injury as bullets slammed into the wall of the building, bracketing the bluejacket on all sides. Armed "with a fresh BAR in his hands," Sands opened fire and emptied the

AOM2c Richard L. Sands, NAS Kaneohe Bay, circa early 1942, and supposed nemesis of Lt. Iida Fusata. (Kennedy)

twenty-round magazine. Again, the fighter pulled up and away and appeared to reform with the others. The Japanese headed for a low notch in the Koʻolaus (dubbed "Gunsight Pass" by the sailors), that lay on a direct line with Pearl Harbor to the west-southwest.[60] The fighter who was engaged in the duel with Sands trailed a thin, white plume of aviation fuel. Near the Armory, AMM1c Woodrow L. Beard exclaimed in delight, "Look, that fireball's got his! He's going down! He's going down!"[61]

The aircraft did not go down, however, but sped away generally to the west, as if to rejoin the rest of the group then assembling over Kāneʻohe Bay. For the Japanese, the smoke that boiled out of Hangar 1 and from various points on the warm-up platform reduced visibility significantly and rendered further attacks on the base impractical. Besides, at long last, after completing at least three strafing runs, the Japanese had run out of targets. With the exception of the three VP-14 machines out on patrol, Kaneohe's entire complement of PBYs was out of action, at least for the present. Of VP-11's dozen planes, seven sat burned, with one wrecked beyond repair by bombs and gunfire. Four other aircraft were repairable, but not immediately flyable. Similarly, VP-12 had eight aircraft completely destroyed, with four severely or moderately damaged. As for VP-14, six of the aircraft at the station were destroyed outright and four others damaged or disabled. Only the three PBY-5's flown by ensigns Tanner, Meyer, and Hillis survived the morning, their crews still facing an anxiety-ridden and uncertain future during their patrols northwest of O'ahu. Aircraft aside, material damage at Kaneohe was extensive, with Hangar 1 "burned completely to the steel structural work." Explosions and fires destroyed the aircraft inside, along with practically all hangar stores and office equipment and records, except for those saved earlier in the morning by the gallant Yeoman Williams.[62]

Accordingly, having accomplished his mission, Lt. Iida summoned the fighters under his command, signaled his men to form, and led them down the coast to Bellows Field. There the fighters executed two quick firing passes, but as the results were unsatisfactory, Iida formed his men for the flight to the rendezvous point.

While passing north toward Kāne'ohe Bay, Lt. (jg) Fujita noticed thin white lines of aviation fuel trailing behind two of the fighters from the lead section, PO1c Atsumi Takashi's, and Lt. Iida's. Damage to the aircraft in the trailing 3rd Section was likewise heavy. Defensive fire had holed Lt. (jg) Fujita's left wing. With the squadron fortunate to have all its pilots alive, Iida directed his group out over Kāne'ohe Bay. Soon after 0930, Iida began climbing, intent on leading his men up to two thousand meters.[63]

During the return flight to Kāne'ohe Bay, however, Iida apparently realized that ground fire had punctured what was likely his main fuel tank. With his *kansen* venting precious fuel aft, and knowing that a return to his carrier was impossible, Iida doubtless remembered a pledge he made back on board the *Sōryū*: were he

disabled and unable to return, he would crash his *kansen* into some suitable target. Flying close to his concerned comrades, Iida pointed to his mouth (meaning fuel) and waved his hand—held straight up, thumb to the face—and waved to the left and right, indicating that his fuel was nearly exhausted. Iida then pointed to himself and then to the ground, an unmistakable signal that he intended to die attacking the target.[64] With that, Iida executed a half roll and dove straight for the station below while his disconsolate subordinates watched in horror. Sick at heart and with hot tears coursing down his cheeks, Lt. (jg) Fujita watched his friend and fellow officer whom he "loved like a brother" plummet toward Kaneohe. Iida's comrades "felt weak and helpless," knowing that there was nothing that could be done to save their leader from his chosen fate.[65]

On the ground, meanwhile, the sailors at the Armory noticed a lone fighter coming back over the

Lt. Fujita Iyozō, second-wave fighter unit, *Sōryū*, seen here later in the war. (Fujita)

station with the apparent intent of attacking that building or those nearby. Alarmed, and seeing that the diving *kansen* vented fuel like the plane that had departed minutes before, one of the sailors shouted, "Hey Sands! That son o' bitch is coming back!"

Sands grabbed a BAR from another sailor and emptied the magazine for a third time at the incoming Mitsubishi, which was "in a constantly descending line of flight," almost as if the pilot intended to crash into the Armory from the south, firing as he came. The fighter ceased fire as it passed overhead and continued in a gradual descent until it struck the ground.[66]

From their position on the south side of the building, the men at the Armory did not see the crash but surmised that the fighter had crashed somewhere to the north. Others, however, had a better vantage point from which to observe. AOM3c Bert Richmond of VP-12, one of another group of sailors that brought Iida under fire, saw the *kansen* as it crossed the hangar line and passed over the Dispensary in a shallow dive at about eight hundred feet, almost level to the ground.[67] Seaman Maltby had no sooner exited the Dispensary from having his wounds dressed than the Zero roared past, "coming straight across the base and getting lower all the time." From Maltby's angle, the plane seemed headed in the direction of the Bachelor Officers Quarters, leading some to conclude that the pilot had targeted the barracks. From the vicinity of Hangar 2, AMM1c Walter Curylo and a number of his VP-14 shipmates saw Iida plunge into the ground at the foot of Pu'u Hawai'iloa near a road that wound around the hill's west face, a bit lower than the front lawns of the Married Officers Quarters on the north side of the hill. At such a low angle, the impact completely demolished the aircraft, with wreckage being strewn over several hundred yards. As the Zero broke apart at high speed, the engine bounced across the ground, coming to rest far from the point of impact—according to one apocryphal tale—in Maj. Donehoo's yard at Quarters "L."[68]

High above Kaneohe, meanwhile, because of the intervening distance and smoke, it was difficult if not impossible for Fujita and his squadron-mates to see precisely what happened. Confident though, that they witnessed the impact, they reported later that Iida dove into "a flaming hangar," committing *jibaku*, or self-destruction. Such was clearly not the case, however, as Iida crashed approximately one mile north of the hangar line. Indeed, it is questionable whether Iida actually intended to crash into a target at that time without first expending his ammunition.[69]

AOM3c Bert Richmond and two or three other sailors sprinted to the crash site and claimed to be first on the scene. Iida's body still lay in what was left of the fuselage, his body almost cut in half by the impact. Richmond admitted later that "it was probably a good thing for all concerned that he was dead." Rummaging through the scattered wreckage, Richmond found what he claimed to be Iida's scarf, stuffed it in his pocket, and departed the scene.[70]

From the Administration Building, when it became obvious that Iida, trailing fuel and weaving erratically, was about to crash, Cdr. Martin ordered 1st Lt. Lockwood, "Get that Jap!" As Iida disappeared from sight, Lockwood and four other Marines boarded his brandnew Packard Clipper and took off down "the roughest corduroy road I have ever experienced." Lockwood reported that Lt. Iida was wearing a "Belt of 1,000 Stitches," that had not brought him particularly good luck. To bystanders, Iida looked like a slaughtered sheep.[71]

A number of "pickers" arrived at the crash scene astonishingly fast, all hoping to liberate a souvenir from the wreckage. Later, even Cdr. Martin's teenaged son, David—a familiar sight speeding around the base on his motor bike—got in on the act, prying instruments from the cockpit and collecting fragments of scalp where Iida's head had crashed into the panel. Elizabeth Martin reportedly "hit the ceiling" when she saw what her son had brought home. There was speculation as to whether the aircraft was inverted when it crashed; Iida's fingers were missing from the corpse, as though Iida were holding onto the canopy at impact.[72]

Other souvenirs came to light as bystanders pulled together the pieces of Iida's torn body. Some swore later (to the totally false notion) that the Japanese pilot wore a Punahou High School class ring. Exhibiting an almost ghoulish fascination, one sailor picked up a finger, still in a piece of the flight glove. Supposedly, Sea2c William L. Bowie and others picked up bits of scalp as trophies. But the most fanciful lore in connection with the men combing through the wreckage was that regarding a Chinese civilian worker who somehow snatched the pilot's flight helmet. After turning the bloodstained helmet inside-out, "the hysterical Chinese ran wildly about the station, bringing down in blood-curdling invective all the traditional hatred of his people upon the heads of the treacherous marauders." Fortunately, perhaps, those interested in collecting intelligence information secured the crash site as best they could, thereby restoring—albeit inadvertently—some dignity to the deceased. For long afterward, however, curious sailors dropped by the site hoping to retrieve at least a bit of the aircraft's skin. Marines appeared and conveyed what remained of Iida's body to the lawn of the Dispensary.[73] There, Seaman Maltby noted that Iida appeared to be wearing civilian clothing underneath his flight suit, prompting speculation that he intended to blend in with the local population had he survived and escaped.[74] Evaluation of the intelligence gleaned from the wreckage would follow shortly, later in the morning.[75]

The most likely flight path taken by Lt. Iida Fusata's aircraft prior to its crash into NAS Kaneohe Bay. (Based on NARA II, 80-G-339895)

**The Crash of Lt. Iida Fusata**
7 December 1941

Crash Site

Armory

Iida's Flight Path

The rear entrance to the Dispensary at NAS Kaneohe Bay, with the detached morgue visible at right, to which sailors transported Lt. Iida's shattered body and deposited it unceremoniously in a garbage can, a decision most likely reflecting a lack of space for his remains than a lack of respect for a slain enemy. View taken on 16 April 1941. (NARA II, 71CA-156B-14237)

Whether there was room for Iida in the small morgue at that time is improbable, but the embittered Americans were in no mood to provide special accommodations for a fallen enemy pilot.[76] Clearing the lawn, men moved the garbage can that contained Iida's corpse to the rear of the Dispensary behind the morgue and transformer room that lay on the northwest side of the Dispensary's drive-through breezeway. Caring for Kaneohe's dead and wounded took priority, so Iida could wait. AMM3c Guy Avery summed up the sentiment among the bluejackets, saying that Iida's disposition was "not entirely out of disrespect—although heaven knows we despised him and his kind to the limit that day—but because we had no more suitable facility at hand . . . besides, there was nothing more that could be done for him then."[77]

Exiting the skies over eastern Oʻahu, the Japanese left behind a military base that, by all appearances, lay hammered into impotence by bombs and gunfire. Even the tumbling wind shears that should have rendered the station a poor target area made little difference. Operationally, Kaneohe had ceased to exist. Although salvage and repair efforts would bring ten of the lesser-damaged PBYs back into service, after the last Japanese planes had departed at the midpoint of the forenoon watch, only the three PBYs still on patrol out were airworthy.[78] Hangar 1 lay demolished and numerous other buildings were machine-gunned and pockmarked. However traumatic those material losses were, they could not match the suffering inflicted on the men of the station and its attached squadrons. Including civilians, nineteen lay dead or dying, with sixty-nine wounded.

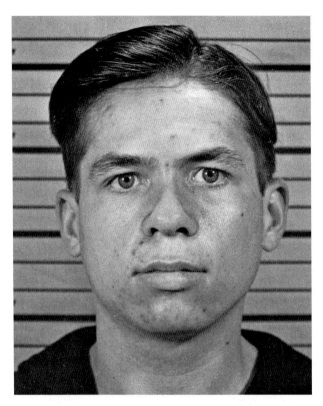

Sea2c James H. Robinson, circa 1941. (NARA, St. Louis)

Sea2c John D. Buckley, circa May 1941. (NARA, St. Louis)

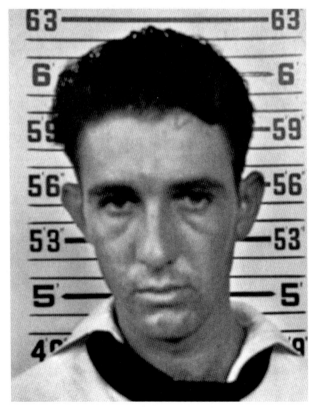

Sea1c Luther D. Weaver of VP-11, victim of the bombing of Hangar 1, NAS Kaneohe Bay. (NARA, St. Louis)

As the casualties streamed into the Dispensary, to everyone's great dismay they found a single, small operating room on the first floor, only two doctors (Lt. Cdr. McCrimmon and Lt. Hutto), a civilian nurse, and a few overworked corpsmen who could only administer morphine. Little could be done for Sea2c James H. Robinson, a victim in the bombing of Hangar 1; a large fragment had carried away the base of his neck. Another man in agony from similar wounds, VP-11's AOM3c John D. Buckley, pleaded with Seaman Petriccione to stay with him until the end. Pete Petriccione had only just finished the grim task of transporting his friend Sea1c Luther Weaver to the morgue, but nonetheless he did what he could to comfort Buckley, who soon

(opposite) "Everyone's Friend," Raphael A. "Ralph" Watson and wife Grace, circa 1938. At this time Mrs. Watson lived in southern Georgia with her two boys while her husband underwent flight training at Pensacola. Photo taken shortly after the birth of their second son, Ralph Jr. (Watson)

died in his friend's arms. Both Robinson and Buckley had joined the Navy without completing high school, searching for a career.[79]

The beleaguered Dispensary staff, however, received assistance from a number of the wives at the station, among them Mynila Billingsley, whose husband returned to the house half an hour after departing for his duty station. With the Dispensary desperately needing help, Lt. Billingsley asked his wife if she would go. Reluctant at first, Mynila replied, "Yes, I will."

Ambulatory sailors also wanted to do their part, with some surrendering their beds to comrades more seriously wounded. With a bullet wound in his left elbow, AMM2c Cecil Malmin allowed good friend AMM1c Ralph Watson, wounded in the chest and right shoulder, to take his bunk. Watson, "a big fellow and one of the best liked people on the base," died later that afternoon after being transferred to the Territorial Hospital, leaving behind a wife and two young sons on base at 444-C Windham Street to be notified of his fate. Malmin set to work immediately, performing odd tasks in the Dispensary that allowed the staff to cope more effectively with the incoming emergencies.[80]

Certainly, one of those was RM3c Richard Moser, critically injured in the attack on Hangar 1, suffering multiple fragment wounds, principally to his left arm and buttocks, the worst being inflicted by a piece of metal that had severed his right femoral artery. Although in shock and woozy from loss of blood, Moser remembered distinctly that Lt. Iida's body had been brought up to the Dispensary at almost the same moment as his own arrival, albeit from a different direction. After that, the "lights went out," with Moser remaining unconscious until later in the afternoon.[81]

Considering the dreadful conditions inside the Dispensary, one would hardly have expected any lighter moments, but there was one regarding RM3c Ray M. Groomer of VP-11, long the object of rough teasing regarding his weight. Shipmates maintained that should a war ever start, Groomer was sure to be hit in the buttocks as no enemy could miss them. Upon his arrival

RM3c Ray M. Groomer. (NARA, St. Louis)

at the Dispensary, Groomer, who blushed quite easily, turned beet red when acquaintances inquired as to the nature of his injury. True to prewar predictions, he had suffered a flesh wound in the posterior. Similarly, Texas native Sea2c Bill J. "Billie Joe" Beard had suffered disparaging remarks all through boot camp regarding the vulnerability of his outsized hindquarters, as there was simply no way to avoid being struck there. The boot camp prognostications proved prophetic, as Beard reported to the Dispensary with a small piece of metal in his backside.[82]

One least one sailor among the wounded decided against treatment after arriving at the Dispensary. ACOM John Finn was finally "persuaded" by a direct order to report from Hangar 2 and seek aid shortly after the attack. Shot through the left arm and foot and with many small cuts and fragment wounds, Finn hobbled into the Dispensary barefooted on one heel as a "walk-in" case. HA1c Robert E. Hoffman attended to Finn when he finally reported for treatment. While none of Finn's injuries seemed life-threatening, many small fragment wounds covered his body—particularly his chest—that necessitated the use of tweezers to extract the tiny bits of metal. Hoffman was just beginning to work on him when Sea2c Earl L. Jones, one of

Sea2c Earl L. Jones, circa 1941. (NARA, St. Louis)

Finn's severely injured shipmates from VP-14 and a victim of the bombing attack south of Hangar 2, arrived with a shattered femur. Naturally, the medical people turned to assist Jones, who required more immediate help. With the Dispensary's corridors "jammed with men," Finn refused further treatment at that time but secured a ride back to his quarters, where his wife Alice dressed his wounds to the best of her abilities. Finn instructed her to gather together all the ladies to make bandages and dressings out of sheets and pillowcases,

With pipe clenched in teeth, an officer strikes a reflective pose beside wreckage of a PBY-5 south of Hangar 2, near the waterfront. Note the unfinished hangar at left. (NARA II, 80-G-77650)

saying, "They need 'em at sick bay." With that, he returned to the hangar line where he posted guards and continued to gather all available ordnance in case the Japanese returned.[83]

As the initial shock of the attack wore off, the survivors were glad to be alive—"counting fingers and toes"—but the morale of some soon reached a low ebb. During the attack, the men had adopted a fatalistic attitude that whatever would be would be. Afterward, however, with lowered adrenaline levels, there was danger of becoming "unglued." For sailors like AMM2c Otto Horky, who had acted in such a clear-headed manner during the attack, the immediate danger had passed, leaving them shaken and anxious. It was indeed fortunate that the magnitude of the required cleanup and preparation of defenses left the men "little time or energy to ponder."

Not all of the sailors, however, proved able to concentrate fully on their work. Sea2c Doyle Bell suffered from a "sickening, helpless feeling," knowing that little could be done to repel any invaders. With no direction or supervision, Ptr3c Henry Retzloff wandered about the base, inquiring about the fates of his friends and wondering just what the future would hold. With no more specific information than any of the sailors, Marines like Pvt. John F. Nichols were "expecting any and everything to happen." Evidence of the overwhelming human and material loss lay in all directions and weighed heavily upon the warriors of Kaneohe, as did the uncertainty of what might lay ahead in the coming hours and days.[84]

# FOUR

## "NO ONE SHIRKED, NO ONE AVOIDED DANGER"

Although the men of Kaneohe did not realize it, they had seen the last of the Japanese. Accordingly, the activities undertaken in the immediate aftermath of the raid combined repairs to the base, its aircraft, and facilities in a frantic race to prepare for the return of the Japanese, either by air or by sea. By any measure it was clear that, operationally, Kaneohe had ceased to exist. If the base were to resurrect itself, however, the first task was to clear aircraft wreckage from the ramps and aprons and to fill in bomb craters to render the apron usable. Immediately after the raid, equipment began pushing the charred remains of PatWing 1's Catalinas into piles east and north of the hangar line. All the men turned to with the single-minded object of putting the base back into operation, but noted that the morning had certainly closed "with none of the peace and quiet with which it dawned."[1]

With arms and ordnance exhausted in the armories, many sailors obtained rifles and ammunition being taken out of storage at the General Storehouse, where a work party spent "a good share of the day" cleaning the 1903 Springfield .30-caliber rifles. Sea2c Robert U. Hanna—one of those reporting to the storehouse after AOM2c Richard Sands had taken charge—watched as Sands supervised the men breaking open crates of weap-

ons packed in Cosmoline. Apparently the men worked too gingerly for Sands' taste, for the burly ordnanceman shouted, "Hell, sailors! Get out of my way!" Soon afterward, crates tumbled onto their sides, some breaking open and spilling their contents onto the concrete. The startled men set about cleaning the rifles immediately, enough to clear the bore and free the bolt action. While engaged in the cleaning detail, some sailors speculated about how long it would take to wipe out the Japanese, with the consensus being about six weeks.[2]

As with other Japanese aircraft crashes across the island of O'ahu, intelligence people converged on the scene of the wreckage of Lt. Iida's *kansen* near Pu'u Hawai'iloa. Expert evaluation of items retrieved came from an unexpected quarter: Lt. (jg) John W. Steele, the station's personnel officer.

Following his graduation from the U.S. Naval Academy in 1925, the young officer's overindulgence in alcohol had almost destroyed his career. Dismissed from flight training at NAS Pensacola, Steele, his health declining, received a medical discharge. With his service at an apparent end, he embarked on a three-year course of Japanese-language study in Honolulu and in Japan, all the while maintaining contact with the Bureau of Navigation. By 1941, the shortage of officers prompted his recall to active duty. Though underweight and par-

The first of four aerial photographs taken at about one thousand feet altitude over NAS Kaneohe Bay on or about 8 December 1941. The images document conditions at the station shortly after the raid. Note that crews have cleared aircraft wreckage from the aprons and have filled most, if not all, of the bomb craters in the pavement. Interestingly, the height from which the photographer worked approximates the relatively low altitude from which Lt. Ichihara Tatsuo approached the station during the bombing attacks of the second wave. Two aircraft are just visible in the shadows of Hangar 1 and the Maintenance Hangar. From this angle it is clear that the latter structure was to form a corner of a hangar identical to Hangars 1 and 2. Note also the unfinished hangar in the foreground. View looks east. (NARA II, 80-G-32942)

Kaneohe's hangar line on or about 8 December. A construction area surrounding the small Maintenance Hangar lies at center, with contractors ready to incorporate the smaller structure as the northwest corner of the new hangar. Note three cranes at center and far left, and two additional PBYs near Hangar 2, one of which has lost its wing fabric to fire damage. View looks northwest. (NARA II, 80-G-32941)

A PBY from VP-14 smolders on Kaneohe's apron south of Hangar 2 shortly after the attack. Note the large hangar still under construction in the distance. (NARA II, 80-G-77613)

Aircraft wreckage, looking northwest toward the squadron office building and the severed bow of 12-P-7 (BuNo 2441). Crews moved the charred remains of this aircraft at least four hundred yards from the location on the other side of the Maintenance Hangar where the machine burned, demonstrating the effort required to clear the aprons sufficiently for air operations to resume. (NARA II, 80-G-77630)

12-P-3 (BuNo 2435), the aircraft launched into the bay in an attempt to save the aircraft from fire, lies on the apron east of Hangar 1. (NARA II, 80-G-77631)

Charred aluminum and concrete shards lie close to the seaplane ramp southeast of Hangar 1. Note 11-P-12 (BuNo 2434), one of the surviving aircraft at left, and the fuel oil tank and cement plant in the far background at right. (NARA II, 80-G-77648)

A PBY from VP-12 (the squadron designator is visible under the starboard wing) rests on the pavement between Hangars 1 and 2. Note the men engaged in repair activities atop the starboard wing and fuselage. (NARA II, 80-G-77628)

tially deaf, Steele passed his physical and reported first to the 14th Naval District, and then to NAS Kaneohe Bay. There he assisted Cdr. Martin in providing accommodations for the many newly arrived officers, men, and their families. While that billet provided him little opportunity to use his Japanese language abilities, those skills now enabled Steele to glean critical intelligence from the wreckage of Lt. Iida's *kansen* on the west slope of Pu'u Hawai'iloa.

Iida's identity and status as a *chūtai-chō*, or division commander, came to light, both from his papers—some loose and some from Iida's pockets—and from the name on his flight suit. More importantly, one of the charts bore Japanese *kanji* characters in a position

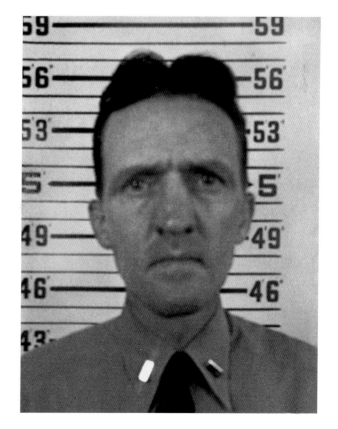

Lt. (jg) John W. Steele, probably at the time of his restoration to active duty and arrival in Hawai'i in January of 1941, a time of high anxiety for the thirty-seven-year-old officer in light of his poor physical condition and past disciplinary issues. (NARA, St. Louis)

approximately ninety miles distant and 223 degrees from Pearl Harbor, suggesting that the enemy, or perhaps a rendezvous point, lay southwest of O'ahu. Judging that Adm. Kimmel might benefit from what Steele had ascertained, Cdr. Martin sent a brief message with that information to CinCPac at noon. Unfortunately, the discovery of Iida's chart and other factors shifted American attention to the southwest and elsewhere rather than to the north, where Vice Adm. Nagumo's carriers were recovering aircraft. Consequently, after midday, the chances that the Americans might launch a significant aerial counterstrike had evaporated.[3]

During midmorning, the Army radioed a message to Bellows Field, saying that they expected Cdr. Martin to assume command of "all defenses and armed troops" on the Mōkapu Peninsula. About thirty minutes after

the Japanese departure, elements of Maj. Kenneth M. Barager's 2nd Battalion of the 98th Coastal Artillery (AA) arrived at Kaneohe's main gate, the vanguard of the 3-inch Batteries F (Capt. Robert O. Thomas) and G (1st Lt. Allen Bennett). Unfortunately, the heavy antiaircraft batteries arrived sans ordnance, causing some of the trucks to backtrack for supplies and ammunition. The sailors turned to and assisted the soldiers in setting up the guns, and by 1315 both batteries were in position and ready for action.[4]

Reinforcements for the defense of Kaneohe's runway arrived during the afternoon. A portion of the Marine Detachment boarded trucks, heading for the strip west of the station. Separating into groups of three, the men dug in, expecting that the Japanese would land and attempt to take Kaneohe at any moment. Men took several of the machine guns recently cleaned at the Supply Department (albeit with insufficient ammunition) and mounted them on either side of the runway, eventually positioning six weapons on each side. Like their Navy counterparts, the Marines dug foxholes, employed sandbags to protect the positions, and installed improvised pipe mountings to allow use of the water-cooled machine guns against high-flying enemy aircraft.[5]

The lower right section of Lt. Iida Fusata's flight chart recovered from the scattered wreckage of his carrier fighter on the morning of 7 December. The Japanese characters noted in the dispatch to CinCPac are circled at lower left. (NARA II, Records of the Pearl Harbor Liaison Office, RG80)

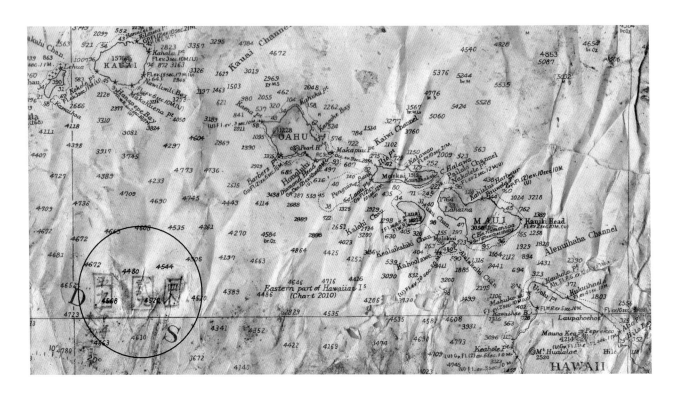

All along the shore, men hewed revetments and rifle pits from the unyielding coral and established numerous strongpoints of .30- and .50-caliber machine guns with three men assigned to each position. One such post was in the Coconut Grove west of the hangar line, the position from which sailors had temporarily driven off the second-wave bombing attacks. Sea2c Desmond V. Hatcher took stock of the available weapons and ordnance. Although the heavier Brownings had been employed elsewhere, he and his fellow defenders counted three Thompson submachine guns, three Springfields, and several thousand rounds of ammunition. The Japanese invaders would not take the Coconut Grove without a fight.[6]

The first report of Japanese landings on the island had emanated from Lt. Col. Kendall J. Fielder (G-2) in the Headquarters, Hawaiian Department, at 1025, when the Army claimed that Japanese paratroopers were dropping near Barbers Point in the vicinity of Jensen and Camel Roads. An hour later, a similar message told of paratroopers jumping into Pearl Harbor.[7]

A report filtered through Oʻahu's communication network late in the morning that would have been far more alarming to Martin, specifically, that Japanese paratroopers were landing on the North Shore. The first mention of the news was a message sent at 1132 by Maj. Gen. Henry T. Burgin, the commanding general of Hawaii's Coastal Artillery Command. "Parachute troops have landed on North Shore and have been identified as wearing blue coveralls with red disc on left shoulder."[8]

The Coconut Grove west of Kaneohe's flight line, a bastion both during and after the air raid. View looking west. (NARA II, 80-G-279362, cropped)

Although the Army eventually disproved the reports—which were due to general confusion, duplicated and misinterpreted messages, and a frightened local population—reports of paratrooper drops persisted through the early afternoon. Companies L and E from one of the battalions of the 21st Infantry passed word up the line at 1235 and 1240, respectively, regarding additional North Shore sightings, all confirmed later by frantic civilian refugees pouring into Haleiwa. As a capstone, despite the clear lack of any aerial activity whatsoever at or near NAS Kaneohe Bay, the Navy contributed to

the "blue coverall" hysteria when, at 1300, it reported "Parachute troops being landed near KANEOHE wearing blue coveralls and a red shield."[9]

Faced with persistent reports of landings along the North Shore and a primitive communications network that prevented Cdr. Martin from gaining a fuller view of unfolding events, the authorities at the station felt compelled to take action. Most of the men on duty earlier in the morning were wearing their blue dungarees, as were most of the men aroused from their sleep during the attack, while those awaiting liberty were dressed in whites. Thus, to avoid confusion, the sailors received orders to change uniforms. Realizing that white uniforms made the men easy targets, the cooks working in the mess hall prepared vats of strong coffee in which the sailors were to immerse two sets of whites. The dyeing process worked admirably, with the whites emerging from the vats dark brown.[10]

AMM1c Joseph C. Engel, one of VP-12's enlisted pilots at the Mess Hall, felt less concern over losing

The bakery for the Enlisted Mess Hall (out of view at left), with quarters for the bakers and cooks atop the second deck. Note the unloading platform at center, the location from which initial efforts moved forward to dye sailors' white uniforms with vats of strong coffee. The platform was also where the station complement reported to secure boiled water. View looking east on 9 April 1941. (NARA II, 71-CA-156B-142320, cropped)

his whites than of having to wear wet clothing. The resourceful NAP hit upon a solution, borrowing a shirt and pair of trousers from a Marine acquaintance. Not all the sailors, however, reported to the Mess Hall. It was not until late in the afternoon that AOM3c Jackson Harris and others on duty in Hangar 1 received the instructions to darken their whites. In order to keep the men near their battle stations, the Mess Hall transported the coffee to the men in large containers. The dyeing activity continued into the next day, albeit with dye packets from the Marines rather than coffee.[11]

Although the station did its best to act upon the conflicting and contradictory information received at the Administration Building, the inevitable confusion made it almost impossible to effectively respond, with the prescribed uniform change being a case in point. Having expended considerable effort to comply with the late directive, word arrived that the "Imperial Marines" were landing—in khaki uniforms. Word went out to go back to whites, "officers and all." Subsequently, at about 1400, it was learned that the Japanese had landed in whites somewhere along the windward shore. Despite the previous alarms, no blue-clad hordes of paratroopers appeared, which resulted in an order to revert to blue shirts and dungarees. Although messmen boiled dungarees in an effort to secure blue dye, it is unknown how many men reported to the Mess Hall for that last change.[12]

One other issue focused attention on the Mess Hall's loading dock. Fearing contamination, the station shut off the water supply during the afternoon. Instructions counseled: "Don't drink any water until we tell you, or get it from the boiled water that's in the can in back of the mess hall." The scare passed quickly, much more so than at NAS Pearl Harbor, but not before elevating the sense of alarm among the sailors and Marines on the windward shore.[13]

Coincidental with directives related to the uniform change, orders emanated from the Administration Building to "defend our station against Japanese paratroopers." The order precipitated a mass exodus to the "big hill"

by those men who had no essential duty to perform in the hangars or whose aircraft had been destroyed. Needing little encouragement, the sailors scattered—some on their own, some under orders but with little organization or direction—and set up defensive positions around the station's perimeter and upon the steep slopes of Puʻu Hawaiʻiloa. Many of the machine guns salvaged from aircraft earlier in the morning found their way into the hands of bluejackets now making their way up the hill, who placed the weapons in hastily dug foxholes. A scarcity of sandbags led the sailors to improvise, reinforcing their positions with dirt-filled cement bags retrieved from contractor trash piles.[14]

That evening, AOM3c Cecil I. Hollingshead headed for Puʻu Hawaiʻiloa along with almost everyone else, but not to man the guns. The sailors were still experiencing difficulty with their weapons, and Hollingshead spent quite some time ensuring that the Brownings would function if and when the rumored landings came. After sunset, he retrieved a pair of flight coveralls to protect himself from the damp, chilly air. VP-14's AOM3c Jackson L. Harris spent the night on Puʻu Hawaiʻiloa with three other men manning a .50-caliber machine gun mounted atop a pipe driven into the hillside. There was a single blanket to keep the four men warm on that "chilly, frightening and sleepless night."[15]

After digging in, inactivity bred fear and spawned the worst possible rumors. Whole sections of Honolulu lay gutted. All ships at Pearl Harbor had been sunk. San Francisco had fallen. Guam, Wake, Midway, and the Philippines were gone, too, while landings were under way in Alaska. Rumors told of landings on Oʻahu and the North Shore, even that the Japanese were going to make a landing at Kaneohe in Ford Tri-Motors. Each report that came in contained precise information regarding landing location and what kind of uniforms the Japanese were wearing. These horrors were mere prologue, however; a huge Japanese task force was under way and would arrive in one week to finish off Hawaiʻi once and for all. With dismal prospects for additional reinforcements and assistance, the defenders waited for nightfall and the Japanese attacks, because according to the Marines five thousand enemy troops were already ashore. Kaneohe's isolation that previously had seemed so idyllic and advantageous might be the station's undoing now.[16]

At the station runway, meanwhile, the Army took measures that complemented the Navy's assistance in setting up the former's antiaircraft batteries. In the afternoon, and working under orders from Cdr. Martin, the artillerists "organized a party to take cars out on the mat . . . to prevent any Jap planes from landing." To provide flexibility and the ability to reposition or clear the field should the need arise, the men gassed up the automotive obstructions and placed a crew of two men on board each of the thirty to thirty-five vehicles. In addition to providing a stationary deterrent to aerial landings, the "crews" had orders from their officers to ram any plane that attempted to land, unless ordered otherwise. At about noon, Kaneohe's Marines took charge of commandeering all private vehicles, and together with soldiers and sailors they set the vehicles in place by middle or late afternoon.[17]

Back at the Dispensary, the surgeons toiled all day long, with no breaks or food, sustained by only coffee. The women on the base played a vital role at the facility, volunteering to take over jobs that would have been performed by nurses or nurse's aides under normal circumstances. One of the volunteers was Lt. Billingsley's wife, Mynila.[18]

Many of the men had fragment wounds and some came in with horrific injuries. Mrs. Billingsley remembered seeing Chief "Skinny" Grisham lying in a cranked-up hospital bed, in a half-sitting position, smoking a cigarette, almost oblivious to the fact that he had lost his left leg above the knee. He had been the first patient Billingsley attended to that morning. ACMM (PA) Harry G. "Duke" Byron arrived with his intestines in his hands, thoroughly disgusted and angry, as "it was his responsibility to be where there action was," not lying inactive in a hospital.[19]

Many men suffering minor wounds did not report to the Dispensary immediately for first aid, and those who did found a long wait ahead of them. It was 1500 before the medical staff stitched up Sea2c Robert W. Ballou's leg, as there was simply no room available. Partly to make space in the cramped Dispensary, and partly to take advantage of more comprehensive hospital facilities elsewhere, shortly before noon, the staff loaded a number of the more seriously wounded sailors on board ambulances for transfer to the Kāne'ohe Territorial Hospital and Insane Asylum. Among those men sent to the larger hospital was Y1c Kenton Nash, who suffered the traumatic amputation of his left arm during the bombing of Hangar 1.[20]

Landing on the operating table at about noon, Nash received a transfusion from an asylum inmate in the operating room. With a low tolerance for ether, the newlywed yeoman did not wake up from the operation until about 2000. The Chinese surgeon who performed the operation, present when Nash awakened, offered him a tin cup with ice and bourbon. "Here son," the physician urged him. "Take a drink of this. It might not help, but it'll make the world look better." The sailor drank gladly. Knowing that his arm was gone the minute he was hit, Nash counted himself fortunate at never having to go through the shock of waking after an operation to find part of his body missing.[21]

Back at the Dispensary, finally finishing his work in the operating room much later in the day, Lt. Cdr. McCrimmon inquired as to whether any Japanese aviators had been killed. Only then did he learn that there was a body in a garbage can back of the Dispensary. McCrimmon set out to investigate and found Iida's body, nearly cut in two. The surgeon pulled out the body to examine the corpse and noted the pair of heavy dark blue woolen trousers to which Sea1c LeRoy Maltby likely referred. Surprisingly, Iida still wore a necklace, which somehow escaped the ghoulish grasp of the souvenir hunters. Fascinated by it, McCrimmon later described it: "Around his neck was a kind of charm necklace I thought made up of many small like trinkets [sic]. As I looked at this charm necklace I thought of the rabbits [sic] foot that is supposed to bring good luck, but never seems to help the rabbit any. This was probably the first aviator that died that day for his Emperor. We buried him in the clean sand on the beach in beautiful Hawaii."²²

During the afternoon, the authorities determined that all dependents should be evacuated, particularly those who resided in wooden structures or in isolated areas within the reservation. Consequently, sailors and Marines circulated among the enlisted housing, rousted out the frightened occupants, placed them in trucks or in their own cars, and assembled an impromptu convoy bound for Kailua School and the Coconut Grove nightclub. From there, the dependents dispersed to the residents of Kailua and Lanikai, with the proviso that the military would supply them with food during their absence.²³

Along with many other Navy wives, Elizabeth Martin, the station commander's wife, pitched in after the attack and assisted with the stressful but necessary evacuation of women and children. Earlier in the day, she had gathered wives and their children together in the lower level of her quarters, doing everything possible to keep them calm. Amid rumors of an impending invasion, one woman's composure faltered, and she asked Mrs. Martin what she would do if a Japanese general walked into the room. "I'd step up," Elizabeth Martin responded bravely, "and I'd spit right in his eye."²⁴

Meanwhile west of O'ahu, the aircraft carrier Enterprise—returning from her mission of ferrying twelve Grumman F4F-3s of VMF-211 to Wake Island—launched patrols during the morning and afternoon hours, searching for the Japanese carrier force. Meanwhile, in one of the SBDs launched that afternoon, Ens. Clifford R. "Bucky" Walters, A-V(N), VB-6's assistant personnel officer, in 6-B-17, proceeded to Ka'ena Point via Kaua'i and after sunset received permission to land at NAS Kaneohe Bay. The station, which showed "a few navigational lights" to guide returning aircraft in (a blackout had been put into effect at sundown), had been notified that Enterprise planes would be coming

in, but apparently short notice had not allowed the station's people to clear the vehicles off the ramp.

Walters, unaware of what obstructions lay in his path, put his SBD down between two automobiles before he saw another in his landing lights and pulled back on the stick to jump over it. He then ground-looped and taxied up the line, weaving between the other parked vehicles, coming to a stop, as Walters later put it, with "a damn cement mixer almost in my lap."²⁵

Even though the sailors and Marines guarding the field were warned of the incoming planes, it was a miracle that no one opened fire. Pfc. Joe M. Trest, unsure of the aircraft's identity and with his blood up, sat at the wheel ready to ram Walters' SBD. Fortunately, at the last second, the order came to stand down, and the plane passed within fifty feet of Trest's vehicle. Trest—more concerned about the SBD crashing into him than anything else—later spoke admiringly of Ens. Walters' skill: "he landed that thing there where nobody but a Navy pilot could have put that plane."²⁶

According to men near the runway, Walters' SBD picked up one car in his landing lights "and jumped over it, ground-looped and taxied up to the line weaving in between the cars." The driver in the car over which he jumped was ACMM (PA) Paul O. Reese, one of the station's plank owners, who admitted later that "he was scared plenty."²⁷

About a half hour after Bucky Walters' feat, Ens. Benjamin H. Troemel, whose day had begun with his aircraft being pushed aside for the morning flight because of a bad spark plug, neared Kaneohe Bay, too, shortly before 1900. After more than five hours of flying, confronted with a pitch-black night and occasional showers, the twenty-six-year-old Troemel and RM3c Alfred R. Stitzelberger, his radio-gunner, felt relieved to be in a position to land. Although the blackout added to the difficulty, Troemel knew it had to be done, because he was almost out of gas. He later called his Kaneohe landing, dodging parked vehicles in the dark, "just about the most stressful maneuver I've made in my life."²⁸

AvCdt. Clifford R. "Bucky" Walters, circa 23 April 1940. (NARA, St. Louis)

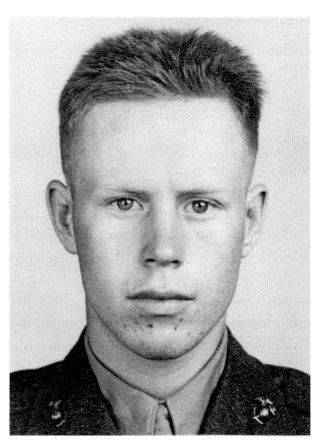

Pvt. Joe M. Trest, USMC—Walters' would-be rammer— seen on 24 August 1940, one week after his enlistment in New Orleans. (NARA, St. Louis)

Walters' and Troemel's approach and landing at Kaneohe proved just as harrowing at ground level. It was just before dark with a light rain falling when Ens. Muckenthaler, ensconced in his position on Pu'u Hawai'iloa, heard engine noise and thought, "This is it!" Fearing that the rumored Japanese Ford Tri-Motor landing was on, at first Muckenthaler could not see the aircraft, though finally the plane became visible during its approach. To his astonishment, however, the aircraft—barely visible—"turned on his landing lights, circled, came around, and landed, zigzagging through all the wreckage and debris thrown out on the runways. The aircraft did not so much as touch a wingtip—a beautiful landing." Despite the best efforts to obstruct the runway, the two scout bomber crews had landed safely, hardly an endorsement of the effectiveness of the barricades.[29]

In the vicinity of the runway, men were spared further drama, at least with regard to aircraft landings. At about the same time as the arrival of the two *Enterprise* SBDs, the trio of PBYs from the dawn patrols landed without incident on the water south of the seaplane ramps. Ens. William P. Tanner (14-P-1, BuNo 2419) and Ens. Otto F. Meyer (14-P-3, BuNo 2415) skimmed onto Kāne'ohe Bay at about sunset, with Ens. Thomas W. Hillis (14-P-2, BuNo 2418) returning shortly thereafter at 1900. Crews refueled and rearmed the aircraft, which at that juncture were the only operational PBYs at Kaneohe.[30]

It was dark by the time the "Tri-Motor" scare subsided, and word passed up the slopes of Pu'u Hawai'iloa that the squadron commanders wanted all officer pilots to report to the BOQ wardroom. In the light rain, Ens. Muckenthaler bid farewell to the pair of enlisted fellow defenders with whom he had spent most of the day and groped his way down

AvCdt. Benjamin H. Troemel, circa 7 November 1939. (NPRC, St. Louis)

the back side of Puʻu Hawaiʻiloa in the misty murk, a dangerous proposition considering that the men at the station were nervous and armed to the teeth. The familiar environs of the BOQ offered little comfort, however, as absolute chaos reigned inside, with the occupants startled and annoyed by "noise and shouts, [and] running into other men in the dark."[31]

When Muckenthaler reached the wardroom, he found that fellow officers had rigged curtains over the windows in observance of the blackout conditions, using only a few candles for lighting. The young ensign had not eaten since the previous evening and was famished. Remembering that he had consumed strawberries the night before, Muckenthaler groped his way toward the galley, bumping into people on the way in. Following his nose in the darkness, he found the large steel kettle containing the berries and dug in . . . with about ten other hands. Standing his ground in the shov-

ing match, Muckenthaler managed to grab a generous mouthful of the fruit, his only supper for the evening.[32]

Eventually, more candles came out and the pilots' meeting finally began. Lt. Cdr. Slim Johnson gathered his men from VP-14 and said, "We need some volunteers." Muckenthaler's hand went up. Then Johnson informed the pilots that Kaneohe had lost all of its aircraft. For a brief moment the idea came to Muckenthaler he might escape from Oʻahu altogether, as a temporary retreat to the West Coast would be necessary to pick up new aircraft, but Johnson quickly dashed those hopes. The skipper had orders for the pilots to be transported to NAS Pearl Harbor, where they were to conduct flight operations from there with the few PBYs left on the island.[33]

A light rain continued to fall, presaging a cheerless and danger-filled evening. In the face of the perceived threat of invasion—foremost in the minds of almost everyone—the men received orders to fire on any light. MAtt1c Walter Simmons summed up the law of the land that night at Kaneohe: "If it moves, shoot it."

There were, however, men who needed to move about in the dark, but they did so at great risk. At about midnight, Platoon Sgt. Theodore F. Wade took charge of a "strike force" of sixteen to twenty Marines. Driver Pvt. John F. Nichols stood by with his truck, ready to transport the group at a moment's notice to the runway without benefit of any lights, leaving Nichols wondering what he was going to bump into. Wade's group got under way to reinforce Marines already at the runway, and when they approached their objective, a group of defenders—presumably from the 98th Coastal Artillery—opened fire at the truck, forcing Nichols to duck behind the steering wheel. Tracers passed over the heads of Marines already in place. Pvt. Victor P. Jacoby—earlier broken in rank from sergeant for awarding extra points on the firing range—was acting sergeant for the Marines caught by the firing from behind. Turning a machine gun 180 degrees, he fired over the heads of those threatening the Marines and bellowed, "The next time I won't go above you!" The firing stopped.[34]

Platoon Sgt. Theodore F. Wade, USMC, on 1 August 1940. (NARA, St. Louis)

A glum Pvt. Victor P. Jacoby, USMC, sits for the photographer four days after being released from confinement, reduced in rank from sergeant for "submitting a false report for rifle practice." (NARA, St. Louis)

One of the most serious firing incidents occurred when a soldier open up on what he thought was a boat light in Kāne'ohe Bay. At the bungalow west of the station's runway, AMM1c Avery thought that a nearby sentry initiated the incident, screaming "Halt!" and opening fire at a movement in the dark. Whatever the cause, it seemed as if everyone on the peninsula opened up, including a "crazy spree of firing by both [antiaircraft] batteries," which went on for about fifteen minutes. Having a clear field of fire from his position in the Coconut Grove, Sea2c Desmond V. Hatcher claimed to have fired ninety rounds from his Springfield.[35]

Among the incidents during the night, an officer on a Cushman scooter drove by several sailors and took fire, not hearing the order to halt over the vehicle's put-put racket. In the revetment next to Sea2c Herschel H. Blackwell Jr. lay a young radioman who decided that he had seen something moving in the brush just

ahead. Leaping forward to challenge the interloper, he bumped into one of the horses that were known to prowl the base, resulting in a much-startled steed and radioman. Elsewhere, on the big hill, after surviving the harrowing ordeal of Ens. Tanner's early-morning attacks and subsequent search for the invading Japanese fleet, AMM3c C. W. "Duck" Mallard, determined not to succumb to the imagined Japanese soldier in his front, left his revetment with fixed bayonet and wildly charged a tree stump in the stygian murk, which flipped over the 220-pound machinist in the process.[36]

During the night of 7 December, for most of the civilians, servicemen, and their families stationed at Kaneohe, the sunny halcyon days of peace seemed a sad and distant memory. It hardly seemed possible that the troubled absence of daylight was a prelude to positive developments, at least in the short term. Sea2c Samuel H. Bussell summed up the experience of the Kaneohe warriors that evening in a terse observation. "It was a dark and dreary suspense-filled night . . . and the morning could not come quickly enough."[37]

Cdr. Martin ordered a funeral service to be held on the afternoon of 8 December for the men killed in action during the previous morning. The conditions in the morgue at the Dispensary—where bodies lay stacked without refrigeration, one atop the other—justified the decision. Martin also thought it best to move past the events of the previous day as soon as possible. Accordingly, he ordered the ceremony to begin in the lengthening shadows of the late afternoon. As Kaneohe did not have a cemetery, the site selected for burial was the sand dunes along the north beach in the far northeast corner of the station.[38]

Lt. Iida's corpse—still in the garbage can outside the morgue—was to be buried in a grave adjacent to that of the Americans, a prospect that incensed quite a few officers and men at the station. Subsequently, newspapers raised a "big fuss" about the incident, but Martin always defended his position on the full military funeral accorded the Japanese aviator. "He deserved it," Martin said, "and that was that."[39]

HA1c Robert E. Hoffman had duty on Monday and was responsible for Lt. Iida's remains and those of the Navy men. There was little room in the morgue, with only four trays and one preparation table for the bodies. At some point during the day, a set of large pine boxes arrived, fashioned by the station's three carpenters, ChCarp Eugene F. Smith, CM1c (F-4-C) Arnold A. Leuthard, and CM3c Norvan R. Fulton. There was one deceased ensign—an aviator (either Fox or Smartt)—being transferred to a box, with Hoffman taking the feet and his partner taking the shoulders. While laying the corpse, gently and reverently, into the coffin, they slipped and inadvertently allowed the officer's head to drop and hit the bottom of the box. Mortified, Hoffman apologized: "I'm sorry, sir."[40]

The decisions regarding the particulars of the funeral came so quickly and so late in the day that the authorities made provision for the Marine honor guard

only at the last minute. In midafternoon, Pfc. Wesley H. Bott and other Marines returned to the barracks for a brief respite, spent, "really tired out," and grateful for a few moments of rest. Suddenly, Sgt. Charles H. Roberts burst in: "Get everybody out," he said, "Put your uniform on. We're going out."

Roberts and the others clambered onto a truck, driven by Pvt. Nichols, with no one knowing where they were going. Eventually, Nichols drove to the sand dunes north of the station, where the Marines were to fire volleys over the graves of the men who had been killed the previous morning. Roberts was NCO-in-charge of the detail.[41]

The ceremony began at about 1600, with an honor guard of eight Marines standing in front of the open grave that was to receive the fifteen coffins, with one corporal, three privates first class, and four privates, under the command of Maj. Donehoo. Drawn up in a rank behind the honor guard were Cdr. Martin and several officers from his staff, including Lt. Cdr. Robert C. Warrack (executive officer) and Lt. Cdr. Wilbur E. Kellum (chief medical officer). Other groups in attendance included a detachment from the station complement, a Navy labor detail, at least one civilian, a Navy bugler (presumably Bug1c Theodore J. Moss), and pallbearers to convey the caskets to the grave. Even a portion of the Army contingent on Mōkapu Peninsula was present, arriving via truck from the east.[42]

After the parties arrived, two stake trucks from the station pulled up from the west along the beach, and groups of six pallbearers for each dead sailor bore the fifteen caskets to the open grave. The first truck then pulled forward after unloading, allowing a second vehicle to gain the entrance to the cemetery site. Although four officers and fourteen seamen and ratings perished as a result of the raid, three of the men were missing; the bodies of two plane guards—AMM1c (NAP) Daniel T. Griffin and AMM2c Walter S. Brown—had not yet washed ashore, and AMM3c Milburn A. Manning, who died early on 8 December across the bay at the Territorial Hospital, still lay in the morgue there. With the dead placed in the grave, in fifteen caskets side by side, the men placed a large American flag over seven caskets in the middle and a Springfield rifle atop the flag over the fourth casket from the sea side end of the row.[43]

No detailed written description of the ceremony was preserved, although from the photography, it appears that Lt. (jg) Wallace L. Kennedy, Ch–V(G), the base's Protestant chaplain, offered remarks and led those present in a prayer. Then the honor guard fired its salute, Bugler Moss sounded taps, and a bulldozer covered the graves. The ceremony followed a similar routine for Lt. Iida, who was buried alone in an adjacent grave, far from his homeland.[44]

No available records indicate when the Navy interred Griffin and Brown, but the burials most likely occurred on 12 December or later, at which time both bodies had finally washed up on the shore of the bay. Circumstances of their burial are not known beyond Brown's reported burial time during the first half of the afternoon watch on 12 December. One account stated that the police of Kāne'ohe town reported that Griffin's body had washed ashore later. With the interment of Brown, Griffin, and Manning on the south end of the mass grave, a very sad chapter from Kaneohe's history came to an end.[45]

The sand dunes northeast end of NAS Kaneohe Bay at 1600 on 8 December. Navy men place the caskets containing the bodies of Kaneohe's slain side by side in a mass grave. Five of the coffins are in place with AMM1c Raphael A. Watson being closest to the photographer. The men work with the coffin of AMM3c Robert K. Porterfield, struggling to set it in place alongside his comrades. The pallbearers for Sea2c George Washington Newman are just about to make the turn to the gravesite, while workers have just removed the body of Sea1c Laxton G. Newman from the stake truck on the beach. (NARA II, 80-G-32852)

Kaneohe's chaplain, Lt. (jg) Wallace L. Kennedy, Ch-V(G), offers remarks just before the honor guard fires a salute. Note the civilian with his round identity tag at far right. (NARA II, 80-G-77634)

At some point after the attack, as the soldiers, sailors, and Marines at Kaneohe finally drew a collective cleansing breath, the men set aside the fear of 7 December. To a man, all in uniform nursed a seething anger and bitterness toward the Japanese and could not wait for an opportunity to exact a fully justified retribution. Kaneohe was a relatively small installation, and there was hardly a man who did not know one or more of the fallen or wounded. In conversations at mess and at night, most comments were along the vein "that the perpetrators of the attacks would eventually pay for it." Exact quotations of the remarks were not printable at the time.[46]

Considering the men's anger and sense of loss, it is understandable that their opinions and conversations sometimes referred to conspiracy and negligence at many levels, sentiments that mirrored those of many on O'ahu, and indeed of the civilian population stateside. At least one nasty rumor making the rounds maintained that responsibility for the surprise lay quite close to home, specifically regarding Ens. Tanner and the midget sub affair south of Pearl Harbor. Sea2c Robert W. Ballou bemoaned the poor use of the critical information radioed in by Tanner, and what was worse (it was said) was that VP-14's duty officer was at the BOQ drinking coffee and had taken the code books with him. Although this story was clearly and demonstrably false, it is significant in that it showed how quickly some of the men had felt betrayed.[47]

Under the command of Maj. John C. Donehoo Jr., the honor guard drawn from Kaneohe's Marine Detachment fires a volley over the open grave. (NARA II, 80-G-32854)

After Maj. Donehoo takes a position in front of the honor guard, Bug1c Theodore J. Moss at left blows "Taps" at the ocean side end of the grave. (NARA II, 80-G-32855)

Chaplain Kennedy offers up suitable words at the grave of Lt. Iida Fusata. Cdr. Martin (in a overseas cap) stands at the (viewer's) far left end of the rank of officers behind the honor guard, with Lt. Cdr. Wilbur E. Kellum, Kaneohe's senior medical officer, alongside to his left. Martin's executive officer, Lt. Cdr. Robert C. Warrack, stands at the end of the rank. (NARA II, 80-G-32956)

The honor guard fires a volley over Lt. Iida, offering begrudging tribute at the behest of Cdr. Martin. Ironically, the grave markers for the Americans lie on the ground behind the honor guard. (NARA II, 80-G-77611)

With the honor guard standing at "present arms," the Navy bugler blows "Taps" on the north side of Lt. Iida's grave, while an unnamed Navy photographer takes a picture of his own shadow. (NARA II, 80-G-32857)

LIEUTENANT IIDA
Imperial Japanese Navy

KILLED IN ACTION
7 DECEMBER 1941

Grave marker for Lt. Iida Fusata. (Prange)

On a sunny afternoon in May 1944, Grace Watson and sons Billie (l) and Ralph Jr. (r) mourn their beloved husband and father, buried in the sand dunes north of the station, overlooking the Pacific Ocean. (NARA II, 80-G-419203, cropped)

Similarly, many of the men could not help feeling that the services had been "set up" by higher commands, particularly with respect to the PBYs being lined up in rows on the apron, although some dispersal of aircraft had taken place during the previous week within feasible limits. The base, however, set the stage for disaster on 5–6 December by lining up all the aircraft on the aprons, just in time for the Japanese. "We set ourselves up like sitting ducks."[48]

It is significant that the anger, fear, frustration, and second guessing of the men at the base had little negative effect on morale, which was high after the attack and remained so. In 1945, Kaneohe's unit historian noted that "the spirit of Kaneohe is an intangible but powerful tradition." From the earliest days of the base, when Cdr. Martin literally "rolled up his sleeves, [and led] by example," the men of Kaneohe exhibited energy, dedication, and resourcefulness. These qualities only intensified in the officers and men during their first taste of battle on 7 December 1941. Reflecting on the spirit of Kaneohe that day, Cdr. Martin later wrote, "After the seventh of December it was my duty to recommend individuals for commendation. I thought a great deal about it. No one shirked, no one avoided danger, everyone did the job he was supposed to do. It suddenly occurred to me that we were not individuals but the NAS Kaneohe Bay and that the station, not individuals, had conducted themselves in a manner which was in keeping with the best traditions of the Navy. I'd like to feel that this station will always be that way."[49]

# Notes

### Chapter 1. "It Was Like the Time of Your Life"

1. "Naval Air Station Kaneohe Bay History, 1 Aug 39–1 Aug 45" (hereinafter Kaneohe History), n.d., 15–17, Aviation Commands, 1941–1952, Box 233, History and Archives Division, Naval History and Heritage Command, Washington Navy Yard (hereinafter HAD, NHHC).

2. With its cottages and coconut palms, the area of Heleloa on the bay's north shore came to be known as the "Coconut Grove," a locale that figured prominently in the station's defense on 7 December 1941. It should not be confused, however, with the club of the same name in the nearby town of Kailua.

3. Kaneohe History, 15–16.

4. Kaneohe History, 15–16, 24; John S. Kennedy, *The Forgotten Warriors of Kaneohe* (Oakland, Calif.: East Bay Blue Print & Supply Co., 1996), account of Gordon Poling (hereinafter Poling account), 172–73. Kennedy's privately published work is a collection of documents and wartime reminiscences by Kaneohe veterans of all services, principally from the 7 December 1941 attack on O'ahu. Eventually Maj. Donehoo and his family would occupy Quarters "L" south of the BOQ.

5. "Commodore Harold Montgomery Martin Re: service of," 3 January 1945, Officer Biography Files, HAD, NHHC; letter from Walter J. Curylo (hereinafter Curylo letter), 3 March 1964, 1, Prange papers in the Goldstein Collection, Archives Service Center, University of Pittsburgh, UA-90/F-78, Box 23, FF-21; Kaneohe History, 24.

6. Analysis of Muster Roll for NAS Kaneohe Bay, 31 March 1941 and Report of Changes, 28 February 1941, www.fold3.com.

7. Kaneohe History, 26–27; Kennedy, *Forgotten Warriors*, 15–16.

8. Kaneohe History, 11, 30; Kennedy, *Forgotten Warriors*, 283–84.

9. Michael D. Roberts, *Dictionary of American Naval Aviation Squadrons, Volume 2: The History of VP, VPD, VP(HL) and VP(AM) Squadrons* (Washington, D.C.: Government Printing Office, 2000), 583; Aircraft History Cards (Microfilm), PBY-5, Various BuNos, 1911–1949, Reel 10, HAD, NHHC, copies courtesy of Eric Mitchell on www.pby.com; Pearl Harbor Muster Rolls at www.footnote.com, Muster Rolls, VP-26, 30 June 1941, Report of Changes, VP-14, 15 April 1941 and VP-26, 1 July 1941. Roberts' *Dictionary* should be used with caution and the content should be confirmed with relevant records where possible. In particular, the histories of VP-12 and VP-24 during the months preceding the attack on Hawaii are jumbled together, possibly owing to confusion surrounding the squadron redesignation ongoing at that time.

10. Muster Rolls, VP-23, 30 June 1941, www.fold3.com.

11. Delivery schedules followed the Navy's priority of sending new aircraft and parts to the Atlantic. In addition, Consolidated delivered an undetermined, though significant, number of PBYs to the Dutch, British, and Australians.

12. CO, VP-11, "Completed Itinerary," 3–28 October, Harry George Byron, Official Military Personnel File (hereinafter OMPF), RG24, NARA, St. Louis; logbook entries, October 1941, Howard J. Spreeman, then an RM3c with VP-11, courtesy of Eric Mitchell on www.pby.com; Bureau of Aeronautics, Aircraft History Cards (Microfilm) (hereinafter Aircraft History Cards, via Mitchell), PBY-5, Various BuNos, 1911–1949, Reel 10, HAD, NHHC, copies courtesy of Eric Mitchell on www.pby.com.

13. *Wright* (AV-1) deck log, 17–27 October 1941, RG24, NARA II; *Ballard* (AVD-10) deck log, 20–29 October 1941, RG24, NARA II; Capt. Charles P. Muckenthaler, USN (Ret.), telephone interview with J. Michael Wenger (hereinafter Muckenthaler interview), 20 December 2009. The B-17 crews flying B-17Es from Hamilton Field to O'ahu harbored similar concerns over Boeing's fuel consumption curves. The departure of VP-12 (the future VP-24) is based on the deck log entry for the *Wright* during the mid-watch of 28 October. Effective 1 September, CNO reduced VP-12's operating strength from twelve aircraft to six, although the Bureau of Aeronautics' "Monthly Status of Naval Aircraft" indicate that the squadron did not lose

its aircraft until October, prior to its departure for Hawai'i as the new VP-24. See page 27A of CNO to Bureaus and Offices and Divisions of the Office of the Chief of Naval Operations, et al., "Operating Force Plan, Fiscal Year 1942," 21 June 1941, RG 313, Records of Naval Operating Forces (Pre–World War II), Entry 299, United States Fleet; Scouting Force: Commander Aircraft; General Correspondence, 1937–1942, File A4-3, Employments, Box 33, NARA I.

14. Muckenthaler interview, 3, 6; Charles P. Muckenthaler, flight log entry for 27–28 October 1941; Microfilmed Movement Card, PatWing 1, HAD, NHHC. Later in his career, Raborn developed the Polaris missile project and served subsequently as director of the Central Intelligence Agency under President Lyndon B. Johnson. Ironically, nothing is known of the activities of Cdr. McGinnis during the events of 7 December 1941.

15. Analysis of NARA II photos 80-G-32839, 77614, 77621, 77627, 77647, 77648, and 279381. See ComAirScoFor dispatches 130526 of 13 October 1941 and 261945 of 26 November 1941. Little is known regarding the application of this experimental camouflage. It is possible that the 10 October 1941 date of photo 80-G-279381 might be in error, which would render the authors' interpretation invalid. It is certain, however, that six aircraft from VP-11 were in the alternate configuration on 7 December. Photos of three surviving aircraft exist, as well as wreckage of two others during and after the attack.

16. CO, VP-12, "Temporary Additional Duty," Thomas W. Helm, III, OMPF, RG24, NARA, St. Louis; Report of Changes, VP-24, 28 October 1941, www.fold3.com; Dispatch 282031, Serial 10-804, ComPatWing 2 to PatWing 1 and PatWing 2, 28 October 1941, RG80, Formerly Security-Classified CNO Documents, NARA II; Aircraft History Cards, via Mitchell, PBY-1 and PBY-5, Various BuNos 1911–1949, Reels 7, 10. Presumably, at this time old VP-12, then based at NAS Pearl Harbor, changed its designation to VP-24.

17. PatWing 2 Watch and Duty Schedules (hereinafter PatWing 2 Schedules), Exhibit 113-C, Exhibits of the Joint Committee, *Pearl Harbor Attack: Hearings Before the Joint Committee on the Investigation of the Pearl Harbor Attack* (hereinafter *PHA*) (Washington, D.C.: Government Printing Office, 1946), Part 26, 2563; Aircraft History Cards, via Mitchell, PBY-5, Various BuNos, 1911–1949, Reel 10; Analysis by Wenger and James Sawruk; Bureau of Aeronautics, "Monthly Status of Naval Aircraft," 31 August 1941, HAD, NHHC.

18. PatWing 2 Schedules, 2547–2567; correspondence with Mr. James Sawruk, 12 February 2009, regarding his research in the microfilmed records of the Bureau of Aeronautics; testimony of Patrick N. L. Bellinger before the Hart Inquiry, 15 March 1944, *PHA*, Part 26, 125.

19. Jamie R. Murphy, interview with Dr. Ronald Marcello, 15 May 1976, OH#0326 (hereinafter Murphy NTU interview), 6, University of North Texas Oral History Collection, Denton, Texas.

20. Kenton and Minnie Nash, interview with Dr. Ronald Marcello, 15 October 1977, OH#0397 (hereinafter Nash NTU interview), 24–25, University of North Texas Oral History Collection, Denton, Texas.

21. Robert E. Hoffman, interview with Dr. Ronald Marcello, 9 May 1974, OH#0193 (hereinafter Hoffman NTU interview), 6, University of North Texas Oral History Collection, Denton, Texas; Herman W. Barber, interview with Dr. Ronald Marcello, 14 October 1974, OH#0392 (hereinafter Barber NTU interview), 8, University of North Texas Oral History Collection, Denton, Texas; Herschel E. Blackwell, interview with Dr. Ronald Marcello, 26 April 1986, OH#0975 (hereinafter Blackwell NTU interview), 18, University of North Texas Oral History Collection, Denton, Texas; Randolph S. D. Lockwood, interview with Dr. Ronald Marcello, 24 August 1974, OH#0250 (hereinafter Lockwood NTU interview), 19, University of North Texas Oral History Collection, Denton, Texas.

22. An affectionate and popular name for the vicinity of NAS Kaneohe Bay.

23. Dispatch 272337, Serial 11-856, OpNav to CinCPac and CinCAF, 28 November 1941, RG80, Formerly Security-Classified CNO Documents, NARA II.

24. Otto V. Horky, interview with Dr. Ronald Marcello, 17 May 1974, OH#0203 9 (hereinafter Horky NTU interview), 30, University of North Texas Oral History Collection, Denton, Texas; Kennedy, *Forgotten Warriors*, 87, 146.

25. Letter from Guy C. Avery (hereinafter Avery letter), 1 December 1963, 3, Prange papers in the Goldstein Collection, Archives Service Center, University of Pittsburgh, UA-90/F-78, Box 23, FF-2; testimony of Harold M. Martin before the Roberts Commission, 3 January 1942, *PHA*, Part 23 (hereinafter Martin testimony, Roberts Commission), 738; Kaneohe

History, 197. For years thereafter, Avery wondered about the aborted inspection and whether the skipper ever intended to inspect the men.

26. "Story of Task Force NINE Activities on December 7, 1941" (hereinafter Task Force NINE Activities), 11–12, enclosure to ComPatWing 2 to CinCPac, "Task Force NINE (Patrol Wings ONE and TWO) Activities on December 7, 1941—Story of," n.d., Ramsey Papers, Box 2 (uncataloged) Pearl Harbor folder, HAD, NHHC. Ens. Edmond M. Jacoby D-V(G), USNR, prepared this narrative for Bellinger, who in turn forwarded it to Kimmel; Martin testimony, Roberts Commission, 738; letter from Donald B. Alexander (hereinafter Alexander letter), 10 July 1956, 1, Lord Collection, HAD, NHHC.

27. For the full text of Pacific Fleet Confidential Letter No. 2CL-41 Revised, see CinCPac to Pacific Fleet, "Security of Fleet at Base and in Operating Areas," 14 October 1941, Proceedings of the Roberts Commission, *PHA*, Part 23, 1115–1120. For comparison to the original 2CL-41, see CinCUS to Fleet, "Security of Fleet at Base and in Operating Areas," 15 February 1941, Proceedings of the Roberts Commission, *PHA*, Part 22, 335–39.

28. PatWing 2 Schedules; chart of aerial searches from 7 December 1941, RG80, Roberts Commission Exhibits, NARA II; Kennedy, *Forgotten Warriors*, account of Jackson L. Harris (hereinafter Harris account), 351.

29. Map of searches and patrols from 7 December 1941, *PHA*, Part 25, Exhibits of the Roberts Commission, Exhibit 44, Item 51.

30. Barber NTU interview, 11; Thomas E. Roth, interview with Dr. Ronald Marcello, 15 October 1977, OH#0400 (hereinafter Roth NTU interview), 9, University of North Texas Oral History Collection, Denton, Texas.

31. Testimony of Patrick N. L. Bellinger before the Navy Court of Inquiry, 25 August 1944, *PHA*, Part 32, 504; Patrol Wing 2, War Diary, entry from 7 December 1941, NHHC.

32. The precise location of the four PBYs from VP-12 and VP-14 is unclear. Although NARA II photo 80-G-418994 shows an anchorage in the bay west of the aprons and hangar line, it is uncertain whether this area was intended for use only by VP-14 or by all squadrons. That the area was in use on 7 December is undisputed, although it is not known whether the two VP-12 machines lay further east, closer to Hangar 1.

    At that time, Christian "Chris" Holmes II, heir to the Fleischmann yeast fortune, owned Coconut Island (sometimes referred to as "Chris Holmes Island"), along with the aged sailing vessel *Seth Parker* (used by Holmes for entertaining), which lay in a small slip at the island. Currently administered by the state of Hawai'i, Coconut Island (Mokuolo'e) is home to a marine biology laboratory. The island also provided the location of the long shot in the opening scene of the television series *Gilligan's Island*.

33. Martin testimony, Roberts Commission, 738–39; Kennedy, *Forgotten Warriors*, account of Harry W. Haase (hereinafter Haase account), 252; Alexander letter, 10 July 1956, 1. The hangar assignments were as follows: VP-11, VP-12 to Hangar 1; VP-14 to Hangar 2. The station allocated parking space on the warmup platform (going west to east) to VP-14 south of Hangar 2; VP-12, south of the Maintenance Hangar; and VP-11 (due to cramped conditions on the warmup platform), both south and east of Hangar 1. Kaneohe's numbering of its hangars is a bit confusing as Hangar 2 ultimately became Hangar 3 following the erection of a new Hangar 2 around the structure of the small Maintenance Hangar in 1942. Indeed, this process was just under way at the time of the attack as photography from 7 December shows footings for the new hangar (future Hangar 2) having been recently excavated. See photo 80-G-77638 in RG80, Still Picture Branch, NARA II. For clarity and consistency, an "apron" refers to the parking area on either side of the hangars, while the "warmup platform" specifies the paved area south of the hangar line. A "ramp" will always refer to one of the five sloping paved thoroughfares by which the aircraft accessed either the water or warmup platform. Confusing matters, the reports from the attack often use "ramp" and "apron" interchangeably to refer to any paved area where aircraft lay parked.

34. The identity of the units placed at Kaneohe during the alert is uncertain, although after the attacks of 7 December, Batteries F and G went into "war position" at the base. See the 98th Coastal Artillery's microfilmed Morning Reports, December 1941, Box 831, RG64, Records of the National Archives and Records Administration, NARA, St. Louis.

35. Commander, Patrol Squadron Eleven to CinCPac, "December 7, 1941 Air Raid: Report of" (hereinafter VP-11 Report), 13 December 1941, RG38, NARA II; Commander, Patrol Squadron Twelve to CinCPac, "Report of Raid of December 7, 1941" (hereinafter VP-12 Report), 14 December 1941, RG38, NARA II; Martin testimony, Roberts Commission, 739;

Testimony of Harold M. Martin before the Army Pearl Harbor Board, 29 August 1944, *PHA*, Part 28, 968; War Diary, Patrol Wing 2, 7 December, 1941, RG38, NARA II; Kennedy, *Forgotten Warriors*, account of John S. Kennedy (hereinafter Kennedy account), 88; Kennedy, *Forgotten Warriors*, Haase account, 252.

## Chapter 2. "This Is the First Time I've Ever Seen the Army Working on Sunday"

1. Ens. Tanner's radioman sent the message from 14-P-1 at 0700.

2. Before his appointment to the U.S. Naval Academy (Class of 1933), Hanson attended École Nouvelle in Lausanne, Switzerland, and the New Mexico Military Institute.

3. It is likely that Lt. Hanson commanded the 2nd Division. He was in VP-14's communications office, which lay near the southeastern corner of the hangar's bayside mezzanine, between the office of Lt. Thurston B. Clark (squadron commander) on the corner to the east and the Yeoman Office and filing room to the west. See Architectural Drawing 1406-45-49, "U.S. Naval Air Station Kaneohe (Oahu) T.H. Extension to Maintenance Hangar," in the microfilmed records of the Bureau of Yards and Docks, RG71I, Series I, Reel 1174, NARA II.

4. ComPatWing 1 to CinCPac, "Report of Japanese Air Attack of Kaneohe Bay, T.H., December 7, 1941" (hereinafter ComPatWing 1 Report), 1 January 1942, 1, RG38, NARA II; ComTF9 to CinCPac, "Operations on December 7, 1941," 20 December 1941, 2, RG38, NARA II; Kennedy, *Forgotten Warriors*, account of Murray Hanson (hereinafter Hanson account), 354.

5. Harold M. Martin, interview, 10 November 1970, 2–3, Prange Collection, University of Maryland, Box 23 (hereinafter Martin interviews); Martin testimony, Roberts Commission, 739.

6. Letter from Dr. Herman P. McCrimmon, 20 March 1956 (hereinafter McCrimmon letter), 1, Lord Collection, HAD, NHHC; e-mail correspondence, Joseph P. McCrimmon, son of Herman P. McCrimmon, 15 August 2009, Wenger Collection. McCrimmon's sons were Jerome and Joseph, the latter being dubbed "Packy" after his middle (and mother's maiden) name "Paxton."

7. Arthur R. Grace Jr., interview with Dr. Ronald Marcello, 14 October 1977, OH#0394 (hereinafter Grace NTU interview), 21, University of North Texas Oral History Collection, Denton, Texas; Cecil I. Hollingshead, interview with Dr. Ronald Marcello, 22 October 1983, OH#0609 (hereinafter Hollingshead NTU interview), 15–16, University of North Texas Oral History Collection, Denton, Texas; Barber NTU interview, 12–13.

8. Kennedy, *Forgotten Warriors*, account of Joseph C. Engel (hereinafter Engel account), 297; Service Record, Dale S. Lyons, OMPF, RG24, NPRC, St. Louis.

9. George Poulos, "At War: Recollections of a VP Pilot," *Naval Aviation News*, 9 August 1982 (hereinafter Poulos account), 29; Kennedy, *Forgotten Warriors*, Haase account, 252; Horky NTU interview, 39–40, 45; Biographical data sheet, 19 July 1941, Rodney S. Foss, OMPF, RG24, NARA, St. Louis.

10. Avery letter, 16 December 1963, 1.

11. Statement, Muranaka Kazuo, 17 December 1949, 3, Prange Collection, University of Maryland, Box 19; statement, Okajima Kiyokuma, 19 January 1951, 2, Prange Collection, University of Maryland, Box 19; *Shōkaku* Detailed Action Report (hereinafter *Shōkaku* DAR), Yamagata Tsunao, pub., *Kaigun: Kūbo-Kan Sentō Kiroku* (Tōkyō: Atene Shobō, 2002), 208.

    In his interviews with Prange, Fuchida states that the altitude to which the fighters were to ascend was closer to five thousand meters, but the interviews, statements, and articles by the fighter pilots show that the altitude was six thousand. It is apparent from the statements of Okajima and Muranaka that prior to landfall, Itaya decided to deploy on the assumption that the Americans lay in wait north of O'ahu. Accordingly, all the fighter units were ordered to six thousand meters to meet that threat. Okajima and Muranaka's recollections match perfectly the text of the tactical order as preserved in the *Shōkaku*'s report. It was not until Fuchida's flare that Okajima and Muranaka descended to two thousand meters in response to the "no force" flare. As Itaya had all his fighters climbing at the time of the flare, Fuchida possibly misinterpreted the action of the proactive fighter leader as failure to deploy properly, although Itaya's decision seems a prudent precaution.

12. Shiga Yoshio, interview, 9 July 1956, 5, Lord Collection, HAD, NHHC; Shiga Yoshio, "*Seikutai kara Mita Shinjuwan Kōgeki*," in Fujita Iyozō, comp., *Shōgen Shinjuwan Kōgeki* (Tōkyō: Kōjin-sha, 1991), 110; *Shōkaku* DAR, 208. It is not known whether,

during the initial ascent ordered by Lt. Cdr. Itaya, Kaneko's unit passed 4,500 meters. Hence it is not known whether, after seeing Fuchida's second flare, Kaneko's fighters ascended or descended to their appointed altitude.

13. Also known as the Honolulu Flying Club. See *Honolulu Star-Bulletin,* 7 December 1941, 8.

14. *Shōkaku* DAR, 210; correspondence, John W. Lambert with Abe Yasujirō, n.d.; *Hikōkitai no Sentō Kōdōchōsho,* War History Office, Japan Defense Agency (hereinafter *kōdōchōsho*), *Shōkaku* and *Zuikaku,* 8 December 1941; Stephen Harding, "First Planes Down at Pearl," *Aviation History Magazine,* 1 January 2014, 52. From the Japanese deployment, it is obvious that Kaneko's fighters were the culprits in the encounter near the Mormon Temple. But because there is nothing in any Japanese records to indicate the 5th Carrier Division fighters took part in such an "engagement," perhaps Rear Adm. Hara's stern admonition regarding civilian targets accounts for the failure to report the incident. It is inconceivable that Kaneko's subordinates would have attacked the civilian plane without orders. The Aeronca would almost certainly have been far below the Japanese fighters. See *kōdōchōsho*s for the *Shōkaku* and the *Zuikaku,* 8 December 1941; Detailed Action Report No. 1, CarDiv 5 (trans.) (hereinafter CarDiv 5 DAR), Prange Collection, University of Maryland, Box 21; *Shōkaku* DAR; "Lessons (Air Operations) of the Sea Battle off Hawaii," vol. I, August 1942 (est.) (trans.) (hereinafter Battle Lessons), Prange Papers, via Cressman.

15. *Shōkaku* DAR, 210, 212.

16. Kennedy, *Forgotten Warriors,* Hanson account, 354.

17. Puʻu Hawaiʻiloa is a small extinct volcano with a summit of 427 feet. Although roads lay on both the east and west side of the hill, Martin likely drove around to the east, a slightly more direct route to the Administration Building.

18. Martin interviews, 10 November 1970, 2–3; ComPatWing 1 Report, 1; Martin testimony, Roberts Commission, 739.

19. Kennedy, *Forgotten Warriors,* Hanson account, 354–55.

20. Born in New Rochelle, New York, Clark was a 1927 graduate of the U.S. Naval Academy.

21. Kennedy, *Forgotten Warriors,* Hanson account, 355–56.

22. Commendation, Sam Aweau, 18 March 1942, HAD, NHHC; Kaneohe History, 38; Application for Federal Employment, Samuel Kahukumaka Aweau Sr., RG181, NARA, St. Louis.

23. Barber NTU interview, 12.

24. Barber NTU interview, 12–13; Grace NTU interview, 22.

25. Of Bohemian ancestry, Horky was fluent in that language and German.

26. Horky NTU interview, 40–41; Service Records, Walter S. Brown and David T. Griffin, OMPF, RG24, NARA, St. Louis.

27. Horky NTU interview, 43–44.

28. Richmond attended LaGrange College in Hannibal, Missouri, and worked as a telephone lineman and surveyor before enlisting on 10 May 1938.

29. Letter and account, Robertus M. Richmond, 26 November 1963 (hereinafter Richmond account), 5, Prange papers in the Goldstein Collection, University of Pittsburgh, Archives Service Center, UA-90/F-78, Box 23, FF-94; Kennedy, *Forgotten Warriors,* Haase account, 252; Kennedy misspells the name as "Hasse." The account of events at NAS Kaneohe Bay in Gordon W. Prange's *December 7th, 1941: The Day the Japanese Attacked Pearl Harbor* (New York: McGraw-Hill Book Company, 1988) should be used with care as the chronologies of the two attack waves lie jumbled together. The greatest strength of the work lies in its endnotes and bibliography, which are invaluable. Prange's original source material should be consulted, if possible.

30. Questionnaire, Sea2c Robert W. Ballou, circa 31 May 1956 (hereinafter Ballou questionnaire), 1, Lord Collection, HAD, NHHC; Enlistment, U.S. Navy, Robert Warren Ballou, 4 March 1941, OMPF, RG24, NARA, St. Louis; Poulos account, 29.

31. Kennedy, *Forgotten Warriors,* Miscellaneous account, 349; Letter from Rickard R. J. Moser, 23 January 1964 (hereinafter Moser letters), 1, Prange papers in the Goldstein Collection, Archives Service Center, University of Pittsburgh, UA-90/F-78, Box 23, FF-80.

32. The lone exception was Wheeler Field, where, according to Japanese records, attacks there occurred in the vicinity of 0745. See *kōdōchōsho, Zuikaku* dive-bombing group, 8 December 1941.

33. Alexander letter, 10 July 1956, 1.

34. Harry Spiller, *Pearl Harbor Survivors: An Oral History of 24 Servicemen* (Jefferson, N.C.: McFarland & Co., Inc., Publishers, 2002), account of Alfred D. Perucci (hereinafter Perucci account), 146; Service Record, Alfred D. Perucci, NPRC, OMPF, RG24, St. Louis.

35. Japanese records state the attack on Kaneohe started at 0755. Kaneohe's chronology, however, suggests approximately 0750. Although this might seem a small detail, the attack time is important in establishing the time and place of the first Japanese attacks. The authors believe that the *Zuikaku's* dive-bombers opened the attack on O'ahu, although attacks on various civilian aircraft might represent the first air actions.

36. *Zuikaku's kōdōchōsho* claims five PBYs set afire and sunk.

37. ComPatWing 1 Report, 1.

38. Kennedy, *Forgotten Warriors*, account of Armand Petriccione (hereinafter Petriccione account), 255.

39. Malmin, who joined the Navy to "learn a trade," was bilingual (English and Norwegian) and had a brother at NAS Pearl Harbor, AM1c Thomas S. Malmin.

40. Moser letters, 23 January 1964, 2; questionnaire, Cecil S. Malmin, circa 9 March 1956 (hereinafter Malmin questionnaire), 1, Lord Collection, HAD, NHHC.

41. Questionnaire, Henry M. Popko, n.d. (hereinafter Popko questionnaire), 1, Lord Collection, HAD, NHHC; Service Record, Moreno J. Caparrelli, OMPF, RG24, NARA, St. Louis.

42. Robert U. Hanna, interview with Dr. Ronald Marcello, 13 June 1978, OH#0424 (hereinafter Hanna NTU interview), 21–22, University of North Texas Oral History Collection, Denton, Texas; Service Record, Robert U. Hanna, OMPF, RG24, NPRC, St. Louis.

43. Joe M. Trest, interview with Dr. Ronald Marcello, 15 October 1977, OH#0389 (hereinafter Trest NTU interview), 18–20, University of North Texas Oral History Collection, Denton, Texas; Service Record, Joe M. Trest, OMPF, RG127, NARA, St. Louis; Wesley H. Bott, interview with Dr. Larry Bowman, 14 October 1977, OH#0399 (hereinafter Bott NTU interview), 21–22, University of North Texas Oral History Collection, Denton, Texas.

44. Ray Merriam, *World War II Journal 2: Pearl Harbor Special Issue* (Bennington, Vt.: Merriman Press, 2000), 41.

45. Kennedy, *Forgotten Warriors*, account of Doyle A. Bell (hereinafter Bell account, 83); Murphy NTU interview, 15–16; Moser letters, 23 January 1964, 2; Service Record, George W. Lunn, OMPF, RG24, NPRC, St. Louis.

46. Questionnaire, Sea2c Warren G. Kearns, n.d. (hereinafter Kearns questionnaire), 1–3, Lord Collection, HAD, NHHC; Moser letters, 23 January 1964, 2; Service Record, James K. Marshall, OMPF, RG24, NARA, St. Louis. Sadly, though leading a charmed life on 7 December, Marshall would perish nine days later in the crash of a PBY-5 near the island of Niihau.

47. *Kōdōchōshos, Shōkaku* and *Zuikaku* fighter units, 8 December 1941; ComPatWing 1 Report, 1; Popko questionnaire, 1, 3; Muster Rolls, VP-12, www.fold3.com.

48. Correspondence, John S. Kennedy with Wenger, 17 June 2005.

49. Avery letter, 16 December 1963, 1.

50. Records indicate that the OS2U-1 was badly damaged but not destroyed. Intending that the aircraft be repaired, the Navy delivered the Kingfisher to NAS Alameda, where the authorities finally struck the floatplane (deleted it from the list of active aircraft in the Navy's inventory) on 16 October 1943. The BuNo and other information concerning this OS2U-1 was made available courtesy of Mr. James Sawruk.

51. Among the men were BM1c Fred E. Gahan, AMM1c Woodrow W. Beard, AMM1c Eric H. Sorensen, AMM3c Robert J. Leach, Sea1c William H. Branham, Sea2c Desmond V. Hatcher, and Sea2c Alfred R. Jiuliani, all part of the station's complement.

52. Correspondence, John S. Kennedy with Wenger, 17 June 2005; Kaneohe History, 198.

53. Kennedy, *Forgotten Warriors*, account of Francis F. Davis (hereinafter Davis account), 145–46; Service Record, Francis F. Davis, OMPF, RG24, NARA, St. Louis.

54. Kennedy, *Forgotten Warriors*, Harris account, 351.

55. McCrimmon letter, 1; Architectural Drawing 1406-31-3, "U.S. Naval Air Station Kaneohe (Oahu) T.H., Dispensary Second Floor Plan," in the microfilmed records of the Bureau of Yards and Docks, RG71I, Series I, Reel 1173, NARA II.

56. CPhM (AA) Albert A. Blake, or CPhM (PA) Roy A. Bryant.

57. Hoffman NTU interview, 19–21.

58. *Forgotten Warriors*, Kennedy account, 87–88.

59. McCrimmon letter, 1, Lord Collection, HAD, NHHC; Kennedy, *Forgotten Warriors*, account of Adelaide McCrimmon (hereinafter McCrimmon account), 109.

60. Hoffman NTU interview, 21–22.

61. *Kōdōchōshos*, *Shōkaku* and *Zuikaku*, 8 December 1941; Moser letters, 23 January 1964, 2; Certificates of Death, Daniel T. Griffin and Walter S. Brown, OMPF, RG24, NARA, St. Louis; Beneficiary Slip, Daniel T. Griffin, OMPF, RG24, NARA, St. Louis; Kennedy, *Forgotten Warriors*, Kennedy account, 88; correspondence, James Sawruk with Wenger; Wendy M. Coble (then an underwater archaeologist at East Carolina University) letter to JMW (hereinafter Coble letter); Popko questionnaire, 1. Gardner lived through the attack and the war, but the Blacksburg, Virginia, native felt guilty ever afterward for sending a friend to his death. An alternative account of Griffin's death comes from then AMM2c Cecil S. Malmin, who told Griffin's family years later that he saw the plane guard shot dead in the water. See Phonecon, JMW and Donald R. Griffin (son of Daniel T. Griffin), 29 January 2014.

62. Phone conversation notes with Paul B. Van Nostrand Jr., 11 July 2010 (hereinafter Van Nostrand notes), Wenger Collection; Service Record, George C. Wilson, OMPF, RG24, NARA, St. Louis.

63. Van Nostrand notes. Van Nostrand Sr. was the only one of the four plane guards to survive the war, as RM3c Wilson went missing in action when his aircraft failed to return to Henderson Field, Guadalcanal, from an antishipping raid by VB-101 on 5 March 1943.

64. John F. Nichols, interview with Dr. Larry Bowman, 15 October 1977, OH#0405 (hereinafter Nichols NTU interview), 23–24, University of North Texas Oral History Collection, Denton, Texas; David H. Thomas, interview with Dr. Ronald Marcello, 28 April 1990, OH#0796 (hereinafter Thomas NTU interview), 10, University of North Texas Oral History Collection, Denton, Texas; Service Record, John F. Nichols, OMPF, RG127, NARA, St. Louis; Service Record, Lucius C. Melton, OMPF, RG127, NARA, St. Louis.

65. Nichols NTU interview, 24, 28, 30; Service Record, Kenneth A. Little, OMPF, RG127, NARA, St. Louis; Kennedy, *Forgotten Warriors*, Poling account, 179.

66. Thomas NTU interview, 10; Service Record, David H. Thomas, OMPF, RG127, NARA, St. Louis. Thomas' wrist was not attended to until his return to the United States about a year later.

67. The town of Kailua, and particularly Kalaheo Drive (fronting the beach), was the residence of many junior officers at Kaneohe.

68. The daughter's given name was Jane Victoria (hence "Tory") Colestock.

69. Letter from Mrs. Edward [Jane] Colestock to "Connie and Hooper" [family], 9 December 1941 (hereinafter Colestock letter), in Rear Adm. Edward E. Colestock Papers, Emil Buehler Library, National Museum of Naval Aviation, Pensacola, Florida; Service Record, Edward E. Colestock, OMPF, RG24, NPRC, St. Louis.

70. The son's given name was Edward Richard ["Dick"] Colestock.

71. Colestock letter.

72. Questionnaire, Walter W. Simmons, circa March 1956 (hereinafter Simmons questionnaire), 1, Lord Collection, HAD, NHHC; Service Record, Walter W. Simmons, OMPF, RG24, NPRC, St. Louis.

73. Simmons questionnaire, 1.

74. Ann Sherman was the daughter of Cdr. Forrest P. Sherman (then serving with OpNav) and Dolores Bronson Sherman (Elizabeth Martin's sister).

75. Lockwood NTU interview, 30–32.

76. Kennedy, *Forgotten Warriors*, account of William K. Spry (hereinafter Spry account), 85.

77. Alexander letter, 10 July 1956, 1; Kennedy, *Forgotten Warriors*, Spry account, 85; Simmons questionnaire, 2.

78. Muckenthaler interview, 3 March 2010, 1–2; Walter Lord, *Day of Infamy* (New York: Henry Holt & Company, 1957), 84.

79. Kennedy, *Forgotten Warriors*, account of Albert L. Dodson (hereinafter Dodson account), 361; Service Record, Albert L. Dodson, OMPF, RG24, NPRC, St. Louis.

80. Muckenthaler interview, 3 March 2010, 2; Service Record, John L. Genta, OMPF, RG24, NPRC, St. Louis.

81. Questionnaire, Daucy B. Goza, n.d. (hereinafter Goza questionnaire), 1, Lord Collection, HAD, NHHC.

82. Mrs. Curylo delivered a son, James, on 15 December 1941 on NAS Kaneohe Bay's Dispensary.

83. Curylo letter, 1–2; Service Record, Walter J. Curylo, OMPF, RG24, NPRC, St. Louis; Continuous Service Certificate, Walter J. Curylo, supplied by son James W. Curylo.

84. Kaneohe History, 202; *Pearl Harbor-Gram*, No. 91, July 1987, 39; "John Finn, Medal of Honor Winner, Dies at 100," *The New York Times*, 27 May 2010, 2.

85. Nash NTU interview, 48–50.

86. Lorenz served on the Yangtze River as an SC1c on board the *Tutuila* (PR-4) during the spring of 1930.

87. Charles H. Roberts, interview with Dr. Ronald Marcello, 13 October 1977, OH#0384 (hereinafter Roberts NTU interview, Marcello), 33–34, University of North Texas Oral History Collection, Denton, Texas; Service Record, Charles H. Roberts, OMPF, RG127, NPRC, St. Louis.

88. Roberts NTU interview, Marcello, 34–35; Charles H. Roberts, interview with Melinda White, 6 November 1994, OH#1201 (hereinafter Roberts NTU interview, White), 2, University of North Texas Oral History Collection, Denton, Texas; Lockwood NTU interview, 32–33.

89. Roberts NTU interview, Marcello; Roberts NTU interview, White, 5; Lockwood NTU interview, 33.

90. Kennedy, *Forgotten Warriors*, Engel account, 297.

91. Mynila Billingsley, interview with Dr. Ronald Marcello, 13 October 1977, OH#0386 (hereinafter Billingsley NTU interview), 12–15, University of North Texas Oral History Collection, Denton, Texas; Service Record, Oliver L. Billingsley, OMPF, RG24, NPRC, St. Louis.

92. Roberts NTU interview, Marcello, 38–39; Roberts NTU interview, White, 5; Service Record, Walter E. Soboleski, OMPF, RG127, NARA, St. Louis; Service Record, Frank Mindel, OMPF, RG127, NARA, St. Louis.

93. Lockwood NTU interview, 32–33. For the details regarding the lanais that connected the barracks, see Architectural Drawing 1406-30-3, "U.S. Naval Air Station Kaneohe, (Oahu) T.H. Barracks. Elevations" in the microfilmed records of the Bureau of Yards and Docks, RG71I, Series I, Reel 1173, NARA II.

94. Hanna NTU interview, 21–21; Blackwell NTU interview, 25–26.

95. Lockwood NTU interview, 33–34; Bott NTU interview, 22.

96. Bott NTU interview, 23, 25, 27, 37; Service Record, Wesley H. Bott, OMPF, RG127, NARA.

97. Roberts NTU interview, Marcello, 36–37; Roberts NTU interview, White, 4–5; Architectural Drawing 1406-30-3, "U.S. Naval Air Station Kaneohe, (Oahu) T.H. Barracks. Elevations."

98. Evans gained access to the roof via a hatch over the north-south corridor, a passageway by which men could reach other barracks up and down the line. The ladder lay along the corridor's west wall, adjacent to rooms 204–205 (gear and storage rooms). See Architectural Drawing 1406-30-2, "U.S. Naval Air Station Kaneohe (Oahu) T.H. Barracks Second Floor Plan, Roof Plan, Details of Covered Passage," in the microfilmed records of the Bureau of Yards and Docks, RG71I, Series I, Reel 1173, NARA II.

99. Merriam, *World War II Journal 2*, 41.

100. Trest NTU interview, 21–23, 27; Service Record, Joe M. Trest, OMPF, RG127, NARA, St. Louis.

101. There is little information regarding the location of Kaneohe's Armory, which figured so prominently in the attack. This lack of data once made interpretation of certain events almost impossible. Unfortunately, such a building does not appear on any station chart dating from 1940 or 1941. The presence of armories in the two hangars further complicates the interpretation of veterans' accounts, and it is clear that such "subsidiary" armories did exist. At least three veterans speak of recently installed rifle racks and a cinderblock/glass enclosure in Hangar 1. Medal of Honor recipient John L. Finn stated in a postwar conversation with Capt. Charles P. Muckenthaler that a similar armory or armories lay in Hangar 2.

While examining Kaneohe's architectural drawings in RG71 at NARA II in College Park, Maryland, the authors discovered that the station's principal Armory lay in Building 19, the Utilities Shop and Parachute Loft. Interestingly, this building also incorporated the station's photo lab. See Architectural Drawing 1406-29-2, "U.S. Naval Air Station

Kaneohe, (Oahu) T.H. Utilities Shop and Parachute Loft," in the microfilmed records of the Bureau of Yards and Docks, RG71I, Series I, Reel 1173, NARA II.

102. Kennedy, *Forgotten Warriors*, Bell account, 83.

103. Kennedy, *Forgotten Warriors*, Bell account, 85.

104. Billingsley NTU interview, 17.

105. ComPatWing 1 to ComAirScoFor, "Enemy action against the Naval Air Station, Kaneohe Bay, T.H. on December 7, 1941," 12 December 1941, 4, Prange Collection, University of Maryland, Box 24; Kaneohe History, 198; Com-Patron 12 to CinCPac, "Report of Raid of December 7, 1941" (hereinafter VP-12 Report), 14 December 1941, 1, RG38, NARA II; Kennedy, *Forgotten Warriors*, account of Samuel H. Bussell (hereinafter Bussell account), 223; Popko questionnaire, 3.

106. Kennedy, *Forgotten Warriors*, account of Ragnar N. "Scotty" Nilssen (hereinafter Nilssen account), 295; Service Record, Ragnar N. Nilssen, OMPF, RG24, NPRC, St. Louis; interviews, William P. Watson, son of AMM1c Raphael A. Watson, 19–20 August 2009, 1, Wenger Collection.

107. Enlistment, U.S. Navy, John Raymond Bacon, 11 March 1941, OMPF, RG24, NARA, St. Louis; Decoration Citation, John R. Bacon, 10 July 1951, HAD, NHHC; Service Record, William L. Pack, OMPF, RG24, NPRC, St. Louis; questionnaire, Ragnar N. Nilssen, n.d. (hereinafter Nilssen questionnaire), 1–2, Lord Collection, HAD, NHHC.

108. Ballou questionnaire, 1–2, Lord Collection, HAD, NHHC; Service Record, Robert W. Ballou, OMPF, RG24, NARA, St. Louis.

109. Hollingshead NTU interview, 20–23; Grace NTU interview, 25.

110. Hollingshead NTU interview, 23–24.

111. Commendation, AOM1c Robert Schnexnayder, December 1941, HAD, NHHC.

112. Malmin questionnaire, 2; Richmond account, 5; Popko questionnaire, 3.

113. ComPatWing 1 Report, 2; VP-11 Report, 2; Ballou questionnaire, 31 May 1956, 2, Lord Collection, HAD, NHHC; Kennedy, *Forgotten Warriors*, account of Joseph T. Crownover (hereinafter Crownover account), 253–54; Service Record, Harry G. Byron, 31 March 1942, OMPF, RG24, NARA, St. Louis.

114. Horky NTU interview, 46–48.

115. Horky NTU interview, 52–53.

116. Malmin questionnaire, 1.

117. Task Force 9 Activities, 17. Ens. Smartt's location in Hangar 1 provided by Capt. Charles P. Muckenthaler.

118. Perucci account, 146.

119. Commendation, Thomas E. Kerr, 28 March 1942, HAD, NHHC; Service Record, Thomas E. Kerr, OMPF, RG24, NPRC, St. Louis; Perucci account, 146.

120. "Moment of Decision," account by Lyle A. Jackson, n.d. (hereinafter "Moment of Decision"), *The Public's Library and Digital Archive*, http://www.ibiblio.org/phha/Lyle.html, accessed 1 June 2013; Service Record, Lyle A. Jackson, OMPF, RG24, NARA, St. Louis.

121. Perucci account, 146; Decoration Citations, James L. Beasley, James E. Walters, Delbert C. Jones, Robert F. Weston, and Morton N. Frey, all 10 July 1951, HAD, NHHC.

122. Kaneohe History, 202.

123. The time of Lt. Kaneko's departure is uncertain. American sources give 0815, whereas the action report from *Shōkaku* states that the fighters lingered over Kaneohe until 0830. Here, as in other similar instances, the authors decided to adhere to the Japanese timeline.

124. There are discrepancies in the ammunition expenditure figures for Kaneko and Satō's fighters. Ordinarily, although the figures provided in the *kōdōchōsho*s for the two air groups could be regarded as the final word, in the case of the *Shōkaku*, the 20-millimeter expenditure figures actually exceed the capacity of the aircraft. Hence, the authors have chosen the (very different) figures provided in the command level action reports. See *kōdōchōsho*s for the *Shōkaku* and the *Zuikaku*, 8 December 1941; CarDiv 5 DAR, 13.

125. Commanding Officer, Naval Air Station, Kaneohe Bay, T. H. to Commandant, Fourteenth Naval District, "The incidents connected with the air raid at the Naval Air Station, Kaneohe Bay, T.H. on 7 December 1941—Narrative of," 8 December 1941, 1, RG38, NARA II; *kōdōchōshos*, *Shōkaku* and *Zuikaku* fighter units, 8 December 1941; John W. Lambert, *Pineapple Air Force: Pearl Harbor to Tokyo* (St. Paul, Minn.: Phalanx Publishing Company, 1991), 17; Lambert Correspondence with Abe Yasujirō, n.d. To his credit, Rear Adm. Hara later revised Kaneko's claims downward to a more realistic (though still inflated) total of thirty aircraft set afire and five damaged. See Detailed Action Report, CarDiv 5, Prange files.

126. Kennedy, *Forgotten Warriors*, Bell account, 84.

127. Richmond account, 5.

128. Kennedy, *Forgotten Warriors*, Dodson account, 361; Kennedy, *Forgotten Warriors*, VP-14 Flight organization from 21 November 1941, 327; Transcript of VP-14 War Diary, 332, 336.

129. Kennedy, *Forgotten Warriors*, 349; Coble letter; Perucci account, 146–47.

130. Wenger's analysis of still photography in Record Group 80G at NARA II. VP-11 and VP-12's after-action reports are too vague to allow differentiation of losses between the two attacks.

131. Moser letters, 23 January 1964, 2; authors' photographic analysis in collaboration with James Sawruk.

132. Moser letters, 23 January 1964, 3; authors' photographic analysis in collaboration with James Sawruk. Information regarding efforts to save these two PBYs appears in a letter in Prange's papers dated 23 January 1964 from RM3c Richard R. J. Moser.

133. Wenger's analysis of still photography in Record Group 80G at NARA II.

134. Wenger's correspondence with James Sawruk. Though no report details this incident, attack photography chronicles the effort in great detail. See NARA 80-G-32828, 32829, 32830, 32832, 32833, 32837, 77618, and 77622. Sadly, despite efforts to save 11-P-3, after being shipped to California, the aircraft was stricken at NAS Alameda in June 1942 and broken up for spare parts.

135. Kaneohe History, 42; Analysis of attack photography at NARA II.

136. VP-11 Report, 1; Task Force 9 Activities, 17.

137. Commendation, Mrs. Alice Beckley Spencer, 4 March 1942, HAD, NHHC.

138. Horky NTU interview, 54; Task Force 9 Activities, 13; McCrimmon letter, 1–2; Architectural Drawing 1406-31-2, "U.S. Naval Air Station Kaneohe, (Oahu) T.H., Dispensary First Floor Plan," in the microfilmed records of the Bureau of Yards and Docks, RG71I, Series I, Reel 1173, NARA II; Kennedy, *Forgotten Warriors*, Kennedy account, 89; Ballou questionnaire, 2.

139. Death Certificate and Report of Death, Rodney S. Foss, OMPF, RG24, NARA, St. Louis; Letter of Recommendation, George B. Norris, for Rodney S. Foss, n.d., OMPF, RG24, NARA, St. Louis; Letter of Recommendation, J. B. Didier, for Rodney S. Foss, n.d., OMPF, RG24, NARA, St. Louis; CO, U.S. Naval Reserve Midshipmen's School, Northwestern University to SecNav, "Midshipman Rodney Shelton FOSS, U.S. Naval Reserve—Silver Life Saving Medal—recommendation for," 13 March 1942, OMPF, RG24, NARA, St. Louis.

## Chapter 3. "I Would Hit the Targets without Any Misses from This Altitude"

1. CarDiv 5 DAR, 15; *kōdōchōshos*, *Shōkaku* and *Zuikaku*, 8 December 1941; *Shōkaku* DAR, 215–17; map, "Japanese Plan of Attack," Prange files via Goldstein; map, 2nd Attack Wave Deployment, John Di Virgilio; Ōkubo Chūhei, "*Kiseki no Kankō Bakugekitai Futatsu no Sō-wa*," in Fujita Iyozō, comp., *Shōgen Shinjuwan Kōgeki* (Tōkyō: Kōjin-sha, 1991) (hereinafter Ōkubo), 390; tactical analysis by Di Virgilio and Wenger. Although Ichihara provided no explanation in the *Shōkaku*'s action report for his decision, the weather conditions over Kāneʻohe Bay unquestionably influenced his change in tactics.

   Considerable discrepancies exist between Prange's map (based on Fuchida's recollections) and the authors' reconstruction of the deployment using available Japanese records and postwar interviews. Great care should be exercised using Prange's accounts relating to the specifics of deployment and target selection, as he tended to rely upon the collective memories of Fuchida and Genda and used neither the Japanese air group *kōdōchōshos* nor the *Shōkaku*'s action report.

2. It is uncertain what area Ichihara used to make his 2,000-meter descent. South of Kaneohe, the steep slopes of the Koʻolau Range rise to 3,105 feet (Puʻu Konahuanui)—almost 1,000 meters—that would require a descent north of the mountains.

3. *Shōkaku* DAR, 216–17; map, 2nd Attack Wave Deployment, John Di Virgilio; tactical analysis and evaluation of Japanese photography by Di Virgilio and Wenger.

4. Analysis by Di Virgilio. With respect to bombsight capabilities, in answering questions from the authors, Yoshino Haruo—then an experienced senior noncommissioned officer in the *Kaga*'s *kankōtai*—insisted that it was impractical to use the bomber's Type 90 Mk.1 bombsight at such a low altitude. Moreover, the Type 97 naval torpedo sight (the type and model are uncertain) was impossible to use at above a thousand feet. Hence, it appears that Ichihara used guesswork to determine his drop point. See Robert C. Mikesh, *Japanese Aircraft Equipment: 1940–1945* (Atglen, Pa.: Schiffer Publishing Ltd., 2004), 163–69, 181.

5. The precise interval between the two divisions, or *chūtai*s, is not known.

6. Japanese photography taken just prior to the strike; Ōkubo, 390; *Shōkaku* DAR, 216–17; tactical analysis by Di Virgilio and Wenger; chart of Lt. Irikiin's formation in the original copy of the *Shōkaku*'s Detailed Action Report, page 39, which resides in the War History Library, Japan Defense Agency, Tōkyō. Fuchida made the general comment that all of the second-wave horizontal bombers "flew at no more than 2,000 meters in order to bomb from beneath the clouds," which does not square with Ichihara's tactical orders. See Fuchida Mitsuo and Masatake Okumiya, *Midway: The Battle That Doomed Japan* (Annapolis, Md.: Naval Institute Press, 1955), 310. Curiously, Ichihara's bizarre low-altitude bombing run is confirmed in an American document ("Story of Task Force NINE Activities on December 7, 1941"), in which the narrator states that the first bombing commenced from 1,500 feet. For years, the authors considered this specific observation flawed and unsupportable until the 2006 discovery by Kamada Minoru of the *Shōkaku*'s action report. Ōkubo speculates in his account regarding Ichihara's reasoning, namely, that he expected little antiaircraft fire. One wonders whether the crews would even have trained for such an unusual attack, which more resembled glide bombing. The low-altitude release also explains the well-known motion picture footage that depicts bomb detonations south of Hangar 2, as the apparent proximity of the photographer to the ground puzzled the authors for many years.

7. Task Force 9 Activities, 14; Martin testimony, Roberts Commission, *PHA*, Part 23, 741.

8. Kennedy, *Forgotten Warriors*, Haase account, 252; Kaneohe History, 42; Curylo letter, 2; Kearns questionnaire, 3. Note that Kennedy uses the name Harry A. Hasse, rather than Harry W. Haase as specified in VP-11's muster rolls.

9. Ōkubo, 391; *kōdōchōsho*, *Shōkaku*, 8 December 1941; Satō Zenichi, interview (n.d.) with Di Virgilio. It is important to reiterate that each of Ichihara's divisions made two separate and distinct drops.

10. Task Force 9 Activities, 14. The location of the Coconut Grove offered a clear shot at Ichihara's unit as it approached, with the bombers displaying their port beams.

11. Goza questionnaire, 2–3; Service Record, Daucy B. Goza, OMPF, RG24, NPRC, St. Louis.

12. Goza questionnaire, 2–3; Malmin questionnaire, 1.

13. Kennedy, *Forgotten Warriors*, Hanson account, 356–57.

14. Avery letter, 16 December 1963, 3; Service Record, Guy C. Avery, OMPF, RG24, NARA, St. Louis; Kennedy, *Forgotten Warriors*, Haase account, 252; Richmond account, 6; Kennedy, *Forgotten Warriors*, Hanson account, 356; Malmin questionnaire, 1–2; Goza questionnaire, 2; Kennedy, *Forgotten Warriors*, Dodson account, 361.

15. "Moment of Decision."

16. The future Hangar 4. Note that contemporary charts of the stations number the hangars *in order of completion* so that the construction near the Maintenance Hangar (completed last in 1942) became Hangar 4, although situated between Hangars 1 and 2. At some point afterward, to avoid confusion the Navy redesignated the hangars in order from east to west. See NAS Kaneohe Bay chart 1406-3-5 in RG71I, Series I, Microfilm Reel 1173, NARA II. The Japanese motion picture footage taken after Ichihara's attack shows no smoke except for 12-P-7 on the apron and 12-P-3 burning in the water south of the hangar line. Perhaps it is more likely that Fujita's fighters destroyed the three VP-14 machines.

17. Analysis of Japanese motion picture footage and American still photography by Wenger.

18. In *December 7, 1941* (according to page 3 of Genda Minoru, interview 26, 29 December 1947 [hereinafter Genda interview 26], 3, Prange Collection, University of Maryland, Box 19), Prange has Ichihara signaling Nagumo that "We . . . attacked the enemy's airfield with little success." The radio log in the 5th Carrier Division's Detailed Action Report, however, indicates that Ichihara sent no such message. It is almost certain that the message Genda remembered was a dispatch from Lt.

Irikiin's 3rd *Chūtai* regarding bombing results observed over NAS Pearl Harbor. While a minor issue, this highlights the pitfalls of overreliance on the "gospel according to Fuchida/Genda" to the exclusion of contemporary records.

19. *Shōkaku* DAR, 216–17; Ōkubo, 391.

20. *Shōkaku* DAR, 217; Ishikawa Satoki, "Shinjuwan Sakusen ni Sanka Shite," monograph of undetermined date and origin (hereinafter Ishikawa account), 221; tactical analysis by Di Virgilio and Wenger.

21. VP-12 Report, 1; Task Force 9 Activities, 14.

22. Malmin questionnaire, 1.

23. *Kōdōchōsho, Shōkaku* 8 December 1941; Ōkubo, 391. Much can be inferred regarding Ichihara's drop from the Japanese strike photography.

24. McCrimmon letter, 20 March 1956, 1–2.

25. McCrimmon letter, 20 March 1956, 2; Biographical data sheet, 7 January 1942, George M. Hutto, OMPF, RG24, NARA, St. Louis. Byron suffered multiple gunshot wounds to the abdomen.

26. *Kōdōchōsho, Sōryū* and *Hiryū,* 8 December 1941; Genda interview 26; Fujita Iyozō, interview, 2 February 1951 (hereinafter Fujita interview), 4, Prange Collection, University of Maryland, Box 19. The *Hiryū's kōdōchōsho* is unambiguous here, stating that Nōno's unit attacked NAS Kaneohe Bay first with Iida at 0915, and then proceeded south to Bellows. It is unclear, however, whether the *Hiryū's* entire division participated in the attack on Kaneohe, as a portion of the unit well may have proceeded south to Bellows Field immediately. The group's claim of only two PBYs destroyed is indeed low. The specific disposition of the 2nd Carrier Division fighters described by Prange in *December 7, 1941* conflicts with that in the *kōdōchōshos* and other accounts.

27. Kennedy, *Forgotten Warriors,* Bell account, 84.

28. Kennedy, *Forgotten Warriors,* Haase account, 252; Hanna NTU interview, 37.

29. Kennedy, *Forgotten Warriors,* Bussell account, 223; Moser letters, 17 November 1963, 1, and 23 January 1964, 3.

30. Simmons questionnaire, 2; Malmin questionnaire, 2.

31. Muckenthaler interview, 3 March 2010, 2–3; Statement of Naval Service, 4 May 1942, Robert J. Waters, OMPF, RG24, NARA, St. Louis.

32. Nash NTU interview, 51–52, 58; Service Record, Kenton Nash, OMPF, RG24, NARA, St. Louis.

33. Decoration Citation, John William Finn, 30 June 1942, HAD, NHHC; Decoration Citation, Robert James Peterson, 23 April 1942, HAD, NHHC; Kaneohe History, 45; *Pearl Harbor-Gram,* July 1987, 39; "Lieutenant John William Finn, U.S. Navy, Transcript Record Service of," OMPF, RG24, NPRC, St. Louis; "Oldest Medal of Honor recipient, 100, downplays 'hero' talk," http://www.cnn.com/2009/US/09/15/finn.medal.of.honor/index.html; Daniel Martinez, reminiscence of National Geographic interview with John W. Finn, circa December 2001.

34. "John Finn, Medal of Honor Winner, Dies at 100," *The New York Times,* 27 May 2010, 1.

35. Kennedy, *Forgotten Warriors,* Transcript of VP-14 War Diary, 332; Certificate of Death and Service Record, Laxton Gail Newman, OMPF, RG24, NARA, St. Louis; tactical analysis by Di Virgilio and Wenger.

36. Tactical analysis by Di Virgilio and Wenger.

37. *Shōkaku* DAR, 217; *kōdōchōsho, Shōkaku,* 8 December 1941; Chart of Lt. Hagiwara's formation in the original copy of *Shōkaku's* Detailed Action Report, page 39, which resides in the War History Library, Japan Defense Agency in Tōkyō; Kaneohe History, 198. Hatcher enlisted 28 December 1940 in Dallas, Texas, being assigned to Kaneohe on 22 July 1940.

38. Poulos account, 29; Nilssen questionnaire, 1.

39. Analysis by Di Virgilio and Wenger; CarDiv 5 DAR, 15. The bomb crater pattern near Hangar 1 is quite different from that produced by Ichihara's drop south of Hangar 2 and lies along an axis anchored on the aprons south of Hangar 1, extending to the open area northeast of the hangar. Although the existing evidence is fragmentary, it is clear from the crater pattern that the attack on Hangar 1 could only have been delivered from, generally, the northwest. The extremely wide distribution of explosions—although still very tight in the center—suggests strongly that Hagiwara's nine aircraft went into extended order, with the *shōtais* on either side of the formation widening intervals to port and starboard.

40. Reconstruction of coded message based on fragmentary code books recovered from Japanese aircraft wreckage. Sadly, no originals are known to exist, but photostatic copies reside in the Records of the Pearl Harbor Liaison Office, Entry 167F, RG80, NARA II. Dr. Timothy P. Mulligan provided copies to the authors.

41. Ballou questionnaire, 1; Com14 to CNO, "Report on the Battle of Pearl Harbor, 7 December 1941," 24 December 1941, Enclosure B, J. H. McGrann to Lt. Cdr. Thomas L. Davey, CEC, "Report on Damage—Work of Rehabilitation: Kaneohe Naval Air Station," 16 December 1941 (hereinafter Davey Report), RG38, NARA II; analysis of attack photography by Wenger. Hagiwara's lead section scored two hits on the hangar—one of which was a dud—and a miss just outside to the east. The port section missed the building with a hit outside the northeast corner, with two other strikes on or near First Street. The starboard section hit the southern half of the hangar with a dud, along with two bombs that opened large craters on the apron between the hangar and the water.

42. Nash NTU interview, 53–55, 58. Based on the crater pattern northeast of Hangar 1, it is possible that the northernmost bombardier, PO1c Shirai Fukujirō, released the bomb that injured Nash. Although Nash would never know, on 7 May 1942, Ens. Leslie L. B. Knox of VF-42 exacted some measure of retribution, shooting down Shirai's Type 97 *kankō* during the Battle of the Coral Sea. See John B. Lundstrom, *The First Team: Pacific Naval Air Combat from Pearl Harbor to Midway* (Annapolis, Md.: Naval Institute Press, 1984), 212–13, 218; *kōdōchōsho, Shōkaku,* 7 May 1942.

43. Task Force 9 Activities, 14–15, 17; ComPatWing 1 Report, 2; Poulos account, 29; Death Certificates and biographical data sheets, Lee Fox Jr. and Robert W. Uhlmann, OMPF, RG24, NARA, St. Louis; Decoration Citation, Thomas W. Helm, III, 28 March 1942, HAD, NHHC.

44. Muckenthaler interview, 3 March 2010, 3; Death Certificate, Joseph G. Smartt, NPRS. Muckenthaler found out years later that Smartt was a Baptist and therefore did not require last rites. Although the circumstances of Smartt's death would seem consistent with the incident taking place in VP-12's badly damaged north mezzanine, Muckenthaler's account (and the squadron to which these men belonged) indicates clearly that the events transpired in VP-11's south mezzanine.

45. Maltby's account has the only known physical description of the hangar armories.

46. Service Record, LeRoy G. Maltby, OMPF, RG24, NARA, St. Louis; account, LeRoy G. Maltby, n.d. (hereinafter Maltby account), 2, Lord Collection, HAD, NHHC; Kennedy, *Forgotten Warriors*, Engel account, 297. Although months of rehabilitation lay ahead for Lyons, with the aid of prosthesis he would again qualify for flight duty, an extraordinary personal victory against the Japanese.

47. Moser letters, 17 November 1963, 2, and 23 January 1964, 3; Service Record, Cyrenus L. Gillette, OMPF, RG24, NPRC, St. Louis.

48. Muckenthaler interview, 3 March 2010, 3, 5.

49. Kennedy, *Forgotten Warriors*, Petriccione account, 255; Horky NTU interview, 46; Death Certificate, Luther D. Weaver, OMPF, RG24, NARA, St. Louis; Richmond account, 6; There are contradictions in the accounts that relate to Weaver's death. The timeline set forth in Petriccione's graphic account maintains that Weaver died in the second-wave bombing attack, which contradicts the contention in Weaver's death certificate that he died from "Wounds, Multiple/Extreme . . . multiple machine gun wounds of [the] chest." Adding to the confusion, there is another eyewitness account from Otto V. Horky, who stated that he saw Weaver fall during the strafing attacks of the first wave. Countering this alternate story, the extreme nature of Weaver's wounds are consistent with injuries from bomb splinters, and beleaguered staff at the chaotic Dispensary might well have misstated the precise nature of the wounds. In addition, Petriccione states quite clearly that he loaded Weaver's body for transport to the Dispensary. Finally, Horky admitted to being in a frantic state of confusion during the opening minutes of the first wave. In light of these details, the authors side with the Petriccione account.

50. Maltby account, 2–3.

51. Certificate of Death and Service Record, Stanley D. Dosick, OMPF, RG24, NARA, St. Louis; Kennedy, *Forgotten Warriors*, frontispiece.

52. ComPatWing 1 Report, 3; VP-12 Report, 2; Commendation, 27 March 1942, Charles E. Williams, OMPF, RG24, NPRC, St. Louis; Service Record, Charles E. Williams, OMPF, RG24, NPRC, St. Louis.

53. Avery letter, 4 November 1963, 2; Richmond account, 6.

54. It is not clear to what structure Poulos refers, perhaps the pair of squadron magazines between the Maintenance Hangar and the Squadron Office Building on the south side of 2nd Street. See Map OA-N1-334 (File 1406–3), a chart of NAS Kaneohe Bay in the microfilmed records of the Bureau of Yards and Docks, RG71I, Series I, Reel 1173, NARA II.

55. Poulos account, 30.

56. Fujita interview, 4.

57. Muckenthaler interview, 3 March 2010, 7–8.

58. Blackwell NTU interview, 26, 28.

59. Richmond account, 2–3; Avery letter, 1 December 1963, 3; Service Record, Richard Lee Sands, OMPF, RG24, NPRC, St. Louis.

60. This terrain feature was almost certainly the area from which Heʻeia Stream flows and across which the present-day highway H-3 passes over the Koʻolau Range.

61. Avery letter, 4 November 1963, 2; Avery letter, 16 December 1963, 3. One of the puzzling aspects of this incident is the slight possibility that the identity of the pilot that first personally engaged Sands might not have been Iida. Lt. (jg) Fujita recalled later that PO1c Atsumi Takashi's *kansen* likewise vented fuel aft.

62. VP-11 Report, 1–2; VP-12 Report, 1–2; Aircraft History Cards, via Mitchell, PBY-5; CO, NAS Kaneohe Bay to Com14, "The incidents connected with the air raid at the Naval Air Station, Kaneohe Bay, T.H. in 7 December 1941—Narrative of" (hereinafter Kaneohe Bay to Com14), 8 December 1941, 2, RG38, NARA II; ComPatWing 1 Report, 2.

63. *Kōdōchōsho, Sōryū,* 8 December 1941; Battle Lessons, 20; Fujita Iyozō, "Kōnnaru Seikan," in *Rekishi-to Jinbutsu* (Tōkyō: Chūō Kōron-sha, 1983), 263; Fujita interview, 4. It is curious that neither the *Sōryū*'s *kōdōchōsho* nor the Yokosuka Naval Air Corps study makes any mention of the two firing passes at Bellows, which creates some uncertainty as to whether the attacks occurred there. Further, American accounts indicate an attack on Bellows only by a single group of nine Japanese fighters (almost surely the eight from the *Hiryū*). However, as Fujita's various accounts and observations are reasonably consistent, reliable, and straightforward, the authors decided to incorporate the incident. It is worthy of note that Iida's fighters made only two or three strafing runs at Kaneohe. Hence the extended interval from Iida's first attacks on Kaneohe at 0915 until his loss at 0942 seems to allow sufficient time for the short flight down to Bellows and back.

    The circumstances surrounding Lt. Iida's loss and the subsequent air battle over Kaneohe present great difficulties regarding timing and sequencing and with reconciling the American and Japanese accounts, particularly if one accepts that the *Sōryū*'s fighters attacked Bellows Field. Official Japanese documents state that Iida's loss and the air battle occurred at 0942 and 0945, respectively, whereas in most American accounts, events unfold substantially earlier. As the eyewitness accounts and time lines of both sides conflict with each other, for the sake of consistency the authors have adopted the chronology of the second wave set forth in the Japanese air records, modified to affect a union with American records. It is significant, however, that the Task Force 9 narrative places the Iida incident at the very end of the attack, and certainly after Hagiwara's bombing attack that concluded after 0920. In addition, the delay introduced by Iida's supposed detour down to Bellows also supports a later time of engagement.

64. According to Fujita, Iida's hand gesture is used in Japan today to signify one's discomfort and/or inability to render assistance.

65. Fujita Iyozō, interview, *Tora, Tora, Tora: The Real Story of Pearl Harbor,* The History Channel; Fujita interview, 5. It is uncertain whether the *Sōryū* unit ascended to their two-thousand-meter altitude prior to, or subsequent to, Iida's departure, but since only three minutes elapsed between Iida's self-destruction and the arrival of the American fighters, the former scenario appears more probable. See *kōdōchōsho, Sōryū,* 8 December 1941.

66. Avery letter, 4 November 1963, 2. Conflicts between American and Japanese descriptions notwithstanding, the authors have incorporated the story here in accordance with eyewitness accounts of sailors near the Armory.

67. "The sailors that brought Iida under fire" numbered in the hundreds if all accounts are to be believed. In a tongue-in-cheek assessment, Charles P. Muckenthaler claimed, lightheartedly, to have brought down Iida with his .45-caliber pistol. "Everybody claims him, and I claim him, and nobody can refute it!"

68. Avery letter, 16 December 1963, 3; Richmond account, 4; Maltby account, 1; Kennedy, *Forgotten Warriors*, Bell account, 84; Curylo letter, 2; Avery letter, 4 November 1963, 2; Kaneohe History, 199. The account regarding Iida's engine is improbable given the distance from Donehoo's residence to the crash site.

69. Analysis by Di Virgilio and Wenger. There is an intriguing story from fighter ace Tsunoda Kazuo, an enlisted fighter pilot who finished the war as a Special Duty Lt. (jg). Tsunoda flew with Iida in China and admired him a great deal. After reporting to the Tsukuba *Kōkūtai* in 1942, Tsunoda began to inquire into the circumstances surrounding Lt. Iida's death. A former *Sōryū* aviator—probably PO3c Sasaki Takahisa, who was a spare observer during the Pearl Harbor strike—confided in Tsunoda that Iida's damage over Oʻahu was probably not so great as to preclude his safe return. The night before the raid, Iida had lamented that there was no way for Japan to win the war against America and that he had no wish to live in a defeated Japan. Iida's true intentions remained a closely guarded secret among the *Sōryū* aviators. See Tsunoda Kazuo, *Shura no Tsubasa* [The Wings of Fury] (Tōkyō: Kōjin-sha, 2002), 86.

70. Richmond account, 4.

71. Lockwood NTU interview, 35–36.

72. Avery letter, 4 November 1963, 3; Martin interviews, 14 September 1971, 5; Kennedy, *Forgotten Warriors*, Davis account, 147.

73. Iida arrived at the Dispensary either on a pallet or in a garbage can. Versions of this story vary considerably in their details.

74. Actually, Iida donned his best dress blue uniform that morning.

75. Task Force 9 Activities, 18; Kaneohe History, 199; Avery letter, 4 November 1963, 3; Maltby account, 3.

76. According to the architectural drawings for the Dispensary, the "mortuary," as it was called in the plans, was approximately fifteen by eighteen feet and provided only one preparation table. More importantly, the refrigeration facility measured a mere six by eight feet. See Drawing 1406-31-2, U.S. Naval Air Station Kaneohe (Oahu) T.H., Dispensary First Floor Plan, RG71I, Series I, Microfilm Reel 1173, NARA II.

77. Avery letter, 4 November 1963, 3.

78. Maintenance crews repaired three aircraft from VP-11, four from VP-12, and three from VP-14. See microfilmed Aircraft Trouble Analysis cards, Reel 25, at NHHC.

79. Kennedy, *Forgotten Warriors*, Petriccione account, 255. Service Records and Death Certificates, John H. Robinson and John D. Buckley, OMPF, RG24, NARA, St. Louis. Speaking later of his ordeal at the Dispensary, Petriccione said only, "It is something I could never forget."

80. Billingsley NTU interview, 18; Malmin questionnaire, 1; Death Certificate, Raphael A. Watson, OMPF, RG24, NARA, St. Louis.

81. Moser letters, 17 November 1963, 1, and 23 January 1964, 4.

82. Malmin questionnaire, 2; Ballou questionnaire, 3.

83. Kaneohe History, 202; Hoffman NTU interview, 33; Kennedy, *Forgotten Warriors*, miscellaneous account, 343; "John Finn, Medal of Honor Winner, Dies at 100," 2.

84. Blackwell NTU interview, 31; Horky NTU interview, 54–55; Kennedy, *Forgotten Warriors*, Bell account, 84; Kennedy, *Forgotten Warriors*, 65; Henry Retzloff Jr., interview with Dr. Ronald Marcello, 4 August 1978 (hereinafter Retzloff NTU interview), OH#0452, 43, University of North Texas Oral History Collection, Denton, Texas; Nichols NTU interview, 31.

## Chapter 4. "No One Shirked, No One Avoided Danger"

1. Davey Report; Photography of NAS Kaneohe Bay in RG80, NARA II; Alexander letter, 10 July 1956, 1; Kaneohe History, 43.

2. Hollingshead NTU interview, 25; Hanna NTU interview, 32–33.

3. Kaneohe History, 198; Phonecon, JMW and John S. Kennedy, 11 December 2002; classified message, NAS Kaneohe Bay to CinCPac, Serial 072230, RG80, NARA II. The text of Kaneohe's message to CinCPac reads, "Captured enemy chart has marked positions bearing 223 distant 90 miles from Pearl Harbor."

4. "Action and Disposition of 53rd CA Brigade (Anti-Aircraft) on 7 December 1941," Exhibit 5, Section VII, Exhibits of the Joint Committee, *PHA*, Part 12, 324; Jeffrey J. Gudmens, et al., *Staff Ride Handbook for the Attack on Pearl Harbor, 7 December 1941: A Study of Defending America* (Fort Leavenworth, Kan.: Combat Studies Institute Press, 2005), 82; 98th Coastal Artillery's microfilmed morning reports, December 1941, Box 831, RG64, Records of the National Archives and Records Administration, NARA, St. Louis. The battalion's Battery H (3-inch) deployed near Waipahu School, northwest of Pearl Harbor. Battery E had not yet organized. According to the battalion commander, the batteries at Kaneohe brought a number of machine guns as well. See Kennedy, *Forgotten Warriors*, account of Kenneth M. Barager, 365–66.

5. Bott NTU interview, 28–30; Roberts NTU interview, White, 11; Lockwood NTU interview, 44. The men continued digging trenches right up until Christmas.

6. Blackwell NTU interview, 31–32, 34; Kaneohe History, 200.

7. Headquarters, Hawaiian Department, G-2 Messages LAND, *PHA*, Part 19, 3628 (hereinafter G-2 LAND Messages); Headquarters, Hawaiian Department, G-2 Messages AIR, *PHA*, Part 19, 3632; 24th Division Artillery, "Journal," RG407, Entry 427, Box 7879, File 324-ART-0.7, NARA II.

8. G-2 LAND Messages, Message T, 3628. The source of Burgin's information is lost and could have stemmed from the sighting of any individual or group clad in coveralls. The most plausible speculation is that residents along the North Shore might have seen the B-17E crew of 1st Lt. Frank P. Bostrom, just in from Hamilton Field, following their forced landing near the Kahuku Golf Course. In the panic of the moment and seen from a far distance after abandoning their aircraft, the crew might well have been mistaken for enemies, complete with "Japanese insignia" (actually AAF patches) on the left shoulder.

9. Headquarters, 25th Division, "Journal," Serial 60, 15th Airlift Wing History Office, Hickam AFB; 24th Division, "G-2 Journal," Serials 23a, 26, and unnumbered, RG407, Entry 427, Box 7684, File 324–2.2, NARA II; Headquarters, Hawaiian Department, G-2 LAND Messages, Message GG, 3629.

10. Kennedy, *Forgotten Warriors*, Hanson account, 357; Kennedy, *Forgotten Warriors*, Engel account, 297; Avery letter, 16 December 1963, 5.

11. Kennedy, *Forgotten Warriors*, Engel account, 297; Kennedy, *Forgotten Warriors*, Harris account, 351; Hanna NTU interview, 39.

12. Walter W. Simmons questionnaire, 3.

13. Barber NTU interview, 19–20.

14. Kennedy, *Forgotten Warriors*, Hanson account, 357; Avery letter, 16 December 1963, 6; Kennedy, *Forgotten Warriors*, Engel account, 297; Kennedy, *Forgotten Warriors*, Bussell account, 223.

15. Hollingshead NTU interview, 25–26; Kennedy, *Forgotten Warriors*, Harris account, 351.

16. Popko questionnaire, 2; Kennedy, *Forgotten Warriors*, Nilssen account, 295; Simmons questionnaire, 3; Kennedy, *Forgotten Warriors*, Harris account, 351; Maltby account, 3; Muckenthaler interview, 3 March 2010, 8–9; Richmond account, 6; Goza questionnaire, 3; Thomas NTU interview, 20; Grace NTU interview, 31–32.

17. Kaneohe History, 199; Kaneohe Bay to Com14, 3; Trest NTU interview, 27, 29.

18. Billingsley NTU interview, 18–19. The woman who looked after ten-year-old Betty Ann Billingsley was probably Mary Jane Post, the wife of ACOM (PA) Robert W. Post, attached to the station's company and the only known serviceman with a surname of "Post" known to have been present at Kaneohe.

19. Billingsley NTU interview, 20; Roth NTU interview, 33–34.

20. Ballou questionnaire, 1; Nash NTU interview, 59. At least ten other men, all from VP-12, transferred with Nash to the Territorial Hospital.

21. Nash NTU interview, 59, 61.

22. McCrimmon letter, 2.

23. Kaneohe Bay to Com14, 2; Kaneohe History, 37; Roberts NTU interview, White, 8.

24. Martin interviews, 14 September 1971, 3; Lockwood NTU interview, 35, 48.

25. Eugene Burns, *Then There Was One: The U.S.S. Enterprise and the First Year of War* (New York: Harcourt, Brace and Co., 1944), 16.

26. Trest NTU interview, 30.

27. Kaneohe History, 199.

28. Questionnaire, enclosure to letter, Capt. Benjamin H. Troemel, USN (Ret.) to RJC, 7 March 1987.

29. Muckenthaler interview, 3 March 2010, 8. "Bucky" Walters met Muckenthaler shortly thereafter, compared notes on 7 December, and discovered their intersecting mutual experience at Kaneohe. Sadly, Walters, along with his radio-gunner, did not return from a search flight from the *Enterprise* on 13 May 1942.

30. Kennedy, *Forgotten Warriors*, transcription of VP-14 War Diary, 332–34. There is a question of when the surviving PBYs reported to NAS Pearl Harbor. In his 10 July 1956 letter to Walter Lord, Donald B. Alexander of VP-14 stated that on "Sunday evening I went in a plane to Ford Island Sea Plane base." Tanner and Meyer's reports are silent regarding activity after their landing. Neither does PatWing 2's war diary mention the arrival of aircraft from Kaneohe, only that, at 2020, "All search planes returned. Negative results."

31. Muckenthaler interview, 3 March 2010, 10.

32. Muckenthaler interview, 3 March 2010, 10.

33. Muckenthaler interview, 3 March 2010, 10. Muckenthaler learned a hard lesson that night; never did he volunteer again.

34. Nichols NTU interview, 31–34; Service Record, Victor P. Jacoby, OMPF, RG127, NARA, St. Louis.

35. Kaneohe History, 200; Kennedy, *Forgotten Warriors*, account of Guy C. Avery, 91.

36. Blackwell NTU interview, 34–35.

37. Kennedy, *Forgotten Warriors*, Bussell account, 224.

38. Kaneohe Bay to Com14, 3; Avery letter, 12 December 1963, 1; Martin interviews, 14 September 1971, 2. Much of the interpretation of the funeral at Kaneohe is derived from the images of the event in RG80, Still Picture Branch, NARA II.

39. Martin interviews, 10 November 1970, 6.

40. Hoffman NTU interview, 27.

41. Bott NTU interview, 30, 39; Nichols NTU interview, 42; Roberts NTU interview, Marcello, 13.

42. Images of the funeral in RG80, Still Picture Branch, NARA II (hereinafter Funeral Images).

43. Funeral Images; Certificates of Death, Daniel T. Griffin and Walter S. Brown, OMPF, RG24, NARA, St. Louis.

44. Funeral Images; Avery letter, 12 December 1963, 1.

45. Kennedy, *Forgotten Warriors*, 454; Funeral Images; Certificates of Death, Daniel T. Griffin and Walter S. Brown, OMPF, RG24, NARA, St. Louis.

46. Richmond account, 7; Curylo letter, 2.

47. Ballou questionnaire, 3.

48. Alexander letter, 10 July 1956, 2.

49. Kaneohe History, 4.

# Bibliography

**SOURCES**

**Participants Consulted**

AEC John S. Kennedy USN (Ret.) (NAS Kaneohe Bay).

Capt. Charles P. Muckenthaler, USN (Ret.) (VP-11).

Capt. William P. Tanner, USN (Ret.) (VP-11).

Abe Zenji (*Akagi*).

Fujita Iyozō (*Sōryū*).

Harada Kaname (*Sōryū*).

Satō Zenichi (*Zuikaku*).

Ushijima Shizundo (*Zuikaku*).

**Documents**

*Reports in the Japan Defense Agency, Tōkyō*

Detailed Battle Report, Aircraft Carrier *Shōkaku*, 8 December 1941.

*Hikōkitai no Sentō Kōdōchōcho* (Aircraft Group Battle Action Reports).

- *Hiryū*, second-wave fighter unit, 8 December 1941
- *Shōkaku*, first-wave fighter unit, 8 December 1941
- *Sōryū*, second-wave fighter unit, 8 December 1941
- *Shōkaku*, second-wave strike unit, 8 December 1941
- *Zuikaku*, first-wave strike unit, 8 December 1941

*Reports in the Prange Papers*

ComPatWing 1 to ComAirScoFor. "Enemy action against the Naval Air Station Kaneohe Bay, T.H., on December 7, 1941." 12 December 1941.

Detailed Action Report No. 1, CarDiv 5 (trans.) via Cressman.

"Lessons (Air Operations) of the Sea Battle off Hawaii." Vol. I, August 1942 (est.), (trans.) via Cressman.

War Diary, CarDiv 5, 1 December 1941–31 December 1941 (trans.) via Cressman.

*Deck Logs (U.S. Navy), National Archives and Records Administration (II), Modern Military Branch, College Park, Maryland, Records of the Bureau of Navigation (RG 24)*

*Ballard* (AVD-10) (20–29 October 1941).

*Pelican* (AVP-6) (29 September 1941–23 October 1941, 4–24 November 1941).

*Thornton* (AVD-11) (3–10 November 1941, 18–24 November 1941).

*Wright* (AV-1) (25 September–4 October 1941, 17 October–1 November 1941).

*Action Reports (U.S. Navy), National Archives and Records Administration (II), Modern Military Branch, College Park, Maryland (RG 38)*

Com14 to CNO. "Report on the Battle of Pearl Harbor, 7 December 1941." [24 December 1941], Enclosure B, J. H. McGrann to Lt. Cdr. Thomas L. Davey, CEC, "Report on Damage—Work of Rehabilitation: Kaneohe Naval Air Station." 16 December 1941.

Com TF9 to CinCPac. "Operations on December 7, 1941." 20 December 1941.

ComPatWing 1 to CinCPac. "Report of Japanese Air Attack of Kaneohe Bay, T. H., December 7, 1941." 1 January 1942.

NAS Kaneohe Bay to Com14. "The incidents connected with the air raid at the Naval Air Station, Kaneohe Bay, T.H. in 7 December 1941—Narrative of." 8 December 1941.

Commander, Patrol Squadron Eleven to CinCPac. "December 7, 1941 Air Raid: Report of." 13 December 1941.

Commander, Patrol Squadron Twelve to CinCPac. "Report of Raid of December 7, 1941." 14 December 1941.


*War Diaries (U.S. Navy), National Archives and Records Administration (II), Modern Military Branch, College Park, Maryland (RG 38)*
War Diary, Patrol Wing Two, 7 December 1941.


*Operational Plans and Orders (U.S. Navy), National Archives and Records Administration (II),*
*Modern Military Branch, College Park, Maryland (RG 38)*
CinCPac to ComPatWing 2. "Patrol Wing Organization, Hawaiian Area." 14 June 1941.


*Dispatches (U.S. Navy), National Archives and Records Administration (II), Modern Military Branch, College Park,*
*Maryland, Records of the Crane Group (RG 38)*
CNO/OpNav Dispatch Files.


*Unit Journals (U.S. Army), National Archives and Records Administration (II), Modern Military Branch,*
*College Park, Maryland, Division Records (RG 407)*
24th Division. "G-2 Journal."
24th Division Artillery. "Journal."


*Reports and Unit Journals (U.S. Army), 15th Airlift Wing History Office, Hickam AFB*
Headquarters, 25th Division. "Journal."


*Microfilmed Architectural Plans and Drawings (U.S. Navy), National Archives and Records Administration (II), Cartographic*
*Branch, College Park, Maryland, Records of the Bureau of Yards and Docks (RG71I, Series I)*
"U.S. Naval Air Station Kaneohe (Oahu) T.H., Administration and Operations Building" [two plans and two elevations]. Architectural drawings 136521, 136522, 136524, and 136525, via NAVFAC Hawaii.

"U.S. Naval Air Station Kaneohe (Oahu) T.H., Bachelor Officers' Quarters: Detail Plan—Wings A and B." Architectural drawing 1406-30-28.

"U.S. Naval Air Station Kaneohe (Oahu) T.H., Bachelor Officers' Quarters: First [Second, and Third] Floor Plan[s]." Architectural drawings 1406-30-19, -20, and -21.

"U.S. Naval Air Station Kaneohe (Oahu) T.H., Barracks: Foundation Plan; First Floor Plan." Architectural drawing 1406-30-1.

"U.S. Naval Air Station Kaneohe (Oahu) T.H. Barracks Second Floor Plan, Roof Plan, Details of Covered Passage." Architectural drawing 1406-30-2.

"U.S. Naval Air Station Kaneohe, (Oahu) T.H. Barracks. Elevations." Architectural drawing 1406-30-3.

"U.S. Naval Air Station Kaneohe, (Oahu) T.H., Dispensary First Floor Plan." Architectural drawing 1406-31-2.

"U.S. Naval Air Station Kaneohe, (Oahu) T.H., Dispensary Second Floor Plan." Architectural drawing 1406-31-3.

"U.S. Naval Air Station Kaneohe (Oahu) T.H., Extension to Maintenance Hangar." Architectural drawing 1406-45-49.

"U.S. Naval Air Station Kaneohe (Oahu) T.H., Recreation Facilities, Enlisted Men." Architectural drawing 1406-34-55.

"U.S. Naval Air Station Kaneohe (Oahu) T.H., Recreation Facilities, Officers, Floor Plans." Architectural drawing 1406-34-112.

"U.S. Naval Air Station Kaneohe, (Oahu) T.H. Utilities Shop and Parachute Loft." Architectural drawing 1406-29-2.

*Exhibits and Documents for Investigations, National Archive and Records Administration (II)—*
*Modern Military Branch, College Park, Maryland, Records of the Chief of Naval Operations (RG 80)*
Formerly Security-Classified CNO Documents, CinCPac Dispatch Files.
Roberts Commission Exhibits.

*Command Files (U.S. Navy), National Archives and Records Administration (I), Old Military Branch, Washington, D.C.,*
*Records of Naval Operating Forces (RG 313)*
Commander, Aircraft, Battle Force, L11-1 files, 1941.
Commander, Aircraft, Scouting Force, A4-3 files, 1941.
Commander, Aircraft, Scouting Force, A16-3 files, 1941.

*Navy Muster Rolls at www.fold3.com (formerly www.footnote.com)*
NAS Kaneohe Bay
VP-11
VP-12
VP-14
VP-23
VP-24
VP-26

*Marine Muster Rolls, Marine Corps History Division, Marine Corps Base Quantico*
Marine Detachment, NAS Kaneohe Bay, 1–31 December 1941.

*Army Morning Reports and Rosters, Record Group 64, Records of the National Archives and Records Administration—National*
*Archives at St. Louis*
34th Engineer Regiment
98th Coastal Artillery (AA) Regiment

*Interviews by the Authors—American Veterans*
Capt. Charles P. Muckenthaler, USN (Ret.), San Diego, California, 20 December 2009 and 3 March 2010 (JMW telephone
    interview) (VP-11).
Paul B. Van Nostrand Jr. (son of Paul B. Van Nostrand), Chula Vista, California, 11 July 2010 (JMW telephone interview).
William P. Watson (son of Raphael A. Watson), Kailua, Hawaii, 19–20 August 2009 (JMW telephone interview).

*Interviews by the Authors—Japanese Veterans*
Abe Zenji, JFD undated interview (*Akagi*).
Fujita Iyozō, JFD undated interview (*Sōryū*).
Harada Kaname, JFD undated interview (*Sōryū*).
Satō Zenichi, JFD undated interview (*Zuikaku*).
Ushijima Shizundo, JFD undated interview (*Zuikaku*).

*Interviews, North Texas State University Oral History Collection*
Herman W. Barber, 14 October 1977 (NAS Kaneohe Bay).
Mynila Billingsley, 13 October 1977 (NAS Kaneohe Bay).
Herschel H. Blackwell, 26 April 1986 (VP-14).
Wesley H. Bott, 14 October 1977 (MarDet, NAS Kaneohe Bay).

Arthur R. Grace Jr., 14 October 1977 (VP-11).

Robert U. Hanna, 13 June 1978 (NAS Kaneohe Bay).

Robert E. Hoffman, 9 May 1974 (NAS Kaneohe Bay).

Cecil I. Hollingshead, 22 October 1983 (VP-11).

Otto V. Horky, 17 May 1974 (VP-11).

Randolph S. D. Lockwood, 24 August 1974 (MarDet, NAS Kaneohe Bay).

Jamie R. Murphy, 15 May 1976 (NAS Kaneohe Bay).

Kenton and Millie Nash, Texas, 15 October 1977 (VP-11).

John F. Nichols, 15 October 1977 (MarDet, NAS Kaneohe Bay).

Henry Retzloff Jr., 4 August 1978 (NAS Kaneohe Bay).

Charles H. Roberts, 13 October 1977 (MarDet, NAS Kaneohe Bay).

Charles H. Roberts, 6 November 1994 (MarDet, NAS Kaneohe Bay).

Thomas E. Roth, 15 October 1977 (VP-11).

Walter A. Simerson, 12 June 1976 (34th Engineer Regiment).

David H. Thomas, 28 April 1990 (MarDet, NAS Kaneohe Bay).

Joseph M. Trest, 15 October 1977 (MarDet, NAS Kaneohe Bay).

*Interviews and Statements in the Papers of Gordon W. Prange, Goldstein Collection,*
*Archives Service Center, University of Pittsburgh*

Guy C. Avery, 1 December 1963 and 16 December 1963 (letter to GWP) (NAS Kaneohe Bay).

Walter J. Curylo, 3 March 1964 (letter to GWP) (VP-14).

Harold M. Martin, 10 November 1970 (GWP interview) (NAS Kaneohe Bay).

Richard R. J. Moser, 23 January 1964 (letter to GWP) (VP-12).

Robertus M. "Bert" Richmond, 26 November 1963 (letters to GWP) (VP-12).

*Interviews and Statements, Prange Collection, University of Maryland*

Fuchida Mitsuo, various dates (*Akagi*).

Fujita Iyozō, 2 February 1951 (*Sōryū*).

Genda Minoru, various dates (*Akagi*).

Muranaka Kazuo, 17 December 1949 (*Hiryū*).

Okajima Kiyokuma, 19 January 1950 (*Hiryū*).

*Interviews and Statements in the Papers of Walter Lord, History and Archives Division, Naval History*
*and Heritage Command, Washington Navy Yard.*

Donald B. Alexander, 10 July 1956 (letter to WL) (VP-14).

Robert W. Ballou, circa June 1956 (questionnaire to WL) (VP-11).

Daucy B. Goza, n.d. (questionnaire to WL) (VP-14).

Warren G. Kearns, n.d. (questionnaire to WL) (VP-12).

Cecil S. Malmin, circa March 1956 (questionnaire to WL) (VP-12).

LeRoy G. Maltby, n.d. (account to WL) (VP-12).

Herman P. McCrimmon, 20 March 1956 (letter to WL) (NAS Kaneohe Bay)

Ragnar N. Nilssen, n.d. (questionnaire to WL) (NAS Kaneohe Bay).

Henry M. Popko, n.d. (questionnaire to WL) (NAS Kaneohe Bay).

Shiga Yoshio, 9 July 1956 (interview) (*Kaga*).

Walter W. Simmons, circa March 1956 (questionnaire to WL) (VP-12).

*Interview in the Papers of John W. Lambert*

Abe Yasujirō, n.d. circa 1980 (questionnaire to JWL) (*Shōkaku* fighter unit).


*Decoration Citations, History and Archives Division, Naval History and Heritage Command, Washington Navy Yard*

Sam Aweau, 18 March 1942.

John R. Bacon, 10 July 1951.

James L. Beasley, 10 July 1951.

John William Finn, 30 June 1942.

Morton N. Frey, 10 July 1951.

Thomas W. Helm III, 28 March 1942.

Delbert C. Jones, 10 July 1951.

Thomas E. Kerr, 28 March 1942.

Robert James Peterson, 23 April 1942.

Robert L. Schnexnayder, December 1941.

Alice Beckley Spencer, 4 March 1942.

James E. Walters, 10 July 1951.

Robert F. Weston, 10 July 1951.


*Biographical Files, History and Archives Division, Naval History and Heritage Command, Washington Navy Yard*

George S. Clute

John L. Genta

Harold M. Martin

Knefler McGinnis

Charles P. Muckenthaler


*Documents from the Bureau of Aeronautics, History and Archives Division, Naval History and Heritage Command, Washington Navy Yard*

Aircraft History Cards (Microfilm), furnished by Eric Mitchell on www.pby.com.

Aircraft Trouble Analysis cards (Microfilm).

"Monthly Status of Naval Aircraft." August–December 1941.


*Correspondence*

Wendy M. Coble (underwater archaeologist at East Carolina University), letter to JMW.

John B. Lundstrom (JMW telephone interviews and e-mails), regarding the microfilmed CinCPac incoming and outgoing dispatch files, 1941.

Richard A. Rodrigues (JMW letter), regarding Army Air Force pilot George R. Bickell. "Pilot's Statement." Landing accident of P-40B. AC No. 41–5207, 22 September 1941.

James C. Sawruk (JMW telephone interviews and e-mails), regarding analysis of Aircraft History Cards.


*Official Military Personnel Files, Record Group 24, Records of the Bureau of Naval Personnel, Record Group 127; Records of the U.S. Marine Corps; Record Group 181, Records of Naval Districts and Shore Establishments, National Archives and Records Administration—National Archives at St. Louis and National Personnel Records Center.*

Personnel records of 181 officers and men from the U.S. Navy and U.S. Marine Corps and personnel records of civilian contractors working for the Navy.

*Miscellaneous*

Rear Adm. Edward E. Colestock Papers, Emil Buehler Library, National Naval Aviation Museum, Pensacola, Florida.

*Pearl Harbor-Gram*s, various dates.


## Unpublished Diaries, Log Books, and Manuscripts

*Flight Log Books*

Charles P. Muckenthaler.

Howard J. Spreeman (furnished by Eric Mitchell on www.pby.com).

*Manuscripts*

Bellinger, Patrick N. L. "The Gooney Birds." Bellinger papers, History and Archives Division, Naval History and Heritage Command.

ComPatWing 2. "Story of Task Force NINE Activities on December 7, 1941." n.d. Rear Adm. Logan C. Ramsey Papers, History and Archives Division, Naval History and Heritage Command.

"Naval Air Station Kaneohe Bay History, 1 Aug 39–1 Aug 45." n.d. History and Archives Division, Naval History and Heritage Command.


## Photography

National Archives and Records Administration (II), Still Picture Branch

    RG 71—Bureau of Yards and Docks

    RG 72—Bureau of Aeronautics

    RG 80—Chief of Naval Operations

National Naval Aviation Museum, Pensacola, Florida

National Personnel Records Center, St. Louis, Missouri

    Service photography, U.S. Navy and U.S. Marine Corps

Naval History and Heritage Command, Photographic Section, Washington Navy Yard

World War II Valor in the Pacific National Monument, Honolulu, Hawaii

    Historian's Office, Photo Archives

    Curator's Office, 14th Naval District Collection

Private Collections

    James W. Curylo

    Robert J. Cressman

    Russell J. Crownover

    John F. Di Virgilio

    Clifton W. Dohrmann

    Angelina and Stephen Engel

    James F. Evans

    Fujita Iyozo

    Denver Gray

    Ed Horky

    Izawa Kazuo

    John S. Kennedy

    Walter Lord

    *Maru* magazine

    Al Makiel

    Jerome McCrimmon

    Charles P. Muckenthaler

Murakami Fukuji

Michael Perucci

Lisa L. (Petricionne) Neumann

Gordon W. Prange via Wenger

Gordon W. Prange Papers, Goldstein Collection, Archives Service Center,
    University of Pittsburgh

Taigh Ramey

Harriett Tracey

Paul B. Van Nostrand Jr.

William Watson

Kathy Weeks

J. Michael Wenger

## Congressional Hearings

U.S. Congress, 79th Congress, 1st Session. *Pearl Harbor Attack: Hearings before the Joint Committee on the Investigation of the Pearl Harbor Attack.* 39 parts. Washington, D.C.: GPO, 1946.

Testimony

| | |
|---|---|
| Patrick N. L. Bellinger | Joint Committee, 31 January 1946, Part 8 |
| | Hart Inquiry, 15 March 1944, Part 26 |
| | Roberts Commission, 31 December 1941, Part 22 |
| | Navy Court of Inquiry, 25 August 1944, Part 32 |
| Frederick M. Martin | Army Pearl Harbor Board, 29 August 1944, Part 28 |
| Harold M. Martin | Roberts Commission, 3 January 1942, Part 23 |

Documents and Exhibits

"Action and Disposition of 53rd CA Brigade (Anti-Aircraft) on 7 December 1941. Exhibit 5, Section VII, Exhibits of the
    Joint Committee, Part 12.

CinCUS to Fleet. "Security of Fleet at Base and in Operating Areas." 15 February 1941. Proceedings of the Roberts Com-
    mission, appearing as document in Part 22 but not introduced as an exhibit.

CinCPac to Pacific Fleet. "Security of Fleet at Base and in Operating Areas." 14 October 1941. Proceedings of the Roberts
    Commission, annex to Adm. Husband E. Kimmel's testimony in Part 23 but not introduced as an exhibit.

Commander, Naval Base Defense Air Force and Commanding General, Hawaiian Air Force. "Joint estimate covering
    Joint Army and Navy air action in the event of sudden hostile action against Oahu or Fleet Units in the Hawaiian
    area." 31 March 1941, excerpts from war and defense plans, appearing as documents in Part 1 but not introduced as
    exhibits.

ComPatWing 2 to CNO. "Patrol Wing TWO—Readiness of." 16 January 1941, Exhibit 24, Hart Inquiry, Part 26.

Headquarters, Hawaiian Department, G-2 Messages AIR. Exhibit 164, Exhibits of the Joint Committee, Part 19.

Headquarters, Hawaiian Department. G-2 Messages LAND. Exhibit 164, Exhibits of the Joint Committee, Part 19.

*Lexington* (CV-2) deck logs, 5 December 1941, Exhibit 102, Exhibits of the Joint Committee, Part 16.

PatWing 2 Watch and Duty Schedules. Exhibit 113-C, Exhibits of the Joint Committee, Part 17.

Rear Admiral H. E. Kimmel to SecNav, "Report of Action of 7 December 1941." 21 December 1941. Exhibits of the Rob-
    erts Commission, Exhibit 39, Part 24.

## Books and Pamphlets

Bureau of Navigation. *Instructions for Use in Preparation for the Rating of Bugler, U.S. Navy.* Washington: Government Printing
    Office, 1940.

Bureau of Yards and Docks. *Building the Navy's Bases in World War II: History of the Bureau of Yards and Docks and the Civil Engineer Corps 1940–1946*, vol. I. Washington: Government Printing Office, 1947.

Burns, Eugene. *Then There Was One: The U.S.S. Enterprise and the First Year of War*. New York: Harcourt, Brace and Co., 1944.

Creed, Roscoe. *PBY: The Catalina Flying Boat*. Annapolis, Md.: Naval Institute Press, 1985.

Cressman, Robert J. *A Magnificent Fight: The Battle for Wake Island*. Annapolis, Md.: Naval Institute Press, 1995.

Fuchida Mitsuo and Masatake Okumiya. *Midway: The Battle that Doomed Japan*. Annapolis, Md.: Naval Institute Press, 1955.

Fujita Iyozō, comp. *Shōgen Shinjuwan Kōgeki*. Tōkyō: Kōjin-sha, 1991.

Gudmens, Jeffrey J., et al. *Staff Ride Handbook for the Attack on Pearl Harbor, 7 December 1941: A Study of Defending America*. Fort Leavenworth, Kan.: Combat Studies Institute Press, 2005.

Kennedy, John S. *The Forgotten Warriors of Kaneohe*. Oakland, Calif.: East Bay Blue Print & Supply Co., 1996. This work is a collection of reminiscences, including those of the following:

    Guy C. Avery (NAS Kaneohe Bay)

    Kenneth M. Barager (98th Coastal Artillery, 2nd Battalion)

    Doyle A. Bell (NAS Kaneohe Bay)

    Samuel H. Bussell (PatWing 1)

    Joseph T. Crownover (VP-11)

    Frank F. Davis (NAS Kaneohe Bay)

    Albert L. Dodson (VP-14)

    Joseph C. Engel (VP-12)

    Harry A. Haase (VP-11)

    Murray Hanson (VP-14)

    Jackson L. Harris (VP-14)

    John S. Kennedy (NAS Kaneohe Bay)

    Adelaide McCrimmon

    Ragnar N. Nilssen (VP-12)

    Alfred D. Perucci (VP-14)

    Armand Petriccione (VP-11)

    Gordon Poling (Marine Detachment)

    George F. Poulos (VP-11)

    William K. Spry (PatWing 1)

Lambert, John W. *Pineapple Air Force: Pearl Harbor to Tokyo*. St. Paul, Minn.: Phalanx Publishing Company, 1991.

Lord, Walter. *Day of Infamy*. New York: Henry Holt & Company, 1957.

Lundstrom, John B. *The First Team: Pacific Naval Air Combat from Pearl Harbor to Midway*. Annapolis, Md.: Naval Institute Press, 1984.

Meier, Nellie Simmons. *Lion's Paws: The Story of Famous Hands, 1937*. Whitefish, Mt.: Kessinger Publishing, 2004.

Merriam, Ray. *World War II Journal 2: Pearl Harbor Special Issue*. Bennington, Vt.: Merriman Press, 2000.

Mikesh, Robert C. *Japanese Aircraft Equipment: 1940–1945*. Atglen, Pa.: Schiffer Publishing Ltd., 2004.

O'Neill, P. G. *Japanese Names: A Comprehensive Index by Characters and Readings*. New York: John Weatherhill, Inc., 1972.

Prange, Gordon W., et al. *December 7, 1941: The Day the Japanese Attacked Pearl Harbor*. New York: McGraw-Hill Book Company, 1988.

Roberts, Michael D. *Dictionary of American Naval Aviation Squadrons, Volume 2: The History of VP, VPD, VP(HL) and VP(AM) Squadrons*. Washington, D.C.: Government Printing Office, 2000.

Spiller, Harry. *Pearl Harbor Survivors: An Oral History of 24 Servicemen*. Jefferson, N.C.: McFarland & Co., Inc., Publishers, 2002.

Tsunoda Kazuo. *Shura no Tsubasa*. Tōkyō: Kōjin-sha, 2002.

United States Naval Institute. *The Bluejackets' Manual: United States Navy 1940*. Annapolis, Md.: United States Naval Institute, 1940.

Walsh, David I. Chairman, Committee on Naval Affairs, United States Senate. "The Decline and Renaissance of the Navy, 1922–1944." Washington, D.C.: Government Printing Office, 1944.

Yamagata Tsunao, pub. *Kaigun: Kū bo-Kan Sentō Kiroku*. Tōkyō: Atene Shobō, 2002.

**Articles, etc.**

Evans, James. "A Kaneohe Naval Air Station Remembrance." *Pearl Harbor Remembered.* http://my.execpc.com/~dschaaf/evans.html. Accessed 1 June 2013.

Fujita, Iyozō. "Kōnnaru Seikan." *Rekishi-to Jinbutsu* . Tōkyō: Chūō Kōron-sha, 20 January 1983.

"Interview with Iyozō Fujita." In *Tora, Tora, Tora: The Real Story of Pearl Harbor.* The History Channel. Written and directed by Laura Verklan. North Hollywood, Calif.: Greystone Communications, 2000.

Harding, Stephen. "First Planes Down at Pearl." *Aviation History Magazine*, 1 January 2014.

Ishikawa Satoki. "Shinjuwan Sakusen ni Sanka Shite." Monograph of unknown date and origin.

Jackson, Lyle A. "Moment of Decision." *The Public's Library and Digital Archive.* http://www.ibiblio.org/phha/Lyle.html. Accessed 1 June 2013.

"John Finn, Medal of Honor Winner, Dies at 100." *New York Times*, 27 May 2010.

Ōkubo, Chūhei. "Kiseki no Kankō Bakugekitai Futatsu no Sō-wa." *Shōgen Shinjuwan Kōgeki.* Tōkyō: Kōjin-sha, 1991.

Poulos, George. "At War: Recollections of a VP Pilot." *Naval Aviation News*, 9 August 1982.

Von Heiland, Frank A. "Army and Navy Aviation in Hawaii." *Pan-Pacific*, January–March 1937.

# Index

Abe Yasujirō, 23, 29*p*, 29*t* 1, 67
aborted run, 90, 94
action reports, 59, 159n123, 159n124, 161n6
Administration Building, 5, 14, 14*p*, 24*p*, 25, 26,
  32, 33, 34, 46, 54, 56, 59, 80, 121, 137, 155n17
aerial views, 10*p*, 15*p*, 85*p*, 86*p*, 91*p*, 94*p*, 95*p*,
  130*p*
Aeronca 65TC Tandem (NC-38838), 22–23,
  23*p*, 155n14
aftermath, 69, 129; burials, 139, 143, 144, 145,
  163n44; burials 144–149*p*; cleanup, 128;
  defenses, 128, 134–35; medical treatment, 80,
  93–94, 124, 138; salvage work, 70, 72, 73, 97,
  120, 123, 129; transportation, medical, 80, 110,
  112, 113, 115–16, 117
Aichi D3A1 Type 99 carrier bomber (*kanbaku*)
  ("Val"), xii(2), 22, 28
Air Medals, Gardner, William W., 40, 40*p*, 157n61
aircraft statistics, destroyed, 67
aircraft wreckage, 112, 129, 131*p*, 132*p*, 163n40
Akao Akira, 104*t* 4
Alexander, Donald B., 167n30
Allen, Dolph C., 6, 6*p*
altitude, 22, 57, 84, 85*p*, 87, 89, 90, 96, 98, 130*p*,
  154n11, 161n6, 164n65
ambulances, 38, 39, 40, 62, 81, 103
ammunition, 56, 65, 66, 67, 78, 96, 97, 117, 129,
  134, 135, 159n124
anchorages. *See* moorings
antiaircraft batteries, 138, 142; Battery E, 153n34,
  166n4; Battery F, 134, 153n34; Battery G, 134;
  Battery H, 166n4
antiaircraft defenses, 19, 84, 90, 161n6
approaches: bombing attacks, 84, 87; first-wave
  attack, 23, 27; Hagiwara Tsutomu, 90, 98;
  Ichihara Tatsuo, 84, 130*p*; to Kāne'ohe Bay, 23;
  from Ko'olaus, 90; to Mōkapu Peninsula, 23; to
  O'ahu, 22; second-wave attack, 86, 92*p*
aprons, 59, 62, 76*p*, 91*p*, 118; bomb strikes, 88, 89,
  93*p*, 100, 102; burning on, 68*p*, 92*p*, 94*p*, 95*p*,
  102*p*; clearing of, 129, 131*p*; defined, 153n33;
  firefighting, 74, 78; Hangar 1, 61, 78, 97, 132*p*,
  162n39; Hangar 2, 66, 88; parking, 10*p*, 70*p*,
  89; PBYs on, 70, 99*p*, 131*p*, 161n16; as primary
  target, 84; simulated strafing runs, 21; tracer
  strikes on, 32; warmup, 10*p*, 18*p*, 19, 23
aprons, parking, 74
Arkansas, Foss, Rodney, S., 22(2), 27–28, 62, 65,
  81–82
armament, Japanese attack bombers, 250-kg
  bombs, 86*p*, 88, 91*p*, 100, 102, 105*p*

armor, 18–19, 22
armored bomb target boat, 36
armories, subsidiary, 59, 66, 109, 129, 158n101,
  163n45
Armory, 27, 34, 53, 56, 59, 59*p*, 109–10, 118, 119,
  120–21, 122*p*, 158n101, 164n66
armory, subsidiary, 106*p*, 113*p*
Army Air Force, 63, 134, 136; attack mistaken for
  simulations, 32, 33, 37, 38, 41, 44, 46, 48, 51, 52,
  72*p*; simulated strafing runs, 21
Atsumi Takashi, 97*t* 3, 120, 164n61
Avenue B, 105*p*, 107*p*
Avenue C, 52
Avenue D, 2*p*, 52
Avery, Guy C., 14, 22, 88, 123, 142, 153n25
Aweau, Samuel K. "Sam", Sr., 25, 26

B-17E crew, 166n8
Bachelor Officers Quarters (BOQ), xiv, 44, 46,
  48, 48*p*, 49*p*, 51, 52, 54, 121, 141, 151n4
Bacon, John R., 61, 62*p*
Baker 5 readiness conditions, 18
bakery, 136*p*
*Ballard* (AV-10), 8
Ballou, Robert W., 27, 62, 63*p*, 81, 138
BAR (Browning Automatic Rifle). *See* Brown-
  ing Automatic Rifle
Barager, Kenneth M., 134
Barber, Herman W., 21, 26
Barbers Point, 135
barracks, 15*p*, 35, 121
Barracks Building 4 (VP-11), 3*p*, 21, 32
Barracks Building 5 (VP-12), 3*p*, 32
Barracks Building 6 (VP-14), 3*p*
Barracks Building 7 ("Ship's Company), 2, 3*p*,
  33, 34
Barracks Building 8 (Marine Detachment), 3*p*,
  33, 57, 158n98
Battery E, 2nd Battalion of the 98th Coastal
  Artillery (AA), 153n34, 166n4
Battery F, 2nd Battalion of the 98th Coastal
  Artillery (AA), 134, 153n34
Battery G, 2nd Battalion of the 98th Coastal
  Artillery (AA), 134
Battery H, 2nd Battalion of the 98th Coastal
  Artillery (AA), 166n4
battleships, Japanese, 22
Beard, Bill J. "Billie Joe", 126
Beard, Woodrow W., 119, 156n51
Beasley, James L., 66
Bell, Doyle A., 34, 34*p*, 59, 69, 128

Bellinger, Patrick N. L., 7, 11
Bellows Field, 26, 63, 96, 120, 134, 162n26,
  164n63; as secondary target, 22, 23
Belt of 1,000 Stitches, 121
belting machine, 66, 70, 88, 103, 109
Bennett, Allen, 134
Billingsley, Betty Ann, 54, 60, 60*p*, 166n18
Billingsley, Mynila, 53–54, 60, 60*p*, 126, 138
Billingsley, Oliver L., 53–54, 60, 60*p*, 126
Black Cat Café, 12, 13*p*
blackout, 139
Blackwell, Herschel H., Jr., 56, 56*p*, 119, 142
blisters, 60, 61*p*, 66, 88, 96
Bloch, Claude C., 18
Boathouse, 34, 36, 37*p*
boatswain, 35
bomb craters, 90, 102, 112, 129, 162n39, 163n41,
  163n42
bomb detonations, 92*p*, 93*p*, 95*p*, 103*p*, 161n6
bomb drops, 85, 87, 90, 100, 162n23
bomb duds, 92*p*, 103, 103*p*, 163n41
bomb water strikes, 88, 89, 90, 92*p*, 95*p*, 100,
  103*p*
bombardier/observer, 85, 87, 87*t* 2, 89, 90, 100,
  104*t* 4, 163n42
bombing attacks, 85*p*; 1st *Chūtai*, 93*p*; aborted
  run, 90, 94; altitudes, 84, 85*p*, 87, 89, 90, 98,
  130*p*, 161n6; approaches, 84, 86, 87, 90, 92*p*,
  98, 130*p*; bomb water strikes, 88, 89, 90, 92*p*,
  95*p*, 100, 103*p*; bombing course, 85; Hagiwara
  Tsutomu, 98, 100, 104*p*, 105*p*, 109, 116–17,
  116*p*, 164n63; Hangar 1, 113; Hangar 2, 92*p*;
  impact, 89, 93*p*, 106*p*, 107*p*; Nakajimi B5N2
  Type 97 carrier attack plane (*kankō*) ("Kate"),
  102*p*; number of, 161n9; patterns, 87, 91*p*
bombsight capabilities, 84–85, 89, 100, 161n4
Bombsight Workshop (Building 12), 15, 36, 38*p*,
  105*p*, 118
BOQ (Bachelor Officers Quarters. *See* Bachelor
  Officers Quarters
Bostrom, Frank P., 166n8
Bott, Wesley H., 57, 57*p*, 143
Bowie, William L., 122
Branham, William H., 156n51
Brig inspection, 34
Brown, Frank J., 51
Brown, Walter S., 27, 40, 40*p*, 143, 144
Browning Automatic Rifles (BARs), xiv, 50*p*, 58,
  78, 119, 121; defense positions, 87–88
Browning machine guns, 57, 59, 61, 61*p*, 63, 66,
  74*p*, 78, 80*p*, 88, 96, 98, 135, 137

# About the Authors

**J. MICHAEL WENGER** is a military historian who has conducted research since the 1970s in repositories the world over. He received the 2012 U.S. Naval Institute Author of the Year Award. Wenger is the coauthor of ten books and lives in Raleigh, North Carolina.

Naval historian **ROBERT J. CRESSMAN** was the recipient of the John Lyman Book Award in 1999 and the Admiral Arthur W. Radford Award in 2008. He lives in Silver Spring, Maryland.

**JOHN DI VIRGILIO** is the author of two groundbreaking articles related to Pearl Harbor and is recognized for his extensive research on Japanese naval ordnance and for his illustrated Pearl Harbor battleship damage profiles. He lives in 'Ewa Beach, Hawai'i.